THE FRENCH NEW WAVE

THE FRENCH
NEW WAVE

CRITICAL LANDMARKS

New Expanded Edition

Edited by

Peter Graham and
Ginette Vincendeau

THE BRITISH FILM INSTITUTE
Bloomsbury Publishing Plc
50 Bedford Square, London, WC1B 3DP, UK
1385 Broadway, New York, NY 10018, USA
29 Earlsfort Terrace, Dublin 2, Ireland
BLOOMSBURY is a trademark of Bloomsbury Publishing Plc

First edition published 1968 by Martin Secker & Warburg
as a publication of the BFI Education Department
Second edition published 2009 by Palgrave Macmillan on behalf of the BFI

This edition first published in Great Britain 2022 by Bloomsbury
on behalf of the
British Film Institute
21 Stephen Street, London W1T 1LN
www.bfi.org.uk

The BFI is the lead organisation for film in the UK and the distributor of Lottery funds for film.
Our mission is to ensure that film is central to our cultural life, in particular by supporting and
nurturing the next generation of filmmakers and audiences. We serve a public role which covers
the cultural, creative and economic aspects of film in the UK.

Cover design: Louise Dugdale
Cover image: *Cléo de 5 à 7*, Agnès Varda (1961). Photo: Liliane de Kermadec © ciné-tamaris.

A catalogue record for this book is available from the British Library.
A catalog record for this book is available from the Library of Congress.

ISBN: HB: 978–1–8390–2230–2
PB: 978–1–8390–2229–6
ePDF: 978–1–8390–2232–6
eBook: 978–1–8390–2231–9

Project managed and designed by TomCabot/ketchup

Printed and bound in India

To find out more about our authors and books visit
www.bloomsbury.com/bfi and sign up for our newsletters.

CONTENTS

I   THE *POLITIQUE DES AUTEURS*: FOUNDATIONAL TEXTS

II   CRITICAL DEBATES: STATEMENTS, POLEMICS, REVISIONS

III THE MISSING PERSPECTIVE: GENDER, POLITICS AND THE NEW WAVE

Preface to the 2022 Edition

This new, expanded, edition of *The French New Wave: Critical Landmarks*, builds on both the original volume *The New Wave* edited by Peter Graham in 1968, and our joint enlarged edition of 2009, to which we have made further additions. Very sadly, Peter died in July 2020 and he was not able to see this third version of his work to completion. He was however very much involved in the direction the new edition takes and the selection of articles. The spirit of his pioneering work therefore lives on through this volume too.

In 1968, barely ten years after the beginning of the movement, Peter had the prescience to gather important articles about the New Wave in a single volume which quickly went out of print. By the time we produced the expanded edition of 2009, forty years had elapsed and the French New Wave had become both a canonical movement and a fixture on Film Studies and French Studies syllabuses – as a result of which, for example, François Truffaut's now canonical 'A Certain Tendency in French Cinema' was added. This is still true a further ten years on. Many of the films continue to fascinate audiences and several have achieved cult status (*Les Quatre cents coups, Hiroshima mon amour, À bout de souffle* and *Cléo de 5 à 7* in particular). The movement continues to elicit new writing, and titles published since 2009 have been added to the bibliography, the most significant of which are discussed at the end of the updated introduction. All the texts included in the 2009 edition are in this volume, though their order in some cases has been slightly altered; the linking texts that appear throughout the volume were written by Peter Graham for the 1968 and 2009 editions, those for this edition by Ginette Vincendeau, as indicated in their signatures.

While film scholars and students continue to ponder the stylistic, thematic and ideological features of the New Wave films, new types of interrogations have also surfaced, rightly demanding more diversity in films and scholarly approaches. A product of their time, the French New Wave films and the critical material written about them at the time, with few exceptions, were the work of white men, as is evident from the previous two volumes. However, if basic historical facts cannot be altered, it is possible to explore gaps in knowledge, ask different questions and look harder for marginalised contributions. We decided to look more systematically for the contribution of women to the New Wave films and to writing about them, as well as pieces that more generally addressed gender, whether by women or men. The result is the new section called 'The missing perspective', which, to our delight, has ended up more extensive and richer than we had initially expected. This includes articles that examine New Wave and other films from a gender perspective, theoretical and critical pieces by women and reviews of the films of Agnès Varda and the lesser-known Paule Delsol. Interestingly, in some instances, the new work is more political and traces of the social context, such as the colonial wars, appear, even if modestly. We believe this makes our selection of material about the French New Wave richer and more comprehensive, while bringing to light material that had been unjustly marginalised.

Ginette Vincendeau, April 2021

Preface to the 2009 Edition

The original edition of this book, then entitled *The New Wave*, a collection of articles by and interviews with leading members of the Nouvelle Vague, as well as some broadsides from French critics who opposed the movement, was published in an English translation by Secker & Warburg in association with the British Film Institute in 1968. When that edition went out of print, it became clear, with film studies now a fixture in university syllabuses, that a new and enlarged edition of the book could usefully fill a gap. Over the years I realised, after much deliberation, that François Truffaut's polemical article, 'A Certain Tendency in French Cinema', which at the time I had decided not to include in the selection, could no longer be omitted. The piece had become so canonical that no anthology about the New Wave could be without it. A note, however: although the piece has already been anthologised in English, I was unhappy with aspects of the various existing translations. As a result, the reader will find here a brand-new translation of this now classic article. This new edition also includes three other additional articles, by Raymond Borde, Luc Moullet and Georges Sadoul, all of them discussions of Godard's film *À bout de souffle*, as well as a substantial and comprehensive introduction by Ginette Vincendeau that puts the Nouvelle Vague phenomenon into perspective. I decided to retain the bulk of my original linking commentary (which should be seen in its historical context: it was written at a time when film studies and indeed semiotics were still in their infancy). Otherwise, the changes I have made to the original text of the translations and commentary are minimal.

Peter Graham, March 2009

Preface to the 1968 Edition

Almost exactly ten years ago, the Nouvelle Vague burst on to the French film scene. Like the British Angry Young Men movement, it was less a movement than a useful journalistic catchphrase; under it, a very heterogeneous bunch of filmmakers were lumped together, some of them readily, but most of them willy-nilly.

But the Nouvelle Vague did have a nucleus of new directors who shared common cinematic ideals and who had the advantage of being both articulate and in control of a mouthpiece that had a certain prestige: *Cahiers du cinéma*. François Truffaut, Jean-Luc Godard, Claude Chabrol, Jacques Rivette, Eric Rohmer and Jacques Doniol-Valcroze all made their first features in 1958–9, and, naturally enough, one has the impression when reading the austere, august pages of *Cahiers* of that period that they were the Nouvelle Vague. This transition, en bloc, and within the space of a year, of a group of men from criticism (or, if you like, theory

Jean-Pierre Léaud (left) in *Les Quatre cents coups* (1959).

– for their criticism was always theoretical) to creation must be unparalleled in the history of the cinema and perhaps all other arts.

Most of the films of the *Cahiers* directors are well known to British filmgoers. The publication of *Cahiers du cinéma* in English now makes their writing available too. But its place in contemporary French criticism and culture may be less familiar. One of the aims of this book is to fill in some of the gaps: to trace the origins of their aesthetics, to indicate the enormous influence of the late André Bazin, to give examples of the sort of criticism they were writing before they became directors, and to suggest some of the problems of transition.

But I hope also to give a fairer and more representative picture of the currents of French film criticism than the one to be obtained from the pages of *Cahiers*. It has often been assumed, and understandably so because of the Nouvelle Vague, that *Cahiers* represents the only important school of criticism. There are, of course, several other good film magazines in France (such as *Cinéma '68*, for example). But the only one which could be said to form a school, and a school diametrically opposed to that of *Cahiers*, is *Positif*. The critics of *Positif* were not lucky, or adroit, enough to cash in on the Nouvelle Vague phenomenon and pass, as many of them would have liked to have done, from criticism to direction. But they none the less represent a wide section of critical opinion. And so two of their most important articles on the Nouvelle Vague have been included as a foil to the other pieces.

But the phenomenon of the Nouvelle Vague was not purely a question of cinematic ideology. It was above all a revolution in production, in the attitude of the public and, in particular, producers. If it allowed the *Cahiers* group, like skilful surf-riders, to sweep along just ahead of the crest of the wave and give the impression of drawing along with them other new directors, the facts of the situation were that experienced makers of shorts, such as Alain Resnais and Georges Franju, had the chance to make their first features; and it became much easier for young filmmakers such as Alexandre Astruc, Roger Vadim and Louis Malle, who had already made one feature, to go on to make others.

Peter Graham, 1968

Acknowledgments for the 2022 Edition

The first thanks for this book go to Peter Graham who enthusiastically worked on this new edition until his sudden death in July 2020. In addition, Ginette Vincendeau would like to thank Jen Wallace, who, at short notice, translated most of the articles in the new section of this edition and the students, colleagues, friends and family who helped in various ways with the selection and retrieval of articles, the translations and the editing of the book: Antoine de Baecque, Catherine and Jean-Loup Bourget, Sarah Cooper, Marion Hallet, Véronique Liaigre, Elizabeth Miller, Richard Neupert, Rym Ouartsi, Brigitte Rollet, Geneviève Sellier and Belèn Vidal. Special thanks to Simon Caulkin for his help with the translations. Thank you also to the anonymous readers of the proposal for this new version, who all supported it, and pointed us in the direction of Marie-Claire Ropars-Wuilleumier's early work. Finally, I am grateful to Rebecca Barden for her continued support – she had overseen the 2009 edition at BFI Publishing, and it was a joy to discover that she was to be in charge of the new edition at Bloomsbury.

The Editors

Peter Graham was a filmmaker, freelance film and cookery writer and a translator. He was the author of, among other things, *A Dictionary of the Cinema* (Tantivy Press, 1968) and *Mourjou: The Life and Food of an Auvergne Village* (Penguin/Viking, 1998).

Ginette Vincendeau is Professor of Film Studies at King's College, London. Her books include *Stars and Stardom in French Cinema* (Continuum, 2000), *Jean-Pierre Melville, An American in Paris* (BFI, 2003), *La Haine* (I. B. Tauris, 2005) and *Brigitte Bardot* (BFI/Palgrave Macmillan, 2013). She is completing a book on Claude Autant-Lara.

Acknowledgments for the 2009 Edition

Peter Graham and Ginette Vincendeau would like to extend their thanks to all those who helped prepare and bring about this new edition: Rebecca Barden, Charles Barr, Simon Caulkin, Sophia Contento, Sophie, Guy and Pierre Delanoue, Jonathan and Rina Fenby, Susan Hayward, Tony Kitzinger, Min Lee, Andrew Lockett, Michel Marie, Brian Oatley, Valerie Orpen, V. F. Perkins, Alastair Phillips, Geneviève Sellier, Paul-Louis Thirard, Jean-Louis, Odette and Raymond Vincendeau and Leila Wimmer.

Acknowledgments for the 1968 Edition

We should like to thank the editors of *Cahiers du cinéma* and *Positif* for permitting us to translate and reproduce our translation of the articles in this book; for permission to reproduce the article 'The Evolution of Film Language', from André Bazin's *Qu'est-ce que le cinéma?*, we should like to thank the University of California Press who are the holders of the English- language rights of Bazin's book, and published a selection of essays from it, translated by Hugh Gray, under the title *What Is Cinema?*

Stills are by courtesy of Contemporary, Gala, Compton/Cameo, Rank, Connoisseur, Columbia, 20th Century-Fox, Film Traders, Miracle Films, Paramount and Regal.

Introduction: Sixty Years of the French New Wave, from Hysteria to Nostalgia and Beyond

GINETTE VINCENDEAU

'Boy Directors, Some Ex-Film Critics, Dominate Entries at Cannes'
Variety reporting on the 1959 Cannes film festival.[1]

The French New Wave has cast a long shadow over world cinema ever since the legendary 'Young Turks' – François Truffaut, Jean-Luc Godard, Claude Chabrol and others – burst on the scene in the late 1950s and their films entered the cinematic pantheon. Reflecting on the phenomenon barely ten years on in 1968, Peter Graham's pioneering anthology pinpointed the passionate

Jean-Pierre Léaud (left), Jean Cocteau (centre) and François Truffaut (right) at the 1959 Cannes Film Festival.

polemics it generated. In the fifty years since the book, and more than half a century since the New Wave itself, many, many more books and articles on the topic have appeared, as witnessed by the bibliography at the end of this volume. What follows is not yet another history of the French New Wave but a survey of the ways in which it has been received and interpreted down the years. Like all historical phenomena, the New Wave has meant different things to different people at different times, this process of canon formation throwing some light on the fascination the New Wave films have continued to exert on viewers and why the New Wave is such a critical landmark in cinema.

Early polemics

Histories of the cinema all agree that the New Wave represents a radical break: it spread new ways of producing and making films (cheaply, quickly, outside the mainstream), it popularized the use of lighter technologies, made more 'realist' aesthetics fashionable, and introduced a new generation of directors, stars, cinematographers, producers and composers to the world. It also, significantly, transformed the way people saw and analysed films, in particular establishing the centrality of the cinematic auteur as supreme creative force. Behind this consensus, honed over the last sixty years, however, lie fluctuating critical fortunes. While the New Wave was an instant hit with audiences and certain critical factions, others such as the *Positif*-aligned writers who published a violent attack in a 1962 edition of the journal *Premier Plan*, found it 'very vague and not all that new',[2] and the scriptwriter Henri Jeanson sneered about the movement as a ripple 'in a washbasin'.[3] Why such virulence?

The immediate post-war period in France witnessed an unparalleled flourishing of film culture, out of which grew the *ciné-club* movement dominated by the figure of André Bazin, and including other important figures such as Roger Leenhardt. The vibrant new film culture saw the increased role of the Cinémathèque Française, the explosion of new film journals *(La Gazette du cinéma, La Revue du cinéma, Les Cahiers du cinéma, Positif,*[4] as well as important writing on film in other important cultural publications such as *Esprit* and *Les Lettres françaises*)[5] and the popularity of alternative film festivals such as the 'Festival du film maudit' in 1949. Shifting factions of young critics coalesced around these outlets, and an eager audience arose, drawn from the new intellectual middle classes. This cinephile ferment was unique to France, as was the level of passion and polemical fire, in the writing of the new critics, as several articles in this volume illustrate: in particular François Truffaut's notorious 'A certain tendency in French cinema', Robert Benayoun's 'The Emperor has no Clothes', and Gérard Gozlan's 'In Praise of André Bazin'.

Behind the outspoken debates lay hidden rifts, the product of the trauma of the 1940 defeat and German occupation which left long-lasting divisions in all spheres of life,[6] including film criticism. Already before the war, film writing followed sharp political lines: the communist Georges Sadoul vs. the fascist François Vinneuil (a.k.a. Lucien Rebatet) and Robert Brasillach.[7] After the war broad left-right divisions persisted but were complicated by the fact that Resistance-associated papers such as *L'Écran français* had published a spectrum of positions (including communist writers but also Catholics like Bazin) on the one hand, and on the other by the Surrealist-influenced anti-clerical left-wing writers who would form the bulk of *Positif*, explaining, as Peter Graham notes, the recurring references to religion in their texts. From the start, François Truffaut, Eric Rohmer, Jean-Luc Godard, Claude Chabrol and others associated with *Cahiers du cinéma* (founded April 1951), while being close to Bazin, positioned themselves further to the right, and in some cases the extreme right.[8] From their mentor's theories on realism and the ontology of the filmic image they retained the moral, even mystical concerns, but stripped away Bazin's political militancy – in part explaining accusations of fascism levelled at them by *Positif* and *Premier Plan*.

The early film criticism of the *Cahiers du cinéma* group was controversial in other ways too, explaining the extreme reactions against what might seem at first sight 'just' film criticism. Alexandre Astruc's 'caméra-stylo' and Truffaut's 'A certain tendency in French cinema' became the aesthetic manifestos of the *politique des auteurs*; this is why both are included in this volume, even though they are not, strictly speaking, 'about' the New Wave. The *politique des auteurs* as a set of ideas (rather than a 'theory') was iconoclastic in at least three ways – as an attack on mainstream French cinema, as a defence of Hollywood, and as a radical rethinking of the place of cinema within culture. 'A certain tendency in French cinema' is extremely partial,[9] but it targets two key French genres of the time, psychological dramas and costume films, and the directors (Yves Allégret, Jean Delannoy, Claude Autant-Lara, René Clément), scriptwriters (Jean Aurenche, Pierre Bost, Henri Jeanson) and, more or less explicitly, the stars (Michèle Morgan, Jean Gabin, Gérard Philipe, Edwige Feuillère) associated with them. Truffaut's insolent oedipal rebellion against the *cinéma de papa* attacked the hegemonic 'well-made films' that displayed the craft of the French film industry then in its heyday, turning in the process the word quality, as in 'Tradition of Quality' into a term of abuse. From French production, only a select band of great directors such as Jean Renoir found grace in Truffaut's eyes, along with a tiny selection of figures, such as Jacques Tati, Robert Bresson, Jean-Pierre Melville and Agnès Varda, who worked independently outside the mainstream.

The young critics' defence of American cinema was also daring, if paradoxical. Having disparaged French genre cinema, they chose Hollywood models among …

Agnès Varda (standing), Alain Resnais (left), Silvia Monfort and Philippe Noiret (right) on the shoot of Varda's *La Pointe Courte* (1954).

genre filmmakers. But in doing so, the 'Hitchcocko-Hawksians', the 'Mac-mahoni-ans'[10] (worshippers of Raoul Walsh, Fritz Lang, Otto Preminger and Joseph Losey) and the fans of Nicholas Ray flew in the face of both Bazin's humanist theories, and communist criticism, which for different reasons (moral for the former, polit-ical for the latter) privileged films with a social content. One way to achieve this was through the emphasis on *mise-en-scène* as ultimate source of meaning, which enabled them to by-pass social, political and moral concerns. This is the gist of Chabrol's 'Little Themes', also in this volume. Another strategy was to weld these ideas to those of Astruc and Bazin who had earlier, in different ways, propounded romantic notions of the director as artist, the great figures being able to express their world-view within, or against the 'system' – Astruc in the 'caméra-stylo' arti-cle, Bazin in his defence of directors such as Orson Welles and William Wyler.[11] These directors' genius was deemed to be expressed through *mise-en-scène* choices such as long takes, elaborate camera movements and depth-of-field, their tools, akin to a writer's pen or a painter's brush. The power and historical legacy of the *politique des auteurs* was also reinforced by a peculiarly French law (of 11 March 1957) which gave the director unprecedented powers, concurrently diminishing the role of producer or scriptwriter.[12]

Commenting on the animosity between *Cahiers du cinéma* and *Positif*, Michel Ciment, long-time editor of the latter, admits that the '*politique des auteurs* divided the two camps before 1959',[13] a remark well supported by some of the texts in this volume. With hindsight though, we know that *Positif*, like *Cahiers du cinéma*, became one of the prime defenders of auteur cinema (albeit with variations in the directors championed) and that the impact of the *politique* would be long-lasting and universal, relayed in the UK by *Movie* and the USA by Andrew Sarris. Starting with Astruc's literary model in the 'caméra stylo' article, the *politique des auteurs* was the prime force in lifting the cinema off its industrial background and separating it from popular cinema. In the process, it claimed a new cultural legitimacy for film, promoting it fully to the realm of art. Much later, critics like Noël Burch, Antoine de Baecque and Leila Wimmer[14] analysed these tactics as an archetypal search for cultural 'distinction', following the work of Pierre Bourdieu. At the time, the critical manoeuvers were both overshadowed and extended by a momentous move on the part of the young critics: they started directing films.

The transition to filmmaking altered the critics' place within the industry and the French cultural scene – epitomized by Truffaut's banning from the Cannes festival in the wake of 'A certain tendency in French cinema' and then taking it by storm in 1959 with *Les Quatre cents coups*. Nevertheless, the old antagonisms persisted and the attacks against the New Wave films in this volume and elsewhere had more to do with the authors' political positions and friendships (Truffaut admiring the fascist Lucien Rebatet, Godard's connection to the right-wing writer Jean Parvulesco, or Chabrol to Jean-Marie Le Pen[15]) than, in most cases, the films themselves. Although Michel Ciment claims that the journal was not opposed to the New Wave *en bloc*,[16] he admits that there was still 'ferocious hostility from many *Positif* writers towards key New Wave directors' (especially Godard and Chabrol).[17] The three texts on *À bout de souffle* reproduced in this volume are a fair indication of these debates. Among them, Sadoul's piece also illustrates the fact that by the time the New Wave films came out, they paradoxically garnered the approval of communist critics. While noticing the lack of social anchorage in the films, and the privileged background from which most filmmakers came, Sadoul embraced the New Wave, saluting it as a 'breath of fresh air' in French cinema.[18] As Laurent Marie explains, this change of line coincided with the beginning of de-Stalinization: film content no longer reigned supreme and style could be considered. The communist agenda concurrently also shifted to a nationalist defence of French cinema (in the context of the threat from Hollywood) and the 'wish to inscribe the new generation within the national patrimony'.[19]

That the New Wave films immediately provoked huge enthusiasm is manifest in their significant critical and/or box-office success[20] and in the enormous amount of press reaction they elicited. Film journals published special issues, including of course *Cahiers du cinéma* and *Positif*, sparking off lively debates that went beyond the French borders. A typical example is the winter 1959 issue of *Film Quarterly* which includes two radically different views of the New Wave, one by theoretician Noël Burch and the other by historian Eugen Weber, introduced by a note indicating that 'The two articles differ markedly in their basic assumptions and their evaluations of the intentions and merits of these filmmakers. We present them both in the hope that [...] a useful critical debate will ensue.'[21] The prominence of the films was underpinned by a sense of the movement being significant to French society beyond 'mere' cinema. The label *Nouvelle Vague* (New Wave) notoriously came from the pen of journalist Françoise Giroud writing in the fashionable news magazine *L'Express* in 1957,[22] designating a sense of renewal, of a new generation emerging from the devastation of the war. Giroud's insight found an echo in the interest the films elicited in terms of their portrayal of a changing France, in particular young people's new moral and sexual codes. For instance, *L'Express* in October 1960 published an enquiry into the identity of 'Mademoiselle Nouvelle Vague',[23] while the following year a team of sociologists including Evelyne Sullerot and Edgar Morin published a wide-scale comparative study of French mainstream cinema and New Wave films, in the first issue of the journal *Communications*.[24] A separate, and influential, publication by Sullerot derived from the same project explored the 'identikit' of the typical New Wave heroine, a piece now included in section III of this book.[25] André S. Labarthe, in the first 'book' (it is a short pamphlet) on the topic saw the coherence of the New Wave in terms of its mix of documentary and fiction.[26] And Jacques Siclier reflected in 1961, apropos of *À bout de souffle*, 'In the audience's mind, the "New Wave" was defined, then, by particular kinds of characters and a non-conformist universe.'[27] Antoine de Baecque echoed this feeling much later when he characterised the New Wave as 'the first film movement to have stylized, in the present, in the immediacy of its history, the world of its contemporaries'.[28] The New Wave films thus provided a snapshot of the country as it was experiencing the first phase of its post-war economic boom, known as the *trente glorieuses*, under the new political regime of General de Gaulle, in power since 1958. The films showed a country attempting to free itself from the shackles of a predominantly conservative, Catholic and patriarchal culture and, although this was less visible, as it was struggling with decolonisation. Their modernity also chimed with other intellectual concerns. As Guy Gauthier later noted, the period's desire for change was reflected in a series of searches for 'the new', for example in terms of new theatre, new criticism, new novel (*nouveau roman*), new *chanson*, and new realism in painting.[29]

However, just as the French New Wave was becoming a critical sensation abroad (the British critic Raymond Durgnat, published a book about it in 1963[30]), the honeymoon was already over in France. After spectacular early successes, filmmakers like Truffaut and Godard made relatively unpopular second films (*Tirez sur le pianiste, Une femme est une femme*) and a violent backlash unleashed what Antoine de Baecque has called a 'paternal punishment'.[31] The hostility was no longer confined to the pages of *Positif*. A number of directors whom Truffaut had targeted in 'A certain tendency in French cinema', such as Jean Delannoy and Claude Autant-Lara, never forgave him, and nor did the scriptwriter Henri Jeanson. The hallmarks of New Wave cinema – spontaneous dialogue, freewheeling photography, iconoclastic editing, nonchalant performances – now, in turn, became terms of abuse – as summed up by a journalist who railed against the

Roger Duchesne (left) in Jean-Pierre Melville's *Bob le flambeur* (1956).

'improvised kind of filmmaking of this "New Wave" we're tired of hearing about.'[32] Even Jean-Pierre Melville, hailed as a precursor with his thriller *Bob le flambeur* (1956) – to which Godard pays tribute in *À bout de souffle* – became embroiled in a polemic against Truffaut,[33] and he decreed in 1967 that 'The New Wave was an inexpensive way of making films. That's all.'[34] This was not just sour grapes. A key fact is that these arguments took place against a backdrop of dramatically declining audiences. From 354.7m spectators in 1960, French audiences decreased to 184.4m in 1970. Seen as the white hope of French cinema in 1959–60, the New Wave was now accused of having precipitated its downfall: 'what they called the New Wave contributed enormously to the deterioration of French cinema.'[35] These feelings were widespread; for instance, as Richard Neupert discusses, the American trade magazine *Variety* quickly turned to negative views: 'By 1960 nearly every article in *Variety* speaks of the New Wave in the past tense.'[36]

Nevertheless, despite this downturn, in the long run the romantic glamour of the young rebels proved a winning formula, and their fusion of criticism with filmmaking both legitimised the critical positions and enhanced their films' exposure and status. Colin MacCabe may overstate his case in declaring *Cahiers du cinéma* 'the most significant journal of the twentieth-century,'[37] but the fact remains that its writing significantly shaped the field, contributing in the process to the establishment of film studies as an academic discipline and to some of its priorities. For a long time, film historians took Truffaut's polemical cracks in 'A certain tendency in French cinema' at face value (forgetting that he quickly recanted, as can be seen in the 1962 interview reproduced in this volume). Thus 1950s French mainstream cinema is routinely disparaged as 'moribund', and this has for a long time precluded research into popular French genre cinema. Historians like Richard Abel have rightly pointed out that the New Wave was in effect a 'second wave', coming after the 'first wave' of the 1920s,[38] and Geoffrey Nowell-Smith is keen to replace it in the context of other cinematic 'waves', especially in Europe.[39] Nevertheless, one has to agree with Serge Daney that, at the turn of the 1960s in France, 'something unique took place with the New Wave.'[40]

New Wave: diverse or unified? The rise of auteur studies in the 1960s

As soon as the canonical films of 1959–60 came out (*Le Beau Serge, Les Cousins, Les Quatre cents coups, Hiroshima mon amour, À bout de souffle*), the notion that the New Wave was a 'movement' was both self-evident and problematic. In their introductory chapter on French cinema from 1960 to 2004, Michael Temple and Michael Witt ask the rhetorical question, 'Does a New Wave Really

Exist?,[41] citing a survey conducted by the newspaper *Le Monde* in August 1959, which contained interviews with directors such as Astruc, Chabrol and Roger Vadim. Unsurprisingly, since artists detest being labelled as part of a movement, all replied 'No'. In his memoirs Chabrol denied there was such a thing as the New Wave, saying, 'In 1958 and 1959, myself and the whole *Cahiers* team, once we started making films, were promoted like a brand of soap,'[42] and many have echoed the feeling that the New Wave was nothing but a marketing 'gimmick'. Yet, who was 'in' and who was 'out', how they could be classified and according to what criteria, what they had in common, as well as when the New Wave started and when it finished, has exercised virtually single critic or scholar writing on the movement.

As early as February 1958, in an article entitled '40 under 40: the young academy of French cinema',[43] Pierre Billard tried to identify a 'young' generation purely on the grounds of age. His results are limited as his criterion means that, for instance a mainstream director like Henri Verneuil is included in the 'new generation' while many key New Wave directors are absent, since they had not made their first feature yet. More reliable criteria have included the large number of first

Corinne Marchand (left) and Agnès Varda on the shoot of Varda's *Cléo de 5 à 7* (1962).

features made at the turn of the 1960s (reportedly 160 between 1958 and 1963), or the prominence of low-budget films.[44] Nevertheless, a clear consensus emerged rapidly, enshrined in Jacques Siclier's 1961 book *Nouvelle vague?* and in the special issue of *Cahiers du cinéma* of December 1962, namely the supremacy of the *Cahiers du cinéma*, or 'Right Bank' group, organised in a set of concentric circles: Chabrol, Godard and Truffaut at the centre, immediately surrounded by Rohmer and Rivette, and then by Pierre Kast, Jacques Doniol-Valcroze, André S. Labarthe, Jean Douchet and Astruc. Siclier's table of contents, for instance, divides the New Wave into precursors, the *Cahiers du cinéma* team and 'a few others'.[45] Always apart – and routinely marginalised in collective accounts of the New Wave – is the 'Left Bank' group of Varda, Resnais and Chris Marker. Still further afield are the precursors (Melville, Bresson, Louis Malle), the 'satellites' (Jean-Daniel Pollet, Jacques Rozier), the 'unclassifiable' (Jacques Demy), the 'commercial' (Vadim), the novelist-turned-filmmaker (Alain Robbe-Grillet), those connected to documentary and *cinéma vérité* (Jean Rouch, Pierre Schendoerffer), the 'ancestors' and 'uncles' in Serge Daney's expression,[46] while Raymond Durgnat names 35 directors whose films were made between the late 1940s and the early 1950s, casting his net very wide indeed to include other marginal figures such as Peter Brook, Jacques Baratier and Jean-Pierre Mocky.[47]

Clearly, the wider the group, the more diffuse the common traits, and reputations have waxed and waned: for instance debates at the time almost inevitably include Marcel Camus' 1958 *Orfeu Negro*, now largely forgotten. Hence the tendency to reframe the concept to a small unit such as the *Cahiers du cinéma* Young Turks. In 1976 James Monaco wrote the transparently named *The New Wave: Truffaut, Godard, Chabrol, Rohmer, Rivette* in which he argues that its defining feature is the *cerebral* nature of the films: 'all of them see film essentially as a phenomenon of intelligence.'[48] Nevertheless the book immediately breaks down into individual directors, with a clear pecking order: there are five chapters devoted to Godard, four to Truffaut, and one to each of the other three. This hierarchy is confirmed by a quick (non-exhaustive) poll of the number of books in French and in English devoted to New Wave directors up to the present day: Godard and Truffaut win hands down, with over thirty books (in French and English) each, whereas for the others, the numbers are mostly in single figures and often extremely small. A few notable exceptions must be mentioned. Of the 'left bank' group, Resnais was, for a long time, the most frequently studied, from the beginning, because of the complex, literary, and cerebral nature of his work; but over the last ten to fifteen years, Varda and Demy have seen a dramatic surge in their critical reputation – as is discussed at the end of this introduction. On the other hand, a pioneering figure like Chabrol, despite being considered part of the inner circle, is relatively little studied, no doubt because of the heterogeneous nature of his work after his early New Wave trilogy of *Le Beau Serge*, *Les Cousins* and *Les Bonnes femmes*. It will be observed that all the discussions above are based on directors, and indeed the canonization of the New Wave *as a group of directors* has remained hegemonic, although over the years, some widening to other categories of personnel eventually took place. Gradually, work on producers (Anatole Dauman, Georges de Beauregard, Pierre Braunberger, Raoul Lévy, Mag Bodard), cinematographers (Raoul Coutard), composers (Georges Delerue) and critics (Bazin), emerged, in the form of memoirs or biographies (often hagiographies). The same is true of actors (Jeanne Moreau, Anna Karina, Bernadette Lafont, Jean-Pierre Léaud) until the 1990s when star studies began to develop more analytical approaches to the analysis of stars and performance in French cinema.

The emphasis on directors continued nevertheless. Even Michel Marie's ambitious concept of the New Wave as an 'artistic school' in his 1998 book – a 'school' on the model of art history, with a body of theories, manifestoes, a coherent group of artists, promotional strategies, etc.[49] – privileges directors. Back in the 1960s, the accent on directors continued with an instant search for 'heirs' – Jean Eustache, Philippe Garrel, and then André Téchiné were seen in this light, as 'a generation of sons both inspired and crushed [by the New Wave].'[50] More fundamentally, the 1960s, in the wake of the New Wave, was to be the era of auteur studies and in 2002, Richard Neupert still justified the organization of his book *A History of the French New Wave Cinema* as such: 'The bulk of the book remains organized around directors, since this was an auteur-centered era.'[51] Other examples abound. Freddy Buache's survey book *Le Cinéma français des années 60* (whose cover features stills from four New Wave films) is almost entirely organised around directors – New Wave stalwarts like Godard, Truffaut and Chabrol, and a few new figures (Alain Cavalier, Pierre Etaix); only half-a dozen pages entitled 'In the tradition' are devoted to popular cinema. This is a particularly clear example of perhaps the most enduring legacy of the *politique des auteurs,* namely the split between auteur cinema (worthy of interest) and popular genre cinema (beneath contempt). In terms of French (and European) cinema, this has underpinned a large quantity of books, film festivals and film courses, and the perception of the public ever since. This is not to say that there were no challenges. Quite early on, Penelope Houston in the UK and Pauline Kael in the US, took the *politique des auteurs* to task in a number of ways, including along the lines of sexism – these dissenting voices are, as Leila Wimmer points out, interestingly gendered.[52] However, it will take decades for these gender concerns to resurface. In the more immediate period following the New Wave, other challenges took precedence.

The 1970s: the New Wave vanishes

The 'Cinémathèque affair' of February 1968, during which Culture minister André Malraux sacked its director Henri Langlois, is often thought of as a precursor of the May '68 events. After an outcry by New Wave filmmakers, Langlois was reinstated. In May, the union of film technicians gathered film personnel under the banner of the *Etats Généraux du cinéma* (Estates General of the Cinema), the Cannes film festival was boycotted, solidarity with students and strikers was expressed. This gave the impression that New Wave filmmakers were at the forefront of political struggles. Yet, in retrospect, May '68 marks the swansong of the New Wave rather than a new beginning. Things had moved on.

May '68 introduced a break with New Wave issues and concerns, with the rise of the political agenda. *Cahiers du cinéma* moved violently against its own earlier aesthetic approach, as well as against Hollywood.[53] In terms of the filmmakers, a parting of the ways took place. Some became ultra-politicized and/or experimental – Godard, Marker – or worked collaboratively, in a challenge to individual authorship: the Godard-Gorin collaboration, the *Loin du Viêt-nam* portmanteau film (1967, which included Godard, Varda and Resnais but also Claude Lelouch). Others, on the other hand, like Rohmer with *Ma nuit chez Maud* or Truffaut with

Chris Marker (right) in the 1960s.

La Sirène du Mississipi (both 1969), turned their backs on politics. The New Wave had fragmented, and its aesthetic concerns were off the critical agenda. We see this clearly reflected in publications: after the first spate of works in the 1960s (Labarthe, Siclier, Durgnat, Graham), books and articles on the New Wave become thin on the ground. Between 1968 and the 1990s, publications generally take the New Wave as a *landmark* but do not significantly analyse it *per se*. They examine what came before (Bazin's essays, *Le cinéma français de la Libération à la Nouvelle Vague* published in 1983) or after (Claire Clouzot's *Le cinéma français depuis la nouvelle vague* in 1972). Only one book on the New Wave proper came out in the 1970s (by James Monaco), but as discussed above it focuses on a collection of individual filmmakers rather than an overview of the movement. New excitement came from developments such as avant-garde group Zanzibar films[54] and the rise of women's cinema, while trends in literary theory (Roland Barthes) and philosophy (Michel Foucault) were dealing severe blows to the notion of the auteur, going as far as 'killing' him, or her, but mostly him.[55]

Critical interest in the New Wave, such as it was, came in the guise of opposition. Philippe Pilard's discussion of the New Wave and politics in late 1969 indicted its detachment from current events and history.[56] Jean-Pierre Jeancolas' retrospective assessment in 1979 was severe: 'the New Wave replaced the underground and killed any manifestation of it in France for a decade.'[57] Even more severe condemnation came from abroad. In 1971, the British Marxist scholar Terry Lovell wrote a critical account of the apolitical nature of characters in New Wave films, in which she argued that 'The lack of any social dimension is characteristic of the typical New Wave film. Its heroes are neither personally nor socially integrated, and are dissociated from their social roles.'[58] Then, in a celebrated two-part article, John Hess published a long, sustained attack on the apolitical nature of the *politique des auteurs* in the American journal *Jump Cut* in 1974.[59] In some ways Lovell's and Hess' arguments were similar to those made by Borde *et al* in *Premier plan* ten years earlier. True, but while Borde, Gozlan and Benayoun's rhetoric was underpinned by left-wing militancy and fuelled by personal hostility to the filmmakers, Hess and Lovell's analyses were couched in terms of more systematic Marxist theory. Meanwhile the era saw the rise of academic film studies which in its initial phase, was influenced by the work of Christian Metz, and dominated by semiology, structuralism and psychoanalysis. Whether from the Anglo-American or the French camps, auteur studies were, temporarily, off the map. They would resurface in the 1980s, with the arrival of a new generation of filmmakers, critics and scholars, especially as film studies fully entered the academy.

The academic turn (I) – rebuilding the canon

After the fallow 1970s, a reclaiming of the New Wave slowly gathered momentum through the 1980s, and especially the 1990s, with a peak around the 40th anniversary in 1998. The effect was to put it back on a pedestal, albeit in historically more informed ways. For, if the fierce attacks against New Wave cinema in the 1960s were underpinned by falling attendances and a sense of the vulnerability of the French film *industry*, by the 1980s and 1990s, the debate had shifted to more fundamental interrogations about the 'end of cinema'. Against a background of the 'contamination' of cinema from advertising, television, video and computer-generated images, the New Wave cinema, in its heady celebration of 'pure' cinephile pleasure, seemed like the perfect antidote. Four authors emerge from the bulk of new writing on the movement: Serge Daney, Jean Douchet, Michel Marie and Antoine de Baecque. From different institutional perspectives (Daney and Douchet are critics, Marie and de Baecque academics), their four-pronged movement gave the New Wave prime of place again.

An early salvo came from the prominent *Cahiers du cinéma* critic Serge Daney who in a 1988 article entitled 'The New Wave, a genealogical approach'[60] makes the astute point that the novelty and impact of the New Wave derived not from the weakness of a 'moribund' French film industry – as had been argued before, following Truffaut's 'A certain tendency in French cinema' – but on the contrary from its strength. However, his argument, couched as an oedipal rebellion, also displays a strong sense of nostalgia. Daney eulogises about the fact that 'The New Wave filmmakers were able to know personally some of the giants who were in at the start of the cinema' and he subscribes to the romantic view of auteurs as (male) 'loners'.[61] Then in 1997–8 three books came out in rapid succession. In his 1997 concise volume, Michel Marie offered a particularly lucid analysis of the movement in terms of its critical and production context, convincingly arguing for it to be seen, as already mentioned, as an artistic 'school'. The following year, Antoine de Baecque published an excellent socio-cultural analysis of the New Wave as the 'portrait of a young generation', identifying the roots of *cinephilia* in a disenfranchised generation (both writers and audiences) who latched onto the cinema as a substitute for political commitment. However, in concluding that 'we are left with a myth', he himself contributed to an ultimately reverential (re)mythologizing of the New Wave – unsurprisingly, since he, like Daney, had worked for *Cahiers du cinéma*. In 1998 too came out the beautifully produced *Nouvelle Vague* by Jean Douchet. The book is eccentric, biased and hostile to academic film studies, yet a valuable resource for its iconography and inclusion of contemporary reviews. A belated contribution by one of the original (albeit marginal) New Wave critics-turned-filmmakers, Douchet's *Nouvelle Vague* is also the clearest manifestation of the creeping nostalgia for the movement 40 years on, including for *cinephilia* itself, as New Wave practitioners were now men and women in their seventies or older, though most of them still making films (except Truffaut who had died in 1984).

De Baecque and Marie, together with the American scholar Richard Neupert were instrumental in consolidating the position of the French New Wave in the University syllabus. But none of them challenged the bias towards the *Cahiers du cinéma* group; even Neupert's very detailed *A History of the French New Wave Cinema* only acquired a chapter on the 'Left Bank group' in its second edition in 2007. And Peter Graham's decision to balance the *Cahiers du cinéma* views with those emanating from *Positif* (and from the 2009 edition of this book, *Premier Plan* too), thus affording valuable insight into the French debates of the time, was never really taken up. For instance the volumes of selected *Cahiers du cinéma* pieces in English edited by Jim Hillier in 1985 and 1992, and continued by Nick Browne in 1989 and David Wilson in 2000 were never matched by collections from 'the other side'.[62] In terms of the directors, the picture is more balanced, and indeed over time the rise of interest in Varda, Demy and Marker as part of the New Wave canon has been noticeable, as seen for instance in the series of monographs on French directors published by Manchester University Press. Others also extended the range towards the 'Left Bank' New Wave through studies of its links to the *nouveau roman*, such as T. Jefferson Kline (1992), Lynn Higgins (1996) and Dorota Ostrowska (2008) – most of these studies emanating from French and literary studies rather than film studies, as if the *Cahiers du cinéma*'s 'inner circle' remained somehow the preserve of Film Studies. And generally, these works too retain a reverential position. For iconoclastic approaches, we need to turn to different paradigms.

The academic turn (II) – challenging the canon

We have seen how the conjunction of influential critical writing and filmmaking in a select group of directors produced not only a 'brand' for the New Wave cinema (even though not all films were made by critics and not all critics made films), but also an influential body of writing. This has been dominated – from the passionate debates of the late 1950s to the present day – by the formal/aesthetic approaches derived from the *politique des auteurs*, despite sporadic ideologically-based attacks such as those of *Positif* and *Premier Plan* in the 1960s, and John Hess and Terry Lovell in the 1970s. The development of approaches derived from industrial history, cultural studies and gender studies, have produced more sustained and more profound challenges.

Inspired by the historicist approach developed by David Bordwell, Kristin Thompson and Janet Staiger in their seminal 1985 book *The Classical Hollywood Cinema*,[63] the Australian academic Colin Crisp wrote in 1993 a study of the 'classic French cinema' from 1930 to 1960. In a brief chapter at the end of the book, Crisp attacks the idea of the New Wave as a radical break from mainstream French cinema derived from Truffaut's rhetoric. Rejecting the view of French mainstream cinema as in decline, Crisp argues that we should see the New Wave 'not as a displacement of the classic cinema but rather as a logical outcome and continuation of it',[64] insofar as it was a prominent offshoot of existing art cinema, generated by 'a set of processes and mechanisms orchestrated within the classic cinema.'[65] If the argument exaggerates the continuities between the New Wave and mainstream cinema and does little to account for aesthetic differences, it has the merit of suggesting that New Wave cinema should be regarded as part of a continuum and that we should stop fetishizing its uniqueness (*pace* Serge Daney). Crisp's study was also followed by a larger movement in the 1990s which saw a welcome turning of the spotlight onto French popular cinema. This was concurrently facilitated by the increased availability of films on VHS, then DVD and now streaming platforms, these new media working hand-in-hand with new approaches to film history. The study of popular genre cinema of the 1950s and 1960s, especially gangster films, costume dramas and stars expanded, providing at the very least a better contextualization of the New Wave (in particular, work by Sellier and Vincendeau, as well as Susan Hayward, Jean Montarnal, Raphaëlle Moine, Gwénaëlle Le Gras and Thomas Pillard).[66]

Concurrently, sociological and cultural studies made a belated entry into the study of French cinema (and into French cinema studies), dealing a greater blow to the hegemony of aesthetic/auteurist approaches and in the process affecting New Wave studies. Two indicative works here are those of John Orr, whose 1993 book *Cinema and Modernity*, features a still from *À bout de souffle* on the cover (and devotes some space to New Wave films inside), and of the American cultural historian Kristin Ross. Her *Fast Cars, Clean Bodies: Decolonization and the Reordering of French Culture*[67] in 1995 does not deal directly with the New Wave but usefully charts, among other things, the rise of the new intellectual bourgeoisie that formed its audience, and the socio-cultural import of images of modernity in the films (such as cars and couples). After decades of work concentrating on authorship and/or the aesthetics of *mise-en-scène*, it was time to pay attention to the films' *contents*. Thus, ironically recalling the early sociological surveys that surrounded the emergence of the New Wave, scholars began to look at the films' representation of modern France and its new social mores (from language to sexual behaviour). If these concerns were in evidence in a number

Emmanuelle Riva and Bernard Fresson in Alain Resnais's *Hiroshima mon amour* (1959).

of the Anglo-American works cited above, they took longer to reach France. One trail-blazing work in this respect, though not directly on the New Wave, was Burch and Sellier's *La Drôle de guerre des sexes du cinéma français* (1993) in terms of its bold linking of filmic representations with ideology, especially in relation to gender; directly addressing the New Wave are Jean-Pierre Esquenazi's *Godard and French Society in the 1960s* (2004) and Philippe Mary's *La Nouvelle vague et le cinéma d'auteur. Socio-analyse d'une révolution artistique* (2006),[68] who both reinsert their objects of study into their social context not in terms of a 'reflection' of that context in the films, but of a historical understanding of both the films and their critical parameters – for instance Mary reflects back on the early debates around the *politique des auteurs* as 'the construction of a certain *distance from the political*, the practice of a "disengagement"' and he gives a historical perspective to the *Positif-Cahiers du cinéma* duel in the light of the 19th century artistic and literary debates between the "social bohemia" of Courbet and Champfleury and the 'art for art's sake' bohemia of Baudelaire and Flaubert.[69] Following the work of Bourdieu and Andreas Huyssen, Esquenazi and Mary, as well as Sellier and Burch also show the rise of cinephile criticism and New Wave filmmaking in the light

The new screen idol: Jean-Paul Belmondo in the early 1960s.

of the break between modernist art and popular culture, as a strategic position to create a cultural 'distinction'.

But perhaps the greatest challenge to the orthodoxy of formal/aesthetic analyses of the New Wave has come from gender perspectives. Here too Anglo-American works led the way, as feminist approaches to the cinema for a long time were resisted in France.[70] In 1980, the pioneer feminist critic Laura Mulvey wrote a chapter on Godard's representation of women in Colin MacCabe's book *Godard: Images, Sounds, Politics*, in which she argued that his attitude was eminently ambivalent, both critical of, and complicit with patriarchy (she was writing about later Godard, but her argument applies to early New Wave films). In 1995, Yosefa Loshitzky also approached Godard's films from a gender point of view, offering a trenchant critique, for instance, of his treatment of the Brigitte Bardot character in *Le Mépris*. Building on her earlier work on French cinema, Sellier offered, in *La Nouvelle Vague, un cinéma au masculin singulier* (2006)[71] an overall gender critique of the movement, in particular of the links between masculinity, auteurism and representation, as reflected in the book's title. She shows how the Young Turks of the New Wave were indeed modern filmmakers who cast new actresses in taboo-breaking roles (doing away with the passé mother/whore stereotypes of mainstream cinema for instance), yet in their modernist stance they also portrayed women as obstacles to the self-realization (however suicidal) of the male alter-ego leading characters – as in *À bout de souffle* or *Paris nous appartient* – or adopted an 'entomological' attitude towards them as pathetic or comic figures (typically *Les Bonnes femmes*). That these representations chimed with the directors' own stance as breakaway modern(ist) artists against the Tradition of Quality is one of Sellier's other insights of gender and socio-cultural approaches to the New Wave.

A welcome consequence of the gender challenge to studies of the New Wave, coupled with the growth in feminist film studies more generally, has been to reframe the New Wave canon to incorporate, at last, one of its key figures, Agnès Varda. With the rise of women's cinema from the 1970s, Varda attracted attention as one of the few female directors in French cinema at that time, and the only one in the New Wave: see Françoise Audé's early feminist study in particular.[72] Varda had in fact been recognized as a precursor, if not the 'mother' of the New Wave, right from the beginning with her film *La Pointe Courte*, shot in 1954 on location and produced independently. Indeed, in this volume the new section III, 'The missing perspective', includes tributes to *La Pointe Courte* and to *Cléo de 5 à 7* by

Bernadette Lafont (left) and Stéphane Audran in Claude Chabrol's *Les Bonnes femmes* (1960).

eminent critics such as Bazin and Sadoul. And yet, despite these early accolades Varda was subsequently ignored or marginalised in histories of the movement. After Sandy Flitterman-Lewis opened the way with her 1990 seminal study *To Desire Differently: Feminism and the French Cinema*[73] which recognizes Varda's films as important explorations of the nature of femininity, more work followed by Alison Smith, Valerie Orpen and Sellier. In the 2010s, scholarship on Varda has expanded remarkably, with books by, among others, Marie-Claire Barnet, Bernard Bastide, Kelley Conway, Delphine Benezet, Rebecca J. DeRoo and T. Jefferson Kline.[74] Varda is now recognised as unquestionably one of the most exciting practitioners of the New Wave cinema and *Cléo de 5 à 7* (which is the subject of no fewer than four monographs)[75] has taken its rightful place in the canon of great New Wave films.

Worth mentioning here too is the increasing visibility of Jacques Demy over the last ten years, with a significant amount of works written from queer studies perspectives (especially in English) – see in particular books by Ann E. Duggan and Darren Waldron.[76] Together with the writing on Varda, the new scholarship on Demy helps rebalance our view of the New Wave significantly in the direction of the 'Left Bank', even if, as mentioned earlier, Godard, Truffaut and now Rohmer, continue to dominate scholarly attention. Beyond Varda and Demy, the

Agnès Varda and Jean-Luc Godard during the shoot of Varda's *Cléo de 5 à 7* (1962).

Corinne Marchand in Agnès Varda's *Cléo de 5 à 7* (1962).

books produced over the last ten years are also beginning to show a welcome widening of the New Wave canon to more peripheral figures such as Astruc, Marker, Georges Franju and Kast, but also Alain Cavalier, Jean-Pierre Mocky, Jacqueline Audry, Philippe de Broca and Ousmane Sembène – the latter for his 1966 film *La Noire de/Black Girl* (see the piece by Marie-Claire Ropars-Wuilleumier in part III of this book).[77] Also contributing to a wider understanding of the New Wave, a few studies are now turning the spotlight to hitherto unexplored areas, such as sound (Orlene Denice McMahon), the relationship with other arts (Marion Schmid) and screenwriters (Sarah Leahy and Isabelle Vanderschelden).[78]

The New Wave sixty years on: where to now?

Since the 2009 edition of this book, and with the 60th anniversary in 2019 already behind us, writing on the New Wave has thus continued apace, as reflected in the lengthy bibliography at the end of this volume. Together with the steady production of DVDs, film retrospectives, exhibitions[79] and university courses, these numerous volumes confirm the continuing fascination of the New Wave films, notwithstanding the minority, yet persistent, stream of challenges by writers such as Hess, Sellier, Esquenazi, Mary and recently Yannick Rolandeau.[80] This is in no small part because the films are still fresh and seductive, while they continue to exert an influence on subsequent generations of filmmakers. As director Martin Scorsese put it, 'The New Wave has influenced all filmmakers who have worked since, whether they saw the films or not. […] It submerged cinema like a tidal wave.'[81]

At the time of updating this introduction, in 2022, most of the New Wave filmmakers are gone, many of them in the last ten years (Rohmer and Chabrol died in 2010, Marker in 2012, Bernadette Lafont in 2013, Rivette in 2016, Jeanne Moreau and Emmanuelle Riva in 2017; Varda, Mocky, the producer Mag Bodard, the composer Michel Legrand in 2019 and Jean-Paul Belmondo in 2022) – explaining the flourishing of biographies and critical studies. The passing of these figures is also bound to increase our sense of nostalgia, reflected in the critical material produced about the movement. Following in the footsteps of Jean Douchet's opulent 1998 volume, other beautifully produced albums have begun to appear, that indulge in the striking designs and photographs of the time – see in particular Raymond Cauchetier's 2015 book of New Wave photographs and Christopher Frayling, Tony Nourmand and Graham Marsh's 2019 lavish presentation of New Wave poster art.[82] Concurrently, the New Wave continues to feature as a topic in films that celebrate it as a 'golden age' – from Godard's typically oblique *Nouvelle vague* (1990), to Agnès Varda's *Jacquot de Nantes* (1991), Olivier Assayas' *Irma Vep* (1996), Bernardo Bertolucci's *The Dreamers* (2003), Antoine de Caunes' *Désaccord parfait* (2006), Michel Hazanavicius' *Le Redoutable* (2017), and almost any film featuring Jean-Pierre Léaud since Truffaut's death, from *36 fillette* (1988) to *Irma Vep* (1996), *Le Pornographe* (2001), *Le Havre* (2011) and *Le Lion est mort ce soir* (2017).

I have no doubt that the New Wave will continue to provoke debate, analysis, celebration and critique and that future generations will identify further blind spots in the scholarship and again move the debate in new directions. But whether seething with criticism or suffused with nostalgia, the mass of writing and other productions discussed in this introduction, all show that the New Wave has lost none of its filmic, cultural and social relevance and that it has truly cemented its position in the national and international[83] cinematic patrimony.

Notes

1. Cited in Richard Neupert, 'Dead Champagne: *Variety's* New Wave', *Film History* 10, No. 2 (1998), p. 222.

2. Bernard Chardère, 'Note de l'éditeur', in Raymond Borde, Freddy Buache and Jean Curtelin, *Nouvelle Vague* (Lyon: Premier Plan, Serdoc, 1962), p. 5.

3. Henri Jeanson, quoted in Christophe Moussé, 'Un adversaire coriace: Henri Jeanson', *CinémAction* No. 104, 'Flash-back sur la Nouvelle Vague', 3e trimestre 2002, p. 90.

4. For accounts of these developments, see in particular, Michel Marie, *La nouvelle vague: Une école artistique* (Paris: Nathan, 1997). Published in English as *The French New Wave: An Artistic School* (Malden: Mass.: Blackwell, 2002). Translated by Richard Neupert. See also, Antoine de Baecque, *La nouvelle vague: Portrait d'une jeunesse* (Paris: Flammarion, 1998).

5. See section III in this volume for three pieces by Marie-Claire Ropars-Wuilleumier first published in *Esprit*; two pieces by Georges Sadoul in this volume were first published in *Les Lettres françaises*.

6. See Henry Rousso, *The Vichy Syndrome: history and memory in France since 1944* (Cambridge, MA : Harvard University Press, 1991). Translated by Arthur Goldhammer.

7. See Richard Abel, *French Film Theory and Criticism: a history/anthology, 1907–1939. Vol I. 1907–1929* (Princeton, NJ: Princeton University Press, 1988); Richard Abel, *French Film Theory and Criticism: a history/anthology, 1907–1939. Vol II. 1929–1939* (Princeton, NJ: Princeton University Press, 1988).

8. See Antoine de Baecque, *La Cinéphilie: Invention d'un regard, histoire d'une culture, 1944–1968* (Paris: Fayard, 2003); Hélène Liogier, '1960: Vue d'Espagne, La Nouvelle Vague est fasciste, ou la Nouvelle Vague selon Jean Parvulesco', *1895* (AFRHC), No. 26, December 1998, 127–53.

9. Truffaut noticeably ignores thrillers and comedies, although these were important genres at the time, the latter especially being extremely popular at the box office.

10. So called because their headquarters were the Mac-Mahon cinema in Paris, near the Champs-Elysées. For more details on the Mac-Mahon, see Leila Wimmer, 'Parisian Cinephiles and the Mac-Mahon', in Alastair Phillips and Ginette Vincendeau (eds), *Paris in the Cinema, Beyond the Flâneur* (London: BFI/Palgrave, 2018), pp. 113–24.

11. See André Bazin, *Orson Welles* (Paris: Chavanne, 1949), and his discussion of both Welles' and Wyler's films in 'The Evolution of Film Language' in this volume.

12. François Garçon, 'De la notion d'auteur dans le cinéma: effets pervers d'une vanité flattée', *CinémAction* No. 104, 'Flash-back sur la Nouvelle Vague', 3e trimestre 2002, pp. 106–111.

13. Michel Ciment, '*Positif* et la Nouvelle Vague', *CinémAction* No. 104, 'Flash-back sur la Nouvelle Vague', 3e trimestre 2002, p. 84.

14. Noël Burch, 'Cinéphilie et masculinité', *Iris* No. 26, 'Cultural Studies, Gender Studies et études filmiques' (1998); Antoine de Baecque, *La Cinéphilie: Invention d'un regard, histoire d'une culture, 1944–1968* (Paris: Fayard, 2003); Leila Wimmer, Cross-Channel Perceptions. The French Reception of British Cinema (Oxford: Peter Lang, 2009).

15. Hélène Liogier, '1960: Vue d'Espagne, La Nouvelle Vague est fasciste, ou la Nouvelle Vague selon Jean Parvulesco', *1895* (AFRHC), No. 26, December 1998, pp. 127–53.

16. Michel Ciment '*Positif* et la Nouvelle Vague', *CinémAction* No. 104, 'Flash-back sur la Nouvelle Vague', 3e trimestre 2002, pp. 83–7.

17. Ciment, *CinémAction* No. 104, *op. cit.*, p. 86.

18. Laurent Marie, 'Globalement positive', *CinémAction*, No. 104, 2002, pp. 93–9.

19. Michel Marie, *CinémAction*, No. 104, *op. cit.*, p. 96.

20. See Michel Marie, *The French New Wave: An Artistic School. op. cit.*, pp. 66–7, for a comparative table of box-office results of New Wave films and mainstream films.

21. Anon, 'The Nouvelle Vague: Two Views from Paris', *Film Quarterly*, No. 2 (Winter 1959), p. 9.

22. The expression, 'La Nouvelle Vague arrive!' ('The New Wave is coming!') was used as title for a series of surveys published between 3 October and 12 December 1957 in *L'Express*.

23. Madeleine Chapsal, 'Vérités sur les jeunes filles', in *L'Express*, 20 October 1960, cited in Geneviève Sellier, *La Nouvelle Vague, un cinéma au masculin singulier* (Paris: CNRS Editions, 2006), p. 129.

24. Edgar Morin, 'Conditions d'apparition de la Nouvelle Vague', *Communications* 1, 1961, pp. 139–41. Claude Bremond, Evelyne Sullerot, Simone Berton, 'Les héros des films dits 'de la Nouvelle Vague'', *Communications* 1, 1961, pp. 142–77.

25. Eve [sic] Sullerot, 'Portrait Robot de l'héroïne 'Nouvelle Vague'', *France Observateur* [*L'Observateur littéraire*], 27 April 1961, pp. 17–18.

26. André S. Labarthe, *Essai sur le jeune cinéma français* (Paris: Le Terrain Vague, 1960), p. 1.

27. Jacques Siclier, *Nouvelle Vague?* (Paris: Editions du Cerf, 1961), p. 57.

28. Antoine de Baecque, *La Nouvelle Vague, Histoire d'une jeunesse* (Paris: Flammarion, 1998), p. 16.

29. Guy Gauthier, 'Années 50, rayon nouveautés', *CinémAction* No. 104, *op. cit.*, pp. 15–18.

30. Durgnat, Raymond, *Nouvelle Vague, the first decade* (London: A Motion Monograph, Motion Publications, 1963). The reason why Durgnat can talk about a 'decade' of New Wave films in 1963 is that his understanding of the movement is much wider than most, starting in the early 1950s.

31. Antoine de Baecque, *La Nouvelle Vague, Histoire d'une jeunesse. op. cit.*, pp. 133–9.

32. Henri Magnan, *Paris-Jour*, 19 October 1959.

33. See Ginette Vincendeau, *Jean-Pierre Melville, an American in Paris* (London: BFI, 2003) for an account of the complicated relationship between Melville and the New Wave.

34. Rui Nogueira (ed.), *Melville on Melville* (London: Secker & Warburg, in association with the BFI, 1971), p. 77.

35. *Les Lettres françaises*, 1 November 1967.

36. Richard Neupert, 'Dead Champagne: *Variety*'s New Wave', *Film History* 10, No. 2 (1998), pp. 224.

37. Colin MacCabe, *Jean-Luc Godard: a Portrait of the Artist at 70* (London: Bloomsbury, 2003), p. 67.

38. Richard Abel, *French Cinema: the First Wave, 1915–1929* (Princeton; Guilford: Princeton University Press, 1984).

39. Geoffrey Nowell-Smith, *Making Waves: New Cinemas of the 1960s* (New York: Continuum, 2007).

40. Serge Daney, 'La Nouvelle Vague, une approche généalogique', in Jean-Loup Passek (ed.), *D'un cinéma l'autre: notes sur le cinéma français des années cinquante* (Paris: Centre Pompidou, Cinéma/Singulier, 1988), pp. 72–4.

41. Michael Temple and Michael Witt (eds), *The French Cinema Book* (London: BFI, 2004), p. 183.

42. Claude Chabrol, *Et pourtant je tourne, un homme et son métier* (Paris: Robert Laffont, 1976), p. 135.

43. Billard, Pierre, '40 moins de 40: La jeune académie du cinéma français', *Cinéma 58*, 24 (February 1958).

44. See Michel Marie, *The French New Wave: An Artistic School*, *op. cit.*, for the most concise account of the new conditions of production of New Wave films.

45. Jacques Siclier, *Nouvelle vague?* (Paris: Editions du Cerf, 1961).

46. Serge Daney, 'La Nouvelle Vague, une approche généalogique', *op. cit.*, p. 72.

47. Raymond Durgnat, *Nouvelle Vague, the first decade* (London: A Motion Monograph, Motion Publications, 1963).

48. James Monaco, *The New Wave: Truffaut, Godard, Chabrol, Rohmer, Rivette* (New York: Oxford University Press, 1976), p. vii.

49. Michel Marie, *La nouvelle vague: Une école artistique*, *op. cit.*, pp. 42–3.

50. Antoine de Baecque, *La nouvelle vague: Portrait d'une jeunesse*, *op. cit.*, p. 149.

51. Richard Neupert, *A History of the French New Wave Cinema* (Madison, Wisconsin: The University of Wisconsin Press, 2002). Second edition, p. xxvii.

52. Leila Wimmer, *Cross-Channel Perceptions. The French Reception of British Cinema* (Oxford: Peter Lang, 2009), p. 140.

53. For a discussion of *Cahiers du cinéma* in the 1970s, see Bérénice Reynaud's introduction to David Wilson (ed.), *Cahiers du cinéma. Vol. 4 1973–1978: history, ideology, cultural struggle* (London, New York: Routledge, 2000).

54. On the Zanzibar films, see Sally Shafto, *Les Films Zanzibar et les dandys de mai 1968* (Paris: Paris Experimental, 2007).

55. For a discussion of these, see John Caugie (ed.), *Theories of Authorship: A Reader* (London: Boston: Routledge & Kegan Paul, in association with the British Film Institute, 1981).

56. Philippe Pilard, 'Nouvelle Vague et politique', *Image et Son*, No. 188 (November 1969), pp. 90–102.

57. Jean-Pierre Jeancolas, 'Nouvelle vague', in *Le Cinéma des Français, La Ve République (1958–1978)* (Paris: Stock/Cinéma, 1979), p. 128.

58. Terry Lovell, 'Sociology and the Cinema', *Screen*, Spring 1971, p. 20.

59. John Hess, 'La Politique des auteurs part one, World View as Aesthetic', *Jump Cut* I (1974); John Hess, 'La Politique des auteurs part two, Truffaut's Manifesto', *Jump Cut* II (1974).

60. Serge Daney, 'La Nouvelle Vague, une approche généalogique', *op. cit.*

61. Daney, 'La Nouvelle Vague, une approche généalogique', *op. cit.*, p. 72.

62. In France, work on *Positif* came out around the time of the journal's 50th anniversary but this material has not been translated either. See Stéphane Goudet (ed.), *L'Amour du cinéma. 50 ans de la revue Positif* (Paris: Gallimard, 2002); for *Cahiers du cinéma* anthologies in English, see Jim Hillier (ed.), *Cahiers du Cinéma: The 1950s* (Cambridge, Mass.: Harvard University Press, 1985); Jim Hillier (ed.), *Cahiers du Cinéma: The 1960s* (Cambridge, Mass.: Harvard University Press, 1992); Nick Browne (ed.), *Cahiers du cinéma 1969–1972, The Politics of Representation* (London: Routledge- BFI, 1989); David Wilson (ed.), *Cahiers du cinéma. Vol. 4 1973–1978 : history, ideology, cultural struggle*; with an introduction by Bérénice Reynaud (London, New York: Routledge, 2000).

63. David Bordwell, Kristin Thompson, and Janet Staiger, *The classical Hollywood cinema : film style & mode of production to 1960* (New York: Columbia University Press, 1985).

64. Colin Crisp, 'The classic French cinema and the New Wave', in *The Classic French Cinema, 1930–1960* (Bloomington: Indiana University Press, 1993), p. 416.

65. Crisp, *The Classic French Cinema, 1930–1960, op. cit.*, p. 417.

66. Ginette Vincendeau, *Stars and Stardom in French Cinema* (London; New York: Continuum, 2000); Raphaëlle Moine (ed.), *Le Cinéma français face aux genres* (Paris: A.F.H.R.C., 2005); Susan Hayward, *French Costume Drama of the 1950s* (Intellect, 2010); Thomas Pillard, *Le Film noir français face aux bouleversements de la France d'après-guerre (1946–1960)* (Joseph K, 2014); Gwénaëlle Le Gras and Geneviève Sellier (eds.), *Cinémas et cinéphilies populaires: dans la France d'après-guerre (1945–1958)* (Paris: Nouveau Monde éditions, 2015); Jean Montarnal, *La "Qualité française": un mythe critique?* (Paris: L'Harmattan, 2018).

67. John Orr, *Cinema and Modernity* (Cambridge: Polity Press, 1993); Kristin Ross, *Fast Cars, Clean Bodies: Decolonization and the Reordering of French Culture* (Cambridge, MA: MIT University Press, 1995).

68. Noël Burch and Geneviève Sellier, *La Drôle de guerre des sexes du cinéma français* (Paris: Armand Colin, 1996); translated into English as *The Battle of the Sexes in French Cinema, 1930–1956* (Durham, London: Duke University Press, 2013); Jean-Pierre Esquenazi's *Godard and French Society in the 1960s* (2004); Philippe Mary, *La Nouvelle vague et le cinéma d'auteur. Socio-analyse d'une révolution artistique* (Paris: Editions du Seuil, 2006).

69. Mary, *La Nouvelle vague et le cinéma d'auteur, op. cit.*, pp. 116–17.

70. See Bérénice Reynaud & Ginette Vincendeau (eds), *20 ans de théories féministes sur le cinéma, Grande-Bretagne et Etats-Unis, CinémAction* No. 67 (1993).

71. Published in English as *Masculine Singular: French New Wave Cinema* (Duke University Press, 2008). Translated by Kristin Ross.

72. Françoise Audé, *Ciné-modèles, cinéma d'elles: situation des femmes dans le cinéma français 1956–1979* (Lausanne: L'Âge d'homme, 1981).

73. Sandy Flitterman-Lewis, *To Desire Differently: Feminism and the French Cinema* (Urbana: University of Illinois Press, 1990).

74. See bibliography for details.

75. See bibliography for details.

76. See bibliography for details.

77. See bibliography for details.

78. See bibliography for details.

79. For example, the Cinémathèque Française in Paris mounted large exhibitions on Demy (2013) and Truffaut (2014), while the James Hyman Gallery in London featured an exhibition of Raymond Cauchetier New Wave photographs in 2015.

80. The provocatively titled monograph by the French writer Yannick Rolandeau, *Nouvelle vague: Essai critique d'un mythe cinématographique* (2018) at first sight launches a virulent attack on the New Wave cinema as a 'zealous propagandist [...] for the consumer society'. Yet, while the polemical tone harks back to some of the *Premier Plan* and *Positif* texts (there is an interview with *Positif*'s editor Michel Ciment at the end of the book), the analysis does not bring to light any new facts, while it more or less leaves the films unexamined.

81. Martin Scorsese, *Cahiers du cinéma*, 'La nouvelle vague en question' (December 1998), p. 92.

82. See bibliography for details.

83. Of all the national film movements featured in the Criterion DVD list, the New Wave is by far he most numerous (compared to Italian Neo-Realism, New German cinema, etc.).

Filmography

À bout de souffle (Jean-Luc Godard, 1960)

Le Beau Serge (Claude Chabrol, 1959)

Bob le flambeur (Jean-Pierre Melville, 1956)

Les Bonnes femmes (Claude Chabrol, 1960)

Cléo de 5 à 7 (Agnès Varda, 1962)

Les Cousins (Claude Chabrol, 1959)

Désaccord parfait (Antoine de Caunes, 2006)

The Dreamers (Bernardo Bertolucci's 2003)

Le Havre (Aki Kaurismäki, 2011)

Hiroshima mon amour (Alain Resnais, 1959)

Irma Vep (Olivier Assayas, 1996)

Jacquot de Nantes (Agnès Varda, 1991)

Le Lion est mort ce soir (Nobuhiro Suwa, 2017)

Loin du Viêt-nam (Joris Ivens, William Klein, Claude Lelouch, Agnès Varda, Jean-Luc Godard, Chris Marker, Alain Resnais, 1967)

Ma nuit chez Maud (Eric Rohmer, 1969)

Le Mépris (Jean-Luc Godard, 1963)

La Noire de/Black Girl (Ousmane Sembène, 1966)

Orfeu Negro (Marcel Camus, 1958)

Paris nous appartient (Jacques Rivette, 1961)

La Pointe Courte (Agnès Varda, 1954)

Le Pornographe (Bertrand Bonello, 2001)

Les Quatre cents coups (François Truffaut, 1959)

Le Redoutable (Michel Hazanavicius, 2017)

La Sirène du Mississipi (François Truffaut, 1969)

Tirez sur le pianiste (François Truffaut, 1960)

36 fillette (Catherine Breillat, 1988)

Une femme est une femme (Jean-Luc Godard, 1961)

I

THE *POLITIQUE DES AUTEURS*: FOUNDATIONAL TEXTS

One of the first important statements – it might even be called a manifesto – concerning a new approach to film-making that was to pave the way for the Nouvelle Vague was Alexandre Astruc's now legendary article 'La Naissance d'une nouvelle avant-garde: la caméra-stylo' ('The Birth of a New Avant-Garde: La Caméra-Stylo'). Parts of it may seem tame or obvious to us today, but at the time it was written (1948) and in the context of almost all film criticism of the day, it was a veritable call for a revolution.

Peter Graham

1 The Birth of a New Avant-Garde: *La Caméra-Stylo*

ALEXANDRE ASTRUC (1948)*

'What interests me in the cinema is abstraction.'

Orson Welles

One cannot help noticing that something is happening in the cinema at the moment. Our sensibilities have been in danger of getting blunted by those everyday films which, year in year out, show their tired and conventional faces to the world.

The cinema of today is getting a new face. How can one tell? Simply by using one's eyes. Only a film critic could fail to notice the striking facial transformation which is taking place before our very eyes. In which films can this new beauty be found? Precisely those which have been ignored by the critics. It is not just a coincidence that Jean Renoir's *La Règle du jeu* (*The Rules of the Game*), Orson Welles's films, and Robert Bresson's *Les Dames du Bois de Boulogne* (*Ladies of the Park*), all films which establish the foundations of a new future for the cinema, have escaped the attention of critics, who in any case were not capable of spotting them.

But it is significant that the films which fail to obtain the blessing of the critics are precisely those which myself and several of my friends all agree about. We see in them, if you like, something of the prophetic. That's why I am talking about *avant-garde*. There is always an *avant-garde* when something new takes place. ...

To come to the point: the cinema is quite simply becoming a means of expression, just as all the other arts have been before it, and in particular painting and the novel. After having been successively a fairground attraction, an amusement analogous to boulevard theatre, or a means of preserving the images of an era, it is gradually becoming a language. By language, I mean a form in which and by which artists can express their thoughts, however abstract they may be, or translate their

---

* *L'Écran français*, No. 144, 30 March 1948

Alexandre Astruc.

obsessions exactly as they do in the contemporary essay or novel. That is why I would like to call this new age of cinema the age of *caméra-stylo* (camera-pen). This metaphor has a very precise sense. By it I mean that the cinema will gradually break free from the tyranny of what is visual, from the image for its own sake, from the immediate and concrete demands of the narrative, to become a means of writing just as flexible and subtle as written language. This art, although blessed with an enormous potential, is an easy prey to prejudice; it cannot go on for ever ploughing the same field of realism and social fantasy which has been bequeathed to it by the popular novel. It can tackle any subject, any genre. The most philo-sophical meditations on human production, psychology, metaphysics, ideas, and passions lie well within its province. I will even go so far as to say that contempo-rary ideas and philosophies of life are such that only the cinema can do justice to them. Maurice Nadeau wrote in an article in the newspaper *Combat*: 'If Descartes lived today, he would write novels.' With all due respect to Nadeau, a Descartes of today would already have shut himself up in his bedroom with a 16mm camera and some film, and would be writing his philosophy on film: for his *Discours de*

Jean Renoir's *La Règle du jeu* (1939) – Gaston Modot (left), Carette (centre), Marcel Dalio (right).

la méthode (*Discourse on Method*) would today be of such a kind that only the cinema could express it satisfactorily.

It must be understood that up to now the cinema has been nothing more than a show. This is due to the basic fact that all films are projected in an auditorium. But with the development of 16mm and television, the day is not far off when everyone will possess a projector, will go to the local bookstore and hire films written on any subject, of any form, from literary criticism and novels to mathematics, history, and general science. From that moment on, it will no longer be possible to speak of *the* cinema. There will be *several* cinemas just as today there are several literatures, for the cinema, like literature, is not so much a particular art as a language which can express any sphere of thought.

This idea of the cinema expressing ideas is not perhaps a new one. Jacques Feyder has said: 'I could make a film with Montesquieu's *L'Esprit des lois* [*The Spirit of the Laws*].' But Feyder was thinking of illustrating it 'with pictures' just as Sergei Eisenstein had thought of illustrating Karl Marx's *Capital* in book fashion. What I am trying to say is that the cinema is now moving towards a form which is making it such a precise language that it will soon be possible to write ideas directly on film without even having to resort to those heavy associations of images that were the delight of the silent cinema. In other words, in order to suggest the passing of time, there is no need to show falling leaves and then apple trees in blossom; and in order to suggest that a hero wants to make love there are surely other ways of going about it than showing a saucepan of milk boiling over on to the stove, as Henri-Georges Clouzot does in *Quai des Orfèvres* (*Jenny Lamour*).

The fundamental problem of the cinema is how to express thought. The creation of this language has preoccupied all the theoreticians and writers in the history of the cinema, from Eisenstein down to the scriptwriters and adaptors of the sound cinema. But neither the silent cinema, because it was the slave of a static conception of the image, nor the classical sound cinema, as it has existed right up to now, has been able to solve this problem satisfactorily. The silent cinema thought it could get out of it through editing and the juxtaposition of images. Remember Eisenstein's famous statement: 'Editing is for me the means of giving movement (i.e. an idea) to two static images.' And when sound came, he was content to adapt theatrical devices.

One of the fundamental phenomena of the last few years has been the growing realisation of the dynamic, i.e. significant, character of the cinematic image. Every film, because its primary function is to move, i.e. to take place in time, is a theorem. It is a series of images which, from one end to the other, have an inexorable logic (or better even, a dialectic) of their own. We have come to realise that the meaning which the silent cinema tried to give birth to through symbolic association exists within the image itself, in the development of the narrative, in every gesture of the characters, in every line of dialogue, in those camera move-

André Malraux's *L'Espoir* (1945).

ments which relate objects to objects and characters to objects. All thought, like all feeling, is a relationship between one human being and another human being or certain objects which form part of his or her universe. It is by clarifying these relationships, by making a tangible allusion, that the cinema can really make itself the vehicle of thought. From today onwards, it will be possible for the cinema to produce works which are equivalent, in their profundity and meaning, to the novels of William Faulkner and André Malraux, to the essays of Jean-Paul Sartre and Albert Camus. Moreover we already have a significant example: Malraux's *L'Espoir* (*Days of Hope*), the film which he directed from his own novel, in which, perhaps for the first time ever, film language is the exact equivalent of literary language.

Let us now have a look at the way people make concessions to the supposed (but fallacious) requirements of the cinema. Scriptwriters who adapt Honoré de Balzac or Fyodor Dostoevsky excuse the idiotic transformations they impose on the works from which they construct their scenarios by pleading that the cinema is incapable of rendering every psychological or metaphysical overtone. In their hands, Balzac becomes a collection of engravings in which fashion has the most important place, and Dostoevsky suddenly begins to resemble the novels of Joseph Kessel, with Russian-style drinking-bouts in night-clubs and troika races in the snow. Well, the only cause of these compressions is laziness and lack of imagination. The cinema of today is capable of expressing any kind of reality. What interests us is the creation of this new language. We have no desire to rehash those poetic documentaries and surrealist films of twenty-five years ago every time we manage to escape the demands of a commercial industry. Let's face it: between the pure cinema of the 1920s and filmed theatre, there is plenty of room for a different and individual kind of film-making.

This of course implies that the scriptwriter directs his own scripts; or rather, that the scriptwriter ceases to exist, for in this kind of film-making the distinction between author and director loses all meaning. Direction is no longer a means of illustrating or presenting a scene, but a true act of writing. The filmmaker/author writes with his camera as a writer writes with his pen. In an art in which a length of film and sound-track is put in motion and proceeds, by means of a certain form and a certain story (there can even be no story at all – it matters little), to evolve a philosophy of life, how can one possibly distinguish between the man who conceives the work and the man who writes it? Could one imagine a Faulkner novel written by someone other than Faulkner? And would *Citizen Kane* be satisfactory in any other form than that given to it by Orson Welles?

Let me say once again that I realise the term *avant-garde* savours of the surrealist and so-called abstract films of the 1920s. But that *avant-garde* is already old hat. It was trying to create a specific domain for the cinema; we on the contrary are seeking to broaden it and make it the most extensive and clearest language there is. Problems such as the translation into cinematic terms of verbal tenses and logical relationships interest us much more than the creation of the exclusively visual and static art dreamt of by the surrealists. In any case, they were doing no more than make cinematic adaptations of their experiments in painting and poetry.

So there we are. This has nothing to do with a school, or even a movement. Perhaps it could simply be called a tendency: a new awareness, a desire to transform the cinema and hasten the advent of an exciting future. Of course, no tendency can be so called unless it has something concrete to show for itself. The films will come, they will see the light of day – make no mistake about it. The economic and material difficulties of the cinema create the strange paradox whereby one can talk about something which does not yet exist; for although we know what we want, we do not know whether, when, and how we will be able to do it. But the cinema cannot but develop. It is an art that cannot live by looking back over the past and chewing over the nostalgic memories of an age gone by. Already it is looking to the future; for the future, in the cinema as elsewhere, is the only thing that matters.

Astruc's call for a totally independent means of expression is one that no one, of whatever school, would take exception to. The champions of 'specificity' were later to twist his argument to fit their own pet theory that a film can be judged only in so far as it is specific, or differs from the other arts, i.e. visually. But Astruc's own films confirmed what he had said in this article: he conceived of a total cinema in which every component part, whether already existing in the arts, like words and music, or new and specific to the cinema, like visual and spatial movement, should have equal importance.

Another article which greatly influenced the thinking of Nouvelle Vague directors was François Truffaut's 'Une certaine tendance du cinéma français' ('A certain tendency in French cinema'), which appeared in *Cahiers du cinéma* in January 1954 when – astonishingly – he was still only 21. His age may explain the somewhat haphazard organisation of the article (even after Bazin, the editor of *Cahiers*, who had had misgivings about publishing the article, had spent months going through it with a fine-tooth comb). The piece is typical of the vituperative, fearless, and much feared Truffaut who used to demolish films by the dozen when he was a critic on the weekly *Arts* as well as *Cahiers* in the 1950s. What may surprise readers today who are familiar with Truffaut's films is the article's resolutely right-wing stance: he takes a very poor view of anti-clerical, anti-militaristic and anti-bourgeois films, as well as what he sees as blasphemy. But, as he explains in an extensive interview reproduced later on in this book, he had mellowed considerably by 1962, after making three features and coming to grips with the brass tacks of the film industry – distribution, admissions, production budgets, financial constraints and so on.

Peter Graham

2 A Certain Tendency in French Cinema

FRANÇOIS TRUFFAUT (1954)*

'It would be nice to think that the meaning of the word 'art' can make men aware of the greatness they do not recognise in themselves.'

André Malraux, *Le Temps du mépris/Days of Contempt* (Preface)

The sole aim of the notes that follow is to try to define a certain tendency in the French cinema – a tendency known as that of 'psychological realism' – and to suggest its limitations.

Ten to 12 films…

Although the French cinema is represented by 100 or so films per year, it goes without saying that a mere ten to 12 of them deserve to attract the attention of critics and cinephiles, and therefore the attention of *Cahiers du cinéma*.

These ten to 12 movies represent what has been aptly described as 'the Tradition of Quality': their ambitiousness inevitably elicits the admiration of the foreign press, and they defend France's colours twice a year at Cannes and Venice, where they have fairly regularly scooped up awards such as the Grand Prix and the Golden Lion since 1946.

*   *   *

At the beginning of the talkies era, the French cinema was an honest carbon copy of the American cinema. Under the influence of *Scarface*, we made the amusing *Pépé le Moko*. Then French scriptwriting developed significantly thanks to Jacques Prévert: *Le Quai des brumes* (*Port of Shadows*) remains the masterpiece of the so-called 'poetic realism' school.

---

* *Cahiers du cinéma*, No. 31, January 1954, pp. 15–28

Michèle Morgan (left), Pierre Blanchar and Line Noro in Jean Delannoy's *La Symphonie pastorale* (1946).

The Second World War and the post-war period saw a renewal of our cinema, which developed under the effect of internal pressures; and poetic realism – which could be said to have expired when it closed *Les Portes de la nuit* (*Gates of the Night*) behind it – was replaced by 'psychological realism', as illustrated by the films of Claude Autant-Lara, Jean Delannoy, René Clément, Yves Allégret and Marcello Pagliero.

Scriptwriters' films

Remembering that Delannoy once made *Le Bossu* and *La Part de l'ombre* (*Blind Desire*), Autant-Lara *Le Plombier amoureux* (the French-language version of Buster Keaton's *The Passionate Plumber*) and *Lettres d'amour* (*Love Letters*), and Allégret *La Boîte aux rêves* and *Les Démons de l'aube* (*Dawn Devils*), and that it is rightly accepted that those films were strictly commercial enterprises, we have to admit that, since the success or failure of such filmmakers is governed by the scripts they choose, then *La Symphonie pastorale* (*Pastoral Symphony*), *Le Diable au corps* (*Devil in the Flesh*), *Jeux interdits* (*Forbidden Games*), *Manèges* (*The Riding School*) and *Un Homme marche dans la ville* (*A Man Walks in the City*) are essentially *scriptwriters' films*.

René Clément holds Brigitte Fossey, with Jean Aurenche to the right, at the time of Clément's film *Jeux interdits* (1952)

And is it not true that the French cinema's undeniable progress has been due mainly to a *renewal* of scriptwriters and themes, to the *liberties* taken with accepted masterpieces, and, lastly, to confidence that audiences will be receptive to themes generally regarded as difficult?

That is why I will restrict my remarks solely to scriptwriters, those very people who were behind the emergence of poetic realism in the Tradition of Quality movement, namely Jean Aurenche and Pierre Bost, Jacques Sigurd, Henri Jeanson (in his second manner), Robert Scipion, Roland Laudenbach and others.

No one is any longer unaware of the fact that …

After first trying his hand at direction with two now forgotten short films, Jean Aurenche started specialising in adaptations for the screen. In 1936, he and the playwright Jean Anouilh wrote the dialogue of Léo Joannon's *Vous n'avez rien à déclarer?* (*Confessions of a Newly-Wed*) and Christian-Jaque's *Les Dégourdis de la 11ème*.

At about the same time, some excellent little novels by Pierre Bost were being published by the *Nouvelle revue française* (*NRF*).

Aurenche and Bost teamed up for the first time when they adapted and wrote the dialogue of *Douce* (*Love Story*), directed by Autant-Lara.

Everyone now realises that Aurenche and Bost rehabilitated the art of adaptation by challenging the notion of what was generally meant by it, in other words they are said to have replaced the old prejudice that required one to be faithful to the letter by the opposite requirement to be faithful to the spirit – to the point where the following audacious aphorism was coined: 'An honest adaptation is a betrayal' (Carlo Rim, *Travelling et sex-appeal*).

Equivalence...

The touchstone of adaptation as practised by Aurenche and Bost is the so-called process of equivalence. This process takes for granted that in the novel being adapted there are filmable and unfilmable scenes, and that instead of scrapping the latter (as used to be done) you had to think up equivalent scenes, in other words ones that the author of the novel might have written for the screen.

'Inventing without betraying' is the watchword that Aurenche and Bost liked to cite, forgetting that one can also betray by omission.

Aurenche and Bost's system is so appealing in the very formulation of its principle that no one has ever thought of examining in detail how it works. This is more or less what I intend to do here.

*   *   *

Aurenche and Bost's entire reputation is based on two specific points:

    1) *Faithfulness* to the spirit of the works they adapt;

    2) The talent they put into the task.

That celebrated faithfulness...

Since 1943, Aurenche and Bost have together been responsible for the screen adaptation and dialogue of the following novels: Michel Davet's *Douce*, André Gide's *La Symphonie pastorale*, Raymond Radiguet's *Le Diable au corps*, Henri Queffélec's *Un Recteur de l'île de Sein* (*Dieu a besoin des hommes*/*God Needs Men*), François Boyer's *Les Jeux inconnus* (*Jeux interdits*/*Forbidden Games*) and Colette's *Le Blé en herbe*.

In addition they wrote an adaptation of Georges Bernanos's novel, *Le Journal d'un curé de campagne* (*Diary of a Country Priest*), which was never filmed, a

Jean Delannoy.

script about Joan of Arc, only part of which has just been filmed by Delannoy (the 'Jeanne' episode of *Destinées* [*Daughters of Destiny*][1]), and the script and dialogue of *L'Auberge Rouge* (*The Red Inn*), directed by Autant-Lara.

The great diversity of inspiration displayed by the works and writers they have adapted will be obvious to all. Anyone capable of bringing off the *tour de force* required to remain faithful to the spirit of Davet, Gide, Radiguet, Queffélec, Boyer, Colette and Bernanos, would, I imagine, need to possess a most unusual mental agility and a multiple personality, as well as a singular spirit of eclecticism.

It also has to be remembered that Aurenche and Bost have worked with a wide range of directors. Delannoy, for example, likes to see himself as a mystical moralist. But the petty vileness of *Le Garçon sauvage* (*Savage Triangle*), the mean-mindedness of *La Minute de vérité* (*The Moment of Truth*) and the insignificance of *La Route Napoléon* (*Napoleon Road*) demonstrate rather convincingly that he pursued that vocation only intermittently.

Claude Autant-Lara, on the other hand, is well-known for his non-conformism, his 'advanced' ideas and his fierce anticlericalism; we should recognise that he always has the merit of being true to himself in his movies.

Since Bost was the technician of the duo, it would seem that the spiritual aspect of their joint enterprise was Aurenche's responsibility.

Aurenche both felt nostalgic about, and rebelled against, his education at a Jesuit school. While he flirted with Surrealism, he seems to have been drawn to anarchist groups in the 30s. That only goes to show what a strong personality he has, and how incompatible his personality would seem to be with those of Gide, Bernanos, Queffélec and Radiguet. But an examination of his work will probably tell us more about this aspect.

Father Amédée Ayffre is convincing in his analysis of *La Symphonie pastorale* and his definition of the relationship between the book and the film: 'We find faith reduced to religious psychology in Gide, and religious psychology reduced to mere psychology in the film (…). This decline in quality is now, according to a rule familiar to aestheticians, matched by a quantitative increase. New characters are added, such as Piette and Casteran, who are supposed to represent certain feelings. Tragedy becomes drama, or melodrama.' (*Dieu au cinéma*, p. 131)[2].

What bothers me…

What bothers me about this celebrated process of equivalence is that I am by no means convinced that a novel can contain unfilmable scenes, and even less so that scenes decreed to be unfilmable are unfilmable by any director.

Praising Robert Bresson for his faithfulness to Bernanos, André Bazin concluded his excellent article, 'La Stylistique de Robert Bresson' ('Robert Bresson's Stylistics'), as follows: 'After *Le Journal d'un curé de campagne*, Aurenche and Bost are no more than the Viollet-le-Ducs of adaptation.'

All those who admire and are familiar with Bresson's film will remember the wonderful scene in a confessional where, as Bernanos puts it, Chantal's face 'began to appear little by little, gradually'.

When Aurenche, several years before Bresson's movie, wrote an adaptation of *Le Journal d'un curé de campagne* which was turned down by Bernanos, he decided that this scene was unfilmable and replaced it with the one that follows:

'Do you want me to listen to you here?' (pointing to the confessional).

'I never confess.'

'But you must have confessed yesterday since you took communion this morning.'

'I didn't take communion.'

He looks at her with great surprise.

'Excuse me, but I gave you communion.'

Chantal quickly moves over to the prie-dieu she occupied that morning.

'Come and see.'

The priest follows her. Chantal points to the missal she left there.

'Look in the book. I may no longer have the right to touch it.'

The priest is very intrigued. He opens the book and discovers stuck between two pages the host that Chantal had spat into it. He looks astonished and shaken.

'I spat out the host,' Chantal says.

'I can see,' the priest says in a flat tone of voice.

'You've never seen anything like that, have you?' says Chantal, fiercely and almost triumphantly.

'No, never,' says the priest, remaining apparently very calm.

'Do you know what needs to be done?'

The priest closes his eyes briefly. He is thinking or praying. He says:

'It can be repaired very simply. But it's a horrible thing to have done.'

He goes over towards the altar, carrying the open book. Chantal follows him.

'No, it's not horrible. What is horrible is to receive the host in a state of sin.'

'So you were in a state of sin?'

'Less than other people, but they don't care.'

'Don't judge them.'

'I do not judge them, I condemn them,' Chantal says with virulence.

'Keep silent before the body of Christ!'

He kneels before the altar, takes the host out of the book and swallows it.

In the middle of the novel there is a discussion about faith between the priest and an obtuse atheist called Arsène. The discussion ends with Arsène saying: 'When one is dead, everything is dead.' In the adaptation, the discussion, which takes place on the very grave of the priest and is between Arsène and another priest, *brings the film to a close*. The sentence 'When one is dead, everything is dead' was supposed to be the last line of dialogue in the film, one that carries weight, the only one perhaps that the audience will remember. In his book Bernanos did not conclude with 'When one is dead, everything is dead', but with 'What difference does that make? Everything is grace.'

'Inventing without betraying,' I can hear you saying. It seems to me that in this case there is rather little invention and a great deal of betrayal. Let's look at just one or two more details. Aurenche and Bost were unable to make *Le Journal d'un curé de campagne* because Bernanos was still alive, whereas Bresson said that he would have taken greater liberties with the book if Bernanos had still been alive.

So Bernanos hampered Aurenche and Bost because he was alive, but hampered Bresson because he was dead[3].

The mask ripped off...

A simple reading of that extract reveals:

    1) A constant and deliberate determination to be *unfaithful* to both the spirit and the letter[4];

    2) A very marked predilection for profanation and blasphemy.

The same unfaithfulness to the spirit also mars *Le Diable au corps*, a love story which becomes an anti-militaristic, anti-bourgeois film[5]; *La Symphonie pastorale*, which becomes the story of a priest in love, turning Gide into a kind of Béatrix Beck; *Un Recteur de l'île de Sein*, ambiguously retitled *Dieu a besoin des hommes*, in which the islanders are portrayed like the 'cretins' in Luis Buñuel's *Las Hurdes* (*Land without Bread*).

As for a fondness for blasphemy, it is constantly in evidence, to a more or less insidious degree, depending on the subject, the director or even the film star.

I need only cite the confessional scene in *Douce*; Marthe's funeral in *Le Diable au corps*; the profaned hosts in this adaptation of *Le Journal d'un curé de campagne*

Brigitte Fossey (left), Georges Poujouly and Laurence Badie at the funeral in René Clément's *Jeux interdits* (1952).

(a scene transferred to *Dieu a besoin des hommes*); the whole script and the Fernandel character in *L'Auberge Rouge*; and the whole script of *Jeux interdits* (the fight in the cemetery).

Aurenche and Bost would seem ideally cut out to be authors of *out-and-out* anti-clerical films, but since movies portraying men in cassocks are in fashion, they agreed to go along with the trend. But as it is incumbent upon them, or so they believe, not to betray their convictions, themes such as profanation and blasphemy and dialogue full of *double entendres* pop up from time to time so they can prove to their chums that they know how 'to pull the wool over the producer's eyes' while at the same time satisfying him, and how to do the same to an equally satisfied general public.

This device is nothing less than a smokescreen; and recourse to it is necessary at a time when we constantly need to pretend to be stupid in order to work intelligently. But while it is fair enough to 'pull the wool over the producer's eyes', surely it is going a bit far to rewrite Gide, Bernanos and Radiguet in this way?

*   *   *

Truth to tell, Aurenche and Bost go about their job like scriptwriters all over the world, just as Charles Spaak and Jacques Natanson did before the war.

In their view, every story must include characters A, B, C and D. Within that equation, everything is articulated according to criteria known only to themselves. People jump into bed with each other according to a well-organised symmetry, some characters are written out, others are thought up, and the script gradually departs from the original and becomes a shapeless but brilliant whole: a new film, step by step, ceremoniously enters the pantheon of the Tradition of Quality.

Okay, people will say...

People will say: 'Let's assume that Aurenche and Bost are unfaithful. But would you also deny that they are talented?' True, talent has nothing to do with faithfulness, but I cannot conceive of a valid adaptation that was not written by a *filmmaker*. Aurenche and Bost are basically men of letters, and my criticism of them here is that they look down on the cinema because they undervalue it. They approach scripts the way people do when they think they can rehabilitate a delinquent by finding him or her a job; they always believe they have done 'all they can' for a script by embellishing it with subtleties, with the art of nuance that is the tenuous merit of the modern novel. One of the major failings of those who attempt to explain what the cinema is about is that they believe they are doing it a service by using literary jargon. (The work of Pagliero has prompted references to Jean-Paul Sartre and Albert Camus, that of Allégret allusions to phenomenology.)

Aurenche and Bost actually water down the books they adapt, as equivalence always tends to encourage betrayal or timidity. Here is a brief example: in Radiguet's novel *Le Diable au corps*, François meets Marthe on a railway platform, when Marthe jumps off the train while it is moving; in the film, they meet in a school that has been turned into a hospital. What is the purpose of this equivalence? To allow the scriptwriters to bring in certain anti-militaristic elements which they have added to the work with Autant-Lara's agreement.

Now it is quite clear that Radiguet's idea is an idea of *mise-en-scène*, whereas the scene thought up by Aurenche and Bost is literary. I can assure you that such examples are legion.

They will one day have to...

Secrets are kept for only a limited length of time, recipes are broadcast, and new scientific discoveries are the subject of announcements by the Académie des Sciences. Since adaptation, if we are to believe Aurenche and Bost, is an exact science, they will one day have to explain to us what criteria, what system and what internal and mysterious geometry of the masterpiece they are adapting govern the way they cut, add, multiply, divide and 'rectify' it.

I have posited the idea that these 'equivalences' are no more than timid devices aimed at getting round difficulties – using the sound track to solve problems with the images and resorting to a form of *tabula rasa* so that nothing is left on the screen except sophisticated framing, complicated lighting and 'sleek' photography, all of them elements that keep the Tradition of Quality alive. It is now time to start examining the full range of films for which Aurenche and Bost wrote the dialogue and adaptation, and to identify the persistence of certain themes which may explain, without justifying it, the two scriptwriters' constant *unfaithfulness* to the works they use as a 'pretext' and an 'opportunity'.

Here, briefly summarised, is what the scripts produced by Aurenche and Bost boil down to:

La Symphonie pastorale: he is a Protestant minister, and he is married. He loves someone else – something he is not allowed to do.

Le Diable au corps: They go through the motions of love – something they are not allowed to do.

Dieu a besoin des hommes: He gives mass, blesses and administers the last rites – something he is not allowed to do.

Edwige Feuillère and Pierre-Michel Beck in Claude Autant-Lara's *Le Blé en herbe* (1952).

Jeux interdits: They bury someone – something they are not allowed to do.
Le Blé en herbe: They love each other – something they are not allowed to do[6].

It could argued that I am also describing the original book. I do not deny that. But I would simply point out that Gide also wrote *La Porte étroite* (*Strait is the Gate*), Radiguet *Le Bal du Comte d'Orgel* (*Count d'Orgel's Ball*), and Colette *La Vagabonde* (*The Vagabond*), and that none of those novels appealed to Delannoy or Autant-Lara.

It should also be noted that scripts I see no point in discussing here tend to support my argument, such as *Au delà des grilles* (*Beyond the Gates*), *Le Château de verre* (*The Glass Castle*) and *L'Auberge Rouge*.

* * *

We can see how adroitly the champions of the Tradition of Quality choose only those themes that lend themselves to the misunderstandings on which the whole system is based.

Under the cloak of literature – and of course quality – audiences are served up their usual helping of gloom, non-conformism and facile audacity.

Aurenche and Bost's influence is enormous…

Writers who took up writing dialogue for films all followed the same rules; between the dialogue he wrote for *Les Dégourdis de la 11ᵉ* and *Un Caprice de Caroline chérie* (*Caroline Cherie*), Anouilh injected something of his own universe into some more ambitious films – a universe of mercantile vulgarity combined with, in the background, Scandinavian mists transposed to Brittany (*Pattes blanches* [*White Paws*]). Another writer, Jean Ferry, followed the same fashion: the dialogue of *Manon* might just as well been written by Aurenche and Bost: 'He thinks I'm a virgin, and in civilian life he's a professor of psychology!' There is nothing better to be expected of the younger generation of scriptwriters. They have simply taken up the torch, while being careful not to break taboos.

Sigurd, one of the latest to have appeared on the 'script and dialogue' scene, works with Allégret. They have together given the French cinema some of its most darkest masterpieces: *Dédée d'Anvers* (*Woman of Antwerp*), *Manèges*, *Une si jolie petite plage* (*Such a Pretty Little Beach*), *Les Miracles n'ont lieu qu'une fois* (*Miracles Only Happen Once*) and *La Jeune folle* (*Desperate Decision*). Sigurd very quickly got the hang of the formula: he must have an admirable ability to synthesise, for his scripts oscillate ingeniously between Aurenche and Bost, Prévert and Clouzot, in a slightly more up-to-date version. Religion never plays a central role, though blasphemy still gingerly shows its face, as when some choirboys or nuns enter the frame at the most unexpected moment (*Manèges*, *Une si jolie petite plage*).

Michèle Morgan and Jean Gabin in Jean Delannoy's *La Minute de vérité* (1952).

The callousness which, it was hoped, would 'turn the stomachs of the bourgeois' can be seen in such neatly crafted lines as: 'He was old – time for him to pop off' (*Manèges*). In *Une si jolie petite plage*, Jane Marken envies the prosperity of the seaside resort of Berck-Plage, which derives from the tuberculosis sufferers who live there: 'Their relatives come to see them, and that's good for business!' (This is reminiscent of the prayer in *Un Recteur de l'île de Sein*.)[7]

Roland Laudenbach, apparently more gifted than most of his colleagues, worked on some of the films that were most typical of that state of mind: *La Minute de vérité*, *Le Bon Dieu sans confession* (*Good Lord without Confession*) and *La Maison du silence* (*Voice of Silence*).

Robert Scipion is a gifted man of letters. He has written only one book, a selection of pastiches. He is notable for being a daily habitué of the cafés of Saint-Germain-des-Prés and for his friendship with Pagliero, who has been dubbed the Sartre of the cinema, presumably because his films resemble articles in Sartre's review, *Les Temps modernes*. Here is some dialogue from *Les Amants de Bras-Mort* (*The Lovers of Bras-Mort*), a populist movie whose central characters are bargemen, like the dockers in *Un homme marche dans la ville*:

'Friends' wives are there to be slept with.'

'You do what's in your interest; to do that, you'd climb on anyone's back, quite literally.'

In a single reel towards the end of the film, within the space of less than ten minutes, we hear the words 'whore', 'tart', 'bitch' and 'bloody stupid'. Is that realism?

We miss Prévert...

Looking at the uniformity and unrelenting vulgarity of scripts nowadays, we find we miss Prévert. He believed in the devil, and therefore in God, and if it was purely his whim to burden most of his characters with all the sins of creation, there was always room for a couple for whom, like some latter-day Adam and Eve, the story would take a turn for the better once the film was over.

Psychological realism, neither real nor psychological...

There are only seven or eight scriptwriters who work regularly for the French cinema. Each of them has only one story to tell, and as each of them can dream of nothing but becoming as successful as the 'two greats', it is hardly an exaggeration to say that the 100 or so French films made each year tell the same story: there is always a victim, usually a cuckold. (This cuckold would be the only attractive character in the film were he not always infinitely grotesque, like the character played by Bernard Blier in

Manèges. The cunning of those close to him and the mutual hatred of the members of his family prove the undoing of the central character, thanks to the unfairness of life in general and, as local colour, the nastiness of other people (priests, concierges, neighbours, passers-by, the wealthy, the poor, soldiers and so on).

During the long winter evenings, why not have fun trying to come up with the titles of French films which do not fit into this formula and, while you're at it, find the one whose dialogue does not contain the following remark, or its equivalent, made by the film's most abject couple: 'They're always the ones that have money [or are blessed with luck, love or happiness]. When it comes down to it, it's all so unfair.'

* * *

That school of film-making, which aims for realism, always destroys it at the very moment when it finally captures it, because it is more interested in imprisoning human beings in a closed world hemmed in by formulas, puns and maxims than in allowing them to reveal themselves as they are, before our eyes. Artists cannot always dominate their work. They sometimes have to be God, or else His creature. We are all familiar with the genre of modern play whose central character, a normal human being when the curtain rises, ends up a legless and armless cripple by the time the final curtain falls, after losing successively all his limbs with each new act. We live in strange times, when any old failed actor uses the term 'Kafkaesque' to describe his marital problems.

This type of cinema comes straight out of modern literature, half Kafkaesque and half Flaubertian! The authors of any film shot in France nowadays imagine they are doing a remake of *Madame Bovary*.

For the first time in French literature, the author of that novel, Gustave Flaubert, adopted a distanced, external attitude to his subject matter, which thus became like an insect under an entomologist's microscope. But although Flaubert said, when he started his novel: 'I shall roll them all in the same mud – while remaining fair' (a remark which present-day authors would be only too willing to adopt as their epigraph), he was ultimately forced to admit: 'Madame Bovary is me'. I doubt whether those same authors would be able to repeat that remark with reference to themselves!

Mise-en-scène, directors, texts.

These notes aim to do no more than examine a certain type of cinema, from the sole point of view of scripts and scriptwriters. But I believe it needs to be made perfectly clear that directors are and want to be responsible for the scripts and dialogue they illustrate.

Jean Delannoy.

I referred earlier to 'scriptwriters' films', and Aurenche and Bost would certainly
not contradict me. When they hand in their script, the film has already been made:
in their view, the *metteur-en-scène* is the person who decides on the framing...
and unfortunately that is true. I have already mentioned the way filmmakers are
obsessed with sticking in a funeral procession at the drop of a hat. And yet death is
always skated over in such films. It is worth recalling the admirable way Jean Renoir
treated the death of Nana or Emma Bovary; in *La Symphonie pastorale*, death is a
mere exercise for the make-up artist and the cinematographer; compare the close-
ups of the dead Michèle Morgan in that film, of Dominique Blanchard in *Le Secret
de Mayerling* (*The Secret of Mayerling*) and of Madeleine Sologne in *L'Eternel retour*
(*Love Eternal*): it is the same face! Everything takes place *after* death.

Let me finally quote the following remark by Delannoy, which I perfidiously
dedicate to French scriptwriters: 'When it happens that talented writers, either
through a love of money or out of weakness, end up one day allowing themselves
to 'write for the cinema', they do so with a feeling that they are somehow lowering
themselves. They tend rather to make a curious attempt at mediocrity, careful as
they are not to compromise their talent, and convinced that if you write for the
cinema you have to ensure you are understood by the lowest common denomi-

nator.' ('*La Symphonie pastorale,* ou l'amour du métier'/ *La Symphonie pastorale* or love of one's craft,' *Verger* N° 3, November 1947).

I must immediately denounce a sophism that is bound to be levelled against me as an argument: 'Such dialogue is spoken by abject characters, and we put such strong words into their mouths in order all the better to stigmatise their vileness. It's our way of being moralists.'

My reply is as follows: it is untrue that such language is used by the most abject characters. True, films in the vein of 'psychological realism' do not solely portray evil people, but so great is the superiority that scriptwriters wish to exert over their characters that those who happen not to be despicable are at best infinitely grotesque[8].

Lastly, I know of a handful of men in France who would be *incapable* of thinking up abject characters of that kind, characters capable of saying abject things – filmmakers whose *Weltanschauung* is at least as valid as that of Aurenche and Bost or Sigurd and Jeanson. I'm thinking, for example, of Renoir, Bresson, Jean Cocteau, Jacques Becker, Abel Gance, Max Ophüls, Jacques Tati and Roger Leenhardt. And yet they are French filmmakers, and it so happens – by a curious coincidence – that they are *auteurs* who often write their own dialogue and in some cases think up the stories they direct.

I can hear you say too…

'But why – I can hear you say – can one not admire to an equal degree all the filmmakers who strive to work within that Tradition and that Quality which you dismiss so flippantly? Why can one not admire Allégret as much as Becker, Delannoy as much as Bresson, Autant-Lara as much as Renoir?'[9]

I simply cannot bring myself to believe in a peaceful coexistence between the Tradition of Quality and a *cinéma d'auteur.*

Basically Allégret and Delannoy are no more than *caricatures* of Henri-Georges Clouzot and Bresson.

It is not out of a desire to shock that I disparage a cinema which receives such high praise elsewhere. I remain convinced that it is the overlong persistence of *psychological realism* which causes audiences to be bemused by films as novel in their conception as Renoir's *Le Carrosse d'or* (*The Golden Coach*), Becker's *Casque d'or* (*Golden Marie*) and even Bresson's *Les Dames du Bois de Boulogne* (*Ladies of the Park*)[10] and Jean Cocteau's *Orphée* (*Orpheus*).

Long live audacity indeed, but we still need to be able to detect where it really is. As the year 1953 comes to a close, if I had to draw up a list of the audacities of the French cinema, I would not be able to include the vomiting scene in *Les*

Jacques Becker (left) and Jean Renoir in the 1950s.

Orgueilleux (*The Proud Ones*), Claude Laydu's refusal to pick up the holy water sprinkler in *Le Bon Dieu sans confession* or the homosexual relationship between the characters in *Le Salaire de la peur* (*The Wages of Fear*). My preference would go to Monsieur Hulot's way of walking, the maid's soliloquies in *Rue de l'Estrapade* (*Françoise Steps Out*), the *mise-en-scène* of *Le Carrosse d'or*, the direction of actors in *Madame de...* (*The Earrings of Madame de...*), and also Gance's experiments with polyvision. You will have realised that these audacities are the work of men of the cinema, not scriptwriters, of directors, not men of letters.

I find it significant for example that some of the most brilliant scriptwriters and *metteurs-en-scène* of the Tradition of Quality school failed when they tried their hand at comedy: Ferry and Clouzot in *Miquette et sa mère* (*Miquette*), Sigurd and Boyer in *Tous les chemins mènent à Rome* (*All Roads Lead to Rome*), Scipion and Pagliero in *La Rose rouge* (*The Red Rose*), Laudenbach and Delannoy in *La Route Napoléon*, Aurenche, Bost and Autant-Lara in *L'Auberge Rouge* or even *Occupe-toi d'Amélie* (*Keep an Eye on Amelia*).

No one who has ever tried writing a script can deny that comedy is by far the most difficult genre, the one that demands the most effort, the most talent and the greatest humility too.

Bourgeois all of them...

The dominant feature of psychological realism is its determination to be anti-bourgeois. But who are Aurenche and Bost, Sigurd, Jeanson, Autant-Lara and Allégret if not bourgeois? And who are the 50,000 new readers created by a film adaptation of a novel if not bourgeois?

What, then, is the worth of an anti-bourgeois cinema made by bourgeois for the bourgeois? It is well known that workers do not particularly appreciate that kind of cinema even when it attempts to find an affinity with them. They refused to identify with the dockers in *Un Homme marche dans la ville*, or the bargemen in *Les Amants de Bras-Mort*. Perhaps parents, when making love, should tell their children to go out on to the landing, but they do not like words like that put into their mouths in a film, even when they are spoken in a 'kindly' way. While members of the public like to slum it using literature as an alibi, they also like to do it using social issues as an alibi. It is edifying to examine which films are put on in which districts of Paris. It emerges that working-class audiences may prefer naïve little foreign films which depict men 'as they should be' rather than as Aurenche and Bost believe them to be.

As one might pass on a good address to a friend...

It is always a pleasure to wind up a discussion: that way, everyone is happy. It is remarkable that 'great' *metteurs-en-scène* and 'great' scriptwriters all spent a long time making minor little films, and that the talent they put into making them was not enough to set them apart from the rest (those with no talent). It is also noteworthy that they all espoused the quality ethos *at the same time*, just as one might pass on a good address to a friend. Remember that a producer – and even a director – earns more money making *Le Blé en herbe* than *Le Plombier amoureux*. So-called 'courageous' films have turned out to be very profitable. A case in point is Ralph Habib, who, after suddenly ceasing to make semi-pornographic films, shot *Les Compagnes de la nuit* (*Companions of the Night*) and claimed to be walking in André Cayatte's footsteps. So what is there to stop people like André Tabet, Jacques Companeez, Jean Guitton, Pierre Véry, Jean Laviron, Yves Ciampi or Gilles Grangier switching overnight to intellectual films, adapting literary masterpieces (there are still a few left) and, of course, littering their movies with funerals?

When that day comes, we shall be up to our necks in the Tradition of Qual-

Claude Autant-Lara.

ity, and French films, trying to outdo each other in their 'psychological realism', 'harshness', 'rigour' and 'ambiguity', will be nothing more than a long-drawn-out funeral procession, which will be able to emerge from the Billancourt film studios and take a short cut to the cemetery that seems to have been specially located next to them so as to speed up the journey from producer to gravedigger.

The trouble is that, if you keep on repeating to audiences that they identify with the central characters of films, they will end up believing you; and the day they realise that the roly-poly old cuckold whose misadventures are supposed to prompt sympathy (a little) and laughter (a lot) is not, as they had thought, a cousin or a next-door neighbour, but *one of them*, that the abject family portrayed is *their* family, and the religion ridiculed is *their* religion, they may well feel ungrateful towards a cinema that made such efforts to show them life as it is seen from a fourth-floor flat in Saint-Germain-des-Prés.

*   *   *

True, I have to admit that some strong feelings and a good dose of prejudice have gone into my deliberately pessimistic examination of a certain tendency in the French cinema. I am told that without the celebrated 'school of psychological realism' we would never have been graced with *Le Journal d'un curé de campagne, Le Carrosse d'or, Orphée, Casque d'or* or Tati's *Les Vacances de Monsieur Hulot* (*Monsieur Hulot's Holiday*).

But the *auteurs* who wanted to educate audiences should realise that they may have diverted them from their original course into the more subtle channels of psychology. They have shepherded them into the first form celebrated by Marcel Jouhandeau in his book, *Ma classe de sixième*. But you cannot go on repeating a year for ever!

Notes

All the notes below from the original text by François Truffaut

1. An excerpt from Aurenche and Bost's dialogue for the 'Jeanne' episode of *Destinées* was published in *La Revue du cinéma* (N° 8, page 9).

2. *La Symphonie pastorale*. Characters added to the film: Piette, Jacques' fiancée, and Casteran, Piette's father. Characters cut out: the minister's three children. There is no mention in the film of what becomes of Jacques after Gertrude's death. In the book, he takes holy orders. The '*Symphonie pastorale* operation': 1) Gide himself writes an adaptation of his novel; 2) His adaptation is regarded as 'unfilmable'; 3) Aurenche and Delannoy in turn write an adaptation; 4) Gide turns it down; 5) Everyone is reconciled when Bost joins the team.

3. When the man who was lined up to produce *Le Journal d'un curé de campagne* expressed surprise that a character called Dr Delbende had been left out of the adapted version, Aurenche (who was supposed to direct) replied: 'In ten years' time, a script might be able to retain a character who dies halfway through the film, but as far as I'm concerned I don't feel I could do that.' Three years later, Bresson kept the character of Dr Delbende and allowed him to die halfway through the film.

4. Aurenche and Bost never said they were 'faithful'. It was the critics who did so.

5. *Le Diable au corps*. The gist of what Autant-Lara said in the course of a radio programme that André Parinaud devoted to Radiguet was: 'What prompted me to make a film based on *Le Diable au corps* was the fact that I saw it as an anti-war novel.' During the same programme, Radiguet's friend, the composer Francis Poulenc, said that when he saw the film he saw no connection with the book.

6. *Le Blé en herbe*. Aurenche and Bost had already prepared their adaptation of Colette's novel in 1946. Autant-Lara accused Leenhardt of having plagiarised *Le Blé en herbe* in *Les Dernières vacances* (*The Last Vacation*). Maurice Garçon arbitrated and ruled in favour of Leenhardt. Aurenche and Bost filled out Colette's plot by adding an extra character, Dick, a lesbian who lived with Madame Dalleray, a woman known as La Dame

Blanche. A few weeks before shooting began the Dick character was written out of the script by Ghislaine Auboin, when she 'reviewed' the adaptation with Autant-Lara.

7. Aurenche and Bost's characters like to talk in maxims. For example: in *La Symphonie pastorale*, 'Ah, children like that should never have been born', 'Not everyone is lucky enough to be blind', and 'A cripple is someone who pretends to be like anyone else'; in *Le Diable au corps* (when a soldier has just lost a leg): 'He may be the last to have been wounded', 'A fat lot of use that is to him' [literally in French, 'that gives him a fine leg']. *Jeux interdits*: Francis: 'What does it mean, putting the cart before the horse?' Berthe: 'Well, it means what we're doing [they are making love].' Francis: 'I didn't realise that was what it was called.'

8. *Psychological realism* was in fact created at the same time as Charles Spaak and Jacques Feyder's *poetic realism*. Perhaps we ought one day to stir up an ultimate controversy about Feyder, before he sinks permanently into oblivion.

9. 'Taste consists of a thousand distastes.' (Paul Valéry).

10. Aurenche worked on *Les Dames du Bois de Boulogne*, but had to part company with Bresson because of a creative incompatibility.

In his piece, 'In praise of André Bazin' (see section II), Gérard Gozlan cites Bazin's article on the *politique des auteurs* as one of the few by him that he likes. The article indeed is remarkable for showing the gap, narrow on the surface but in fact quite wide, between the critical positions of Bazin and those of his disciples.

The term *politique des auteurs* (literally 'the policy of authors') is a vague one, and has been used to encompass a number of widely differing attitudes. Understood in the sense of a faithfulness to certain directors and a willingness to champion them through the thick and thin of their inspiration, it is a term which applies more accurately to the critics of *Positif* than of *Cahiers*. *Positif*'s favourite directors (Luis Buñuel, Orson Welles, John Ford, John Huston, Vincente Minnelli, Federico Fellini and Michelangelo Antonioni, to mention but a few) have remained more or less constant. But *Cahiers* has a long record of fickle tastes: first there were the grotesquely-styled '*hitch-cockohawksiens*', then the worshippers of Fritz Lang, Joseph Losey, Douglas Sirk and Raoul Walsh, then the fanatics who swore by Edgar G. Ulmer and Riccardo Freda, and so on. Bazin's own tastes, however, always remained constant, personal and both catholic and Catholic.

The term *politique des auteurs* also took on a new shade of meaning. As the cinema in general, but especially the American cinema, tends to be an industry in which the personality of the director can easily be swamped, those directors came to be admired who managed somehow to get their personality across in spite of pressures against it such as an imposed script, imposed sets, imposed stars and so on. As the next step, the quality of a film was sometimes measured solely in terms of the amount of individual personality the director had been clever enough to slip into it, irrespective of whether that personality were interesting in the first place, irrespective of his preoccupations and themes, if any.

Needless to say, Bazin had his feet too firmly on the ground to subscribe to this kind of inane attitude to films. In his article on the *politique des auteurs*, he mounts a convincing attack on the distorters of this theory and, incidentally, on those who are prone, as is *Positif* occasionally, to suppose that a good director can never make a bad film.

Peter Graham

3 De la politique des auteurs

ANDRÉ BAZIN (1957)*

'Goethe? Shakespeare? Everything they put their name to is supposed to be good, and people rack their brains to find beauty in the silliest little thing they bungled. All great talents, like Goethe, Shakespeare, Beethoven and Michelangelo, created not only beautiful works, but things that were less than mediocre, quite simply awful.'

Leo Tolstoy, *Diary 1895–99.*

I realise my task is fraught with difficulties. *Cahiers du cinéma* is thought to practise the *politique des auteurs.* This opinion may perhaps not be justified by the entire output of articles, but it has been true of the majority, especially for the last two years. It would be useless and hypocritical to point to a few scraps of evidence to the contrary, and claim that our magazine is a harmless collection of wishywashy reviews.

Nevertheless, our readers must have noticed that this critical standpoint – whether implicit or explicit – has not been adopted with equal enthusiasm by all the regular contributors to *Cahiers,* and that there might exist serious differences in our admiration, or rather in the degree of our admiration. And yet the truth is that the most enthusiastic among us nearly always win the day. Eric Rohmer put his finger on the reason in his reply to a reader in No. 64: 'When opinions differ on an important film, we generally prefer to let the person who likes it most write about it.' It follows that the strictest adherents of the *politique des auteurs* get the best of it in the end, for, rightly or wrongly, they always see in their favourite directors the manifestation of the same specific qualities. So it is that Alfred Hitchcock, Jean Renoir, Roberto Rossellini, Fritz Lang, Howard Hawks, or Nicholas Ray, to judge from the pages of *Cahiers,* appear as almost infallible directors who could never make a bad film.

* *Cahiers du cinéma,* No. 70, April 1957, pp. 2–11

I would like to avoid one misunderstanding from the start. I beg to differ with those of my colleagues who are the most firmly convinced that the *politique des auteurs* is well founded, but this in no way compromises the general policy of the magazine. Whatever our differences of opinion about films or directors, our common likes and dislikes are numerous enough and strong enough to bind us together; and although I do not see the role of the *auteur* in the cinema in the same way as François Truffaut or Rohmer for example, it does not stop me believing to a certain extent in the concept of the *auteur* and very often sharing their opinions, although not always their passionate loves. I fall in with them more reluctantly in the case of their hostile reactions; often they are fiercely critical of films I find defensible – and I do so precisely because I find that the work transcends the director (they dispute this phenomenon, which they consider to be a critical contradiction). In other words, almost our only difference concerns the relationship between the work and its creator. I have never regretted that one of my colleagues has stuck up for such and such director, although I have not always agreed about the qualities of the film under examination. Finally, I would like to add that although it seems to me that the *politique des auteurs* has led its supporters to make a number of mistakes, its total results have been fertile enough to justify them in the face of their critics. It is very rare that the arguments drawn upon to attack them do not make me rush to their defence.

So it is within these limits, which, if you like, are those of a family quarrel, that I would like to tackle what seems to me to represent not so much a critical mistranslation as a critical 'false nuance of meaning'. My point of departure is an article by my friend Jean Domarchi on Vincente Minnelli's *Lust for Life*, which tells the story of Vincent Van Gogh. His praise was very intelligent and sober, but it struck me that such an article should not have been published in a magazine which, only one month previously, had allowed Rohmer to demolish John Huston. The relentless harshness of the latter, and the indulgent admiration of the former, can be explained only by the fact that Minnelli is one of Domarchi's favourites and that Huston is not a *Cahiers auteur*. This partiality is a good thing, up to a certain point, as it leads us to stick up for a film that illustrates certain facets of American culture just as much as Minnelli's personal talent. I could get Domarchi caught up in a contradiction, by pointing out to him that he ought to have sacrificed Minnelli in favour of Renoir, since it was the shooting of *Lust for Life* that forced the director of *French Cancan* to give up his own project on Van Gogh. Can Domarchi claim that a *Van Gogh* by Renoir would not have brought more prestige to the *politique des auteurs* than a film by Minnelli? What was needed was a painter's son, and what we got was a director of filmed ballets!

But whatever the case, this example is only a pretext. Many a time I have felt uneasy at the subtlety of an argument, which completely failed to camouflage the *naïveté* of the assumption whereby, for example, the intentions and the coherence of a deliberate and well- thought-out film are read into some little B feature.

And of course as soon as you state that the filmmaker and his or her films are one, there can be no minor films, as the worst of them will always be in the image of their creator. But let's see what the facts of the matter are. In order to do so, we must go right back to the beginning.

Of course, the *politique des auteurs* is the application to the cinema of a notion that is widely accepted in the individual arts. Truffaut likes to quote Jean Giraudoux's remark: 'There are no works, there are only *auteurs*' – a polemical sally which seems to me of limited significance. The opposite statement could just as well be set as an exam question. The two formulae, like the maxims of François de La Rochefoucauld and Chamfort, would simply reverse their proportion of truth and error. As for Rohmer, he states (or rather asserts) that in art it is the *auteurs,* and not the works, that remain; and the programmes of film societies would seem to support this critical truth.

But one should note that Rohmer's argument does not go nearly as far as Giraudoux's aphorism, for, if *auteurs* remain, it is not necessarily because of their output as a whole. There is no lack of examples to prove that the contrary is true. Maybe Voltaire's name is more important than his bibliography, but now that he has been put in perspective it is not so much his *Dictionnaire philosophique* that counts nowadays as his Voltairean wit, a certain *style* of thinking and writing. But today where are we to find the principle and the example? In his abundant and atrocious writings for the theatre? Or in the slim volume of short stories? And what about Pierre-Augustin Caron de Beaumarchais? Are we to go looking in *La Mère coupable*?

In any case, the authors of that period were apparently themselves aware of the relativity of their worth, since they willingly disowned their works, and sometimes even did not mind being the subject of lampoons whose quality they took as a compliment. For them, almost the only thing that mattered was the work itself, whether their own or another's, and it was only at the end of the eighteenth century, with Beaumarchais in fact, that the concept of the *auteur* finally crystallised legally, with his or her royalties, duties, and responsibilities. Of course I am making allowances for historical and social contingencies; political and moral censorship has made anonymity sometimes inevitable and always excusable. But surely the anonymity of the writings of the French Resistance in no way lessened the dignity or responsibility of the writer. It was only in the nineteenth century that copying or plagiarism really began to be considered a professional breach that disqualified its perpetrator.

The same is true of painting. Although nowadays any old splash of paint can be valued according to its measurements and the celebrity of the signature, the objective quality of the work itself was formerly held in much higher esteem. Proof of this is to be found in the difficulty there is in authenticating many old pictures. What emerged from a studio might simply be the work of a pupil, and we are now unable to *prove* anything one way or the other. If one goes back even further, one has to take into consideration the anonymous works that have come down to us as the products not of an artist, but of an art, not of a person, but of a society.

I can see how I will be rebutted. We should not objectify our ignorance or let it crystallise into a reality. All these works of art, from the Venus de Milo to the African mask, did in fact have an *auteur*; and the whole of modern historical science is tending to fill in the gaps and give names to these works of art. But did one really have to wait for such erudite addenda before being able to admire and enjoy them? Biographical criticism is but one of many possible critical dimensions – people are still arguing about the identity of William Shakespeare or Molière.

But that's just the point! People *are* arguing. So their identity is not a matter of complete indifference. The evolution of Western art towards greater personalisation should definitely be considered as a step forward, as a refinement of culture, but only as long as this individualisation remains only a final perfection and does not claim to *define* culture. At this point, we should remember the irrefutable

James Stewart in Alfred Hitchcock's *The Man Who Knew Too Much* (1956).

commonplace we learnt at school: the individual transcends society, but society is also and above all *within* the individual. So there can be no definitive criticism of genius or talent which does not first take into consideration the social determinism, the historical combination of circumstances, and the technical background which to a large extent determine it. That is why the anonymity of a work of art is a handicap that impinges only very slightly on our understanding of it. In any case, much depends on the particular branch of art in question, the style adopted, and the sociological context. African art does not suffer by remaining anonymous – although of course it is unfortunate we know so little about the societies that gave birth to it.

But *The Man Who Knew Too Much, Europe '51,* and *Bigger Than Life* are contemporary with the paintings of Pablo Picasso, Henri Matisse, and Gustave Singier! Does it follow that one should see in them the same degree of individualisation? I for one do not think so.

If you will excuse yet another commonplace, the cinema is an art which is both popular and industrial. These conditions, which are necessary to its existence, in no way constitute a collection of hindrances – no more than in architecture – they rather represent a group of positive and negative circumstances which have to be reckoned with. And this is especially true of the American cinema, which the theoreticians of the *politique des auteurs* admire so much. What makes Hollywood so much better than anything else in the world is not only the quality of certain directors, but also the vitality and, in a certain sense, the excellence of a tradition. Hollywood's superiority is only incidentally technical; it lies much more in what one might call the American cinematic genius, something which should be analysed, then defined, by a sociological approach to its production. The American cinema has been able, in an extraordinarily competent way, to show American society just as it wanted to see itself; but not at all passively, as a simple act of satisfaction and escape, but dynamically, i.e. by participating with the means at its disposal in the building of that society. What is so admirable in the American cinema is that it cannot help being spontaneous. Although the fruit of free enterprise and capitalism – and harbouring their active or still only virtual defects – it is in a way the truest and most realistic cinema of all because it shrinks from depicting even the contradictions of that society.

But it follows that directors are swept along by this powerful surge; naturally their artistic course has to be plotted according to the currents – it is not as if they were sailing as their fancy took them on the calm waters of a lake.

In fact it is not even true of the most individual artistic disciplines that genius is free and always self-dependent. And what is genius anyway if not a certain combination of unquestionably personal talents, a gift of the gods, and a moment in

Christopher Olsen (left), James Mason and Barbara Rush in Nicholas Ray's *Bigger Than Life* (1956).

history? Genius is an H-bomb. The fission of uranium triggers off the fusion of hydrogen pulp. But a sun cannot be born from the disintegration of an individual alone unless this disintegration has repercussions on the art that surrounds it. Whence the paradox of Arthur Rimbaud's life. His poetic flash in the pan suddenly died out and Rimbaud the adventurer became more and more distant like a star, still glowing but heading towards extinction. Probably Rimbaud did not change at all. There was simply nothing left to feed the flames that had reduced the whole of literature to ashes. Generally speaking, the rate of this combustion in the cycles of great art is usually greater than the lifespan of a man. Literature's step is measured in centuries. It will be said that genius foreshadows that which comes after it. This is true, but only dialectically. For one could also say that every age has the geniuses it needs in order to define, repudiate, and transcend itself. Consequently, Voltaire was a horrible playwright when he thought he was Jean Racine's successor and a story-teller of genius when he made the parable a vehicle for the ideas which were going to shatter the eighteenth century.

And even without having to use as examples the utter failures which had their causes almost entirely in the sociology of art, creative psychology alone could easily account for a lot of patchiness even in the best authors. Victor Hugo's *Notre-*

Dame-de-Paris is pretty slight compared with *La Légende des siècles,* Gustave Flaubert's *Salammbô* does not come up to *Madame Bovary,* or André Gide's *Corydon* to *Le Journal des faux-monnayeurs.* There is no point in quibbling about these examples, there will always be others to suit everyone's taste. Surely one can accept the permanence of talent without confusing it with some kind of artistic infallibility or immunity against making mistakes, which could only be divine attributes. But God, as Jean-Paul Sartre has already pointed out, is not an artist! Were one to attribute to creative man, in the face of all psychological probability, an unflagging richness of inspiration, one would have to admit that this inspiration always comes up against a whole complex of particular circumstances which make the result, in the cinema, a thousand times more chancy than in painting or in literature.

Conversely, there is no reason why there should not exist – and sometimes they do – flashes in the pan in the work of otherwise mediocre filmmakers. Results of a fortunate combination of circumstances in which there is a precarious moment of balance between talent and milieu, these fleeting brilliancies do not prove all that much about personal creative qualities; but they are not however intrinsically inferior to others – and probably would not seem so if the critics had not begun by reading the signature at the bottom of the painting.

Well, what is true of literature is even truer of the cinema, to the extent that this art, the last to come on to the scene, accelerates and multiplies the evolutionary factors that are common to all the others. In fifty years, the cinema, which started with the crudest forms of spectacle (primitive but not inferior) has had to cover the same ground as the play or the novel and is often on the same level as they are. Within that same period, its technical development has been of a kind that cannot compare with that of any traditional art within a comparable period (except perhaps architecture, another industrial art). Under such conditions, it is hardly surprising that genius will burn itself out ten times as fast, and that a director who suffers no loss of ability may cease to be swept along by the wave. This was the case with Erich von Stroheim, Abel Gance, and Orson Welles. We are now beginning to see things in enough perspective to notice a curious phenomenon: a filmmaker can, within his or her own lifetime, be refloated by the following wave. This is true of Gance and Stroheim, whose modernity is all the more apparent nowadays. I am fully aware that this only goes to prove their quality of *auteur,* but their eclipse still cannot be entirely explained away by the contradictions of capitalism or the stupidity of producers. If one keeps a sense of proportion, one sees that the same thing has happened to people of genius in the cinema as would have happened to a 120-year-old Racine writing Racinian plays in the middle of the eighteenth century. Would his tragedies have been better than Voltaire's? The answer is by no means clear-cut; but I bet they would not have been.

Dorothy Comingore
and Orson Welles
in *Citizen Kane*
(1941).

One can justifiably point to Charles Chaplin, Renoir, or René Clair. But each of them was endowed with further gifts that have little to do with genius and which were precisely those that enabled them to adapt themselves to the predicament of film production. Of course, the case of Chaplin was unique, since, as both *auteur* and producer, he has been able to be both the cinema and its evolution.

It follows, then, according to the most basic laws of the psychology of creation, that, as the objective factors of genius are much more likely to modify themselves in the cinema than in any other art, a rapid maladjustment between the filmmaker and the cinema can occur, and this can abruptly affect the quality of his or her films as a result. Of course I admire Welles's *Confidential Report,* and I can see the same qualities in it as I see in *Citizen Kane.* But *Citizen Kane* opened up a new era of American cinema, and *Confidential Report* is a film of only secondary importance.

But let's pause a moment on this assertion – it may, I feel, allow us to get to the heart of the matter. I think that not only would the supporters of the *politique des auteurs* refuse to agree that *Confidential Report* is an inferior film to *Citizen Kane;*

Orson Welles in his own film *Mr Arkadin* (aka *Confidential Report*, 1955).

they would be more eager to claim the contrary, and I can easily see how they would go about it. As *Confidential Report* is Welles's sixth film, one can assume that a certain amount of progress has already been made. Not only did the Welles of 1953 have more experience of himself and of his art than in 1941, but however great the freedom he was able to obtain in Hollywood *Citizen Kane* cannot help remaining to a certain extent an RKO product. The film would never have seen the light of day without the co-operation of some superb technicians and their just as admirable technical apparatus. Gregg Toland, to mention only one, was more than a little responsible for the final result. On the other hand, *Confidential Report* is completely the work of Welles. Until it can be proved to the contrary, it will be considered *a priori* a superior film because it is more personal and because Welles's personality can only have matured as he grew older.

As far as this question is concerned, I can only agree with my young firebrands when they state that age as such cannot diminish the talent of a filmmaker and react violently to that critical prejudice which consists of always finding the works of a young or mature filmmaker superior to the films of an old director. It has been said that Chaplin's *Monsieur Verdoux* was not up to *The Gold Rush*; people have criticised Renoir's *The River* and *Carrosse d'or*, saying they miss the good old days of *La Règle du jeu*. Eric Rohmer has found an excellent answer to this: 'The history of art offers no example, as far as I know, of an authentic genius who has gone through a period of true decline at the end of his career; this should encourage us rather to detect, beneath what seems to be clumsy or bald, the traces of that desire for simplicity that characterises the 'last manner' of painters such as Titian, Rembrandt, Matisse, or Bonnard, composers such as Beethoven and Stravinsky (*Cahiers du cinéma*, No. 8, 'Renoir américain'). What kind of absurd discrimination has decided that filmmakers alone are victims of a senility that other artists are protected from? There do remain the exceptional cases of dotage, but they are much rarer than is sometimes supposed. When Charles Baudelaire was paralysed and unable to utter anything other than his '*cré nom*', was he any less Baudelairean? Robert Mallet tells us how Valery Larbaud, Joyce's translator into French, struggling against paralysis after twenty years of immobility and silence, had managed to build up for himself a vocabulary of twenty simple words. With these, he was still able to bring out some extraordinarily shrewd literary judgements. In fact, the few exceptions one could mention only go to prove the rule. A great talent matures but does not grow old. There is no reason why this law of artistic psychology should not also be valid for the cinema. Criticism that is based implicitly on the hypothesis of senility cannot hold water. It is rather the opposite postulate that ought to be stated: we should say that when we think we can discern a decline it is our own critical sense that is at fault, since an impoverishment of inspiration is a very unlikely phenomenon. From this point of view, the bias of the *politique des auteurs* is very fruitful, and I will stick up for them against the *naïveté*, the foolishness even, of the prejudices they are fighting.

But, always remembering this, one has nevertheless to accept that certain indisputable 'greats' have suffered an eclipse or a loss of their powers. I think what I have already said in this article may point to the reason for this. The problem has to do with the ageing not of people but of the cinema itself: those who do not know how to age *with* it will be overtaken by its evolution. This is why it has been possible for there to have been a series of failures leading to complete catastrophe without it being necessary to suppose that the genius of yesterday has become an imbecile. Once again, it is simply a question of the appearance of a clash between the subjective inspiration of the creator and the objective situation of the cinema, and this is what the *politique des auteurs* refuses to see. To its supporters *Confidential Report* is a more important film than *Citizen Kane* because they justifiably see more of Orson Welles in it. In other words, all they want to retain in the equation *auteur plus subject = work* is the *auteur*, while the subject is reduced to zero. Some of them will pretend to grant me that, all things being equal as far as the *auteur* is concerned, a good subject is naturally better than a bad one, but the more outspoken and foolhardy among them will admit that it very much looks as if they prefer minor B films, where the banality of the scenario leaves more room for the personal contribution of the *auteur*.

Of course I will be challenged on the very concept of *auteur*. I admit that the equation I have just used is artificial, just as much so in fact as the distinction one learnt at school between form and content. To benefit from the *politique des auteurs* one first has to be worthy of it, and as it happens this school of criticism claims to distinguish between true *auteurs* and *metteurs-en-scène*, even talented ones: Nicholas Ray is an *auteur*, John Huston is supposed to be only a *metteur-en-scène*; Robert Bresson and Roberto Rossellini are *auteurs*, René Clément is only a great *metteur-en-scène*, and so on. So this conception of the author is not compatible with the *auteur*/subject distinction, because it is of greater importance to find out if a director is worthy of entering the select group of *auteurs* than it is to judge how well he or she has used the material to hand. To a certain extent at least, *auteurs* are a subject to themselves; whatever the scenario, they always tell the same story, or, in case the word 'story' is confusing, let's say they have the same attitude and pass the same moral judgements on the action and on the characters. Jacques Rivette has said that an *auteur* is someone who speaks in the first person. It's a good definition; let's adopt it.

The *politique des auteurs* consists, in short, of choosing the personal factor in artistic creation as a standard of reference, and then of assuming that it continues and even progresses from one film to the next. It is recognised that there do exist certain important films of quality that escape this test, but these will systematically be considered inferior to those in which the personal stamp of the *auteur*, however run-of-the-mill the scenario, can be perceived even infinitesimally.

It is far from my intention to deny the positive attitude and methodological qualities of this bias. First of all, it has the great merit of treating the cinema as an adult art and of reacting against the impressionistic relativism that still reigns over the bulk of film criticism. I admit that the explicit or admitted pretension of a critic to reconsider the production of a filmmaker with every new film in the light of his or her judgement has something presumptuous about it that recalls Ubu. I am also quite willing to admit that if one is human one cannot help doing this, and, short of giving up the whole idea of actually criticising, one might as well take as a starting-point the feelings, pleasant or unpleasant, one feels personally when in contact with a film. Okay, but only on condition that these first impressions are kept in their proper place. We have to take them into consideration, but we should not use them as a basis. In other words, every critical act should consist of referring the film in question to a scale of values, but this reference is not merely a matter of intelligence; the sureness of one's judgment arises also, or perhaps even first of all (in the chronological sense of the word), from a general impression experienced during a film. I feel there are two symmetrical heresies, which are: (*a*) objectively applying to a film a critical all-purpose yardstick; and (*b*) considering it sufficient simply to state one's pleasure or disgust. The first denies the role of taste, the second presupposes the superiority of the critic's taste over that of the author. Detachment… or presumption!

What I like about the *politique des auteurs* is that it reacts against the impressionist approach while retaining the best of it. In fact the scale of values it proposes is not ideological. Its starting-point is an appreciation largely composed of taste and sensibility: it has to discern the contribution of the artist as such, quite apart from the qualities of the subject or the technique: i.e. the person behind the style. But once one has made this distinction, this kind of criticism is doomed to beg the question, for it assumes at the start of its analysis that the film is automatically good since it has been made by an *auteur*. And so the yardstick applied to the film is the aesthetic portrait of the filmmaker deduced from his or her previous films. This is all right so long as there has been no mistake about promoting this filmmaker to the status of *auteur*. For it is objectively speaking safer to trust in the genius of the artist than in one's own critical intelligence. And this is where the *politique des auteurs* falls in line with the system of 'criticism by beauty'; in other words, when one is dealing with a genius, it is always a good method to presuppose that a supposed weakness in a work of art is nothing other than a beauty that one has not yet managed to understand. But as I have shown this method had its limitations even in traditionally individualistic arts such as literature, and all the more so in the cinema where the sociological and historical cross-currents are countless. By giving such importance to B films, the *politique des auteurs* recognises and confirms this dependence *a contrario*.

Another point is that as the criteria of the *politique des auteurs* are very difficult to formulate the whole thing becomes highly hazardous. It is significant that our finest writers on *Cahiers* have been practising it for three or four years now and have yet to produce the main corpus of its theory. Nor is one particularly likely to forget how Rivette suggested we should admire Hawks: 'The mark of Hawks's genius is its statement of fact; *Monkey Business* is the work of a genius, and it impresses itself on one's mind through this statement of fact. Some people resist against this, they demand more than simple affirmations. And perhaps the failure to appreciate his talent arises quite simply from this… .' You can see the danger here: an aesthetic personality cult.

But that is not the main point, at least to the extent that the *politique des auteurs* is practised by people of taste who know how to watch their step. It is its negative side that seems the most serious to me. It is unfortunate to praise a film that in no

Cary Grant (left), Ginger Rogers (centre) and Marilyn Monroe (right) in Howard Hawks's *Monkey Business* (1952).

way deserves it, but the dangers are less far-reaching than when a worthwhile film is rejected because its director has made nothing good up to that point. I am not denying that the champions of the *politique des auteurs* discover or encourage a budding talent when they get the chance. But they do systematically look down on anything in a film that comes from a common fund and which can sometimes be entirely admirable, just as it can be utterly detestable. Thus, a certain kind of popular American culture lies at the basis of Minnelli's *Lust for Life,* but another more spontaneous kind of culture is also the principle of American comedy, the Western, and the *film noir.* And its influence is here beneficial, for it is this that gives these cinematic genres their vigour and richness, resulting as they do from an artistic evolution that has always been in wonderfully close harmony with its public. And so one can read a review in *Cahiers* of a Western by Anthony Mann – and God knows I like Anthony Mann's Westerns! – as if it were not above all a Western, i.e. a whole collection of conventions in the script, the acting, and the direction. I know very well that in a film magazine one may be permitted to skip such mundane details; but they should at least be implied, whereas what in fact happens is that their existence is glossed over rather sheepishly, as though they were a rather ridiculous necessity that it would be incongruous to mention. In any case, the supporters of the *politique des auteurs* will look down on, or treat condescendingly, any Western by a director who is not yet approved, even if it is as round and smooth as an egg. Well, what is *Stagecoach* if not an ultra-classical Western in which the art of John Ford consists simply of raising characters and situations to an absolute degree of perfection? And while sitting on the Censorship Committee I have seen some admirable Westerns, more or less anonymous and off the beaten track, but displaying a wonderful knowledge of the conventions of the genre and respecting that style from beginning to end.

Paradoxically, the champions of the *politique des auteurs* admire the American cinema, where production restrictions are heavier than anywhere else. It is also true that it is the country where the greatest technical possibilities are offered to the director. But the one does not cancel out the other. I do however admit that freedom is greater in Hollywood than it is said to be, as long as one knows how to detect its manifestations, and I will go so far as to say that the tradition of genres is a base of operations for creative freedom. The American cinema is a classical art, but why not then admire in it what is most admirable, i.e. not only the talent of this or that filmmaker, but the genius of the system, the richness of its ever-vigorous tradition, and its fertility when it comes into contact with new elements – as has been proved, if proof there need be, in such films as *An American in Paris, The Seven Year Itch,* and *Bus Stop.* True, Logan is lucky enough to be considered an *auteur,* or at least a budding *auteur.* But then when *Picnic* or *Bus Stop* get good reviews the praise does not go to what seems to me to be the essential point, i.e. the social truth, which of course is not offered as a goal that suffices in itself, but is integrated into a style of cinematic narration just as pre-war America was integrated into American comedy.

To conclude: the *politique des auteurs* seems to me to hold and defend an essential critical truth that the cinema is in need of more than the other arts, precisely because an act of true artistic creation is more uncertain and vulnerable in the cinema than elsewhere. But its exclusive practice leads to another danger: the negation of the film to the benefit of praise of its *auteur.* I have tried to show why mediocre *auteurs* can, by accident, make admirable films, and how, conversely, a genius can fall victim to an equally accidental sterility. I feel that this useful and fruitful approach, quite apart from its polemical value, should be complemented by other approaches to the cinematic phenomenon which will restore to a film its quality as a work of art. This does not mean one has to deny the role of *auteurs,* but simply give them back the preposition without which the noun *auteur* remains but a halting concept. *Auteur,* yes, but what *of?*

II

CRITICAL DEBATES: STATEMENTS, POLEMICS, REVISIONS

Much more directly influential than Astruc or Truffaut, though his theories too were later traduced by his disciples, was André Bazin. In 1947 he founded *La Revue du cinéma*, which became *Cahiers du cinéma* in April 1951. He remained one of its editors and its spiritual leader until his death at the age of forty in 1958. A convinced Catholic, he wrote a large number of cogent articles or studies, on such varied subjects as eroticism in the cinema, filmed theatre, Neo-Realism, the Western, and the myth of Stalin in the Soviet cinema. But, as well as the text on *De la politique des auteurs* in the preceding pages, the article of his which probably had the greatest influence over the thinking of the *Cahiers* directors was 'L'évolution du langage cinématographique' ('The evolution of film language').

Peter Graham

4 The Evolution of Film Language

ANDRÉ BAZIN (1951–58)[*]

B y 1928, the art of the silent film was at its height. Many of the best directors were understandably, though not justifiably, sorry to witness the disappearance of this perfect world of images. They felt that the cinema, having taken a certain aesthetic direction, had become an art that was supremely suited to what was known as the 'exquisite unnaturalness' of silence. The realism of sound was bound to upset matters.

In fact, now that the use of sound has satisfactorily proved that far from annihilating the Old Testament of the cinema it has brought it to fulfilment, one might well ask oneself if the technical revolution that resulted from the introduction of sound could really be called an aesthetic revolution. In other words, did the years 1928–30 really witness the birth of a new cinema? As far as the way a film is put together is concerned, the history of the cinema does not in fact reveal as marked a difference as one might expect between the silent and sound cinema. There are many affinities to be found between certain directors of the twenties and others of the thirties and especially the forties – between, for instance, Erich von Stroheim and Jean Renoir or Orson Welles, Carl Theodor Dreyer and Robert Bresson. These more or less marked affinities prove first of all that the dividing line of 1930 was no barrier, that certain qualities of the silent cinema were carried over into the sound era, but above all that instead of contrasting 'sound' with 'silent' films we should examine in what way they differed from *and* resembled each other in conception and style.

---

[*] This translated piece was published in *Qu'est-ce que le cinéma?*, vol. I, in 1958; it was the synthesis of three earlier articles written by Bazin: 'Pour en finir avec la profondeur de champ', in *Cahiers du cinéma* No. 1, April 1951; 'Découpage', in *Vingt ans de cinéma à Venise* (1952); and 'Le Découpage et son évolution', in *L'Age nouveau* No. 93 (July 1955).)

André Bazin.

I am quite aware that the brevity of this essay will oblige me to make some critical simplifications, and I shall regard what I put forward more as a working hypothesis than an objective truth. With this in mind, I would say that by and large there were two opposing schools in the cinema from 1920 to 1940: directors who believed in the image and those who believed in reality.

By 'image', I mean in a general sense anything that can be added to a depicted object by its being depicted on the screen. This addition is complex, but it can be traced back to two factors: the plasticity of the image and the resources of editing (in other words, the organisation of images in time). By plasticity I mean the style of the sets and the make-up, to a certain extent even the acting, and of course the lighting and framing which complete the composition. As for the editing, which, as is well known, had its source in D.W. Griffith's masterpieces, André Malraux wrote in *The Psychology of the Cinema* that it constitutes the birth of the film as an art: editing is what truly distinguishes it from simple animated photography and makes it a language.

The use of editing can be 'invisible'; and this was most frequently the case in the classical pre-war American film. The only purpose of breaking down the shots is to analyse an event according to the physical and dramatic logic of a scene. This analysis is rendered imperceptible by its very logicality. The spectator's mind naturally accepts the camera angles that the director offers him because they are justified by the disposition of the action or the shifting of dramatic interest.

But the neutrality of this 'invisible' breakdown of sequences does not take into account the full possibilities of editing. These are to be found in three devices generally known as 'parallel editing', 'accelerated editing', and 'editing by attraction'. In creating parallel editing, Griffith managed to evoke the simultaneity of two widely separated actions, by a succession of shots of first one, then the other. In *La Roue* (*The Wheel*), Abel Gance creates the illusion of an accelerating locomotive without having recourse to any real images of speed (for all we know, the wheels might as well be revolving on the spot), simply by an accumulation of shorter and shorter shots. Finally, editing by attraction, conceived by Eisenstein and more difficult to describe, might be broadly defined as the reinforcement of the meaning of one image by another image which does not necessarily belong to the same action: for instance, the cascade of light, in *The General Line,* which follows the shot of the bull. In this extreme form, editing by attraction has not been used very frequently, even by its originator, but the much more general practice of ellipse, comparison, or metaphor is basically very similar: for instance, stockings thrown on to the chair at the foot of the bed, or even spilt milk (in Henri-Georges Clouzot's *Quai des Orfèvres* [*Jenny Lamour*]).

Naturally there exist various combinations of these three devices. But whatever they are, they have a common recognisable feature (which could serve as the very definition of editing): the creation of a meaning which is not contained objectively in the individual images themselves, but which arises from their collocation. Lev Kuleshov's famous experiment with the same shot of Ivan Mozhukhin, whose

The bull and 'the cascade of light' in Grigori Aleksandrov and Sergei Eisenstein's *The General Line* (1929).

smile seemed to change in implication according to the shot that preceded it, is a perfect summary of the properties of editing.

Kuleshov, Eisenstein, and Gance do not show the event through their editing; they allude to it. True, they take most of their elements from the reality they are supposed to be describing, but the final meaning of the film lies much more in the organisation of these elements than in their objective content. The substance of the narrative, whatever the realism of the individual shots, arises essentially from these relationships (Mozzhukhin smiling plus dead child = pity); that is to say there is an abstract result whose origins are not to be found in any of the concrete elements. In the same way, one could imagine that young girls plus apple trees in blossom = hope. The combinations are innumerable. But they all have one thing in common: they suggest an idea by means of a metaphor or an association of ideas. And so between the scenario proper – the ultimate object of the narrative – and the raw image, a supplementary link is inserted, a kind of aesthetic 'transformer'. The meaning is not *in* the image, but is merely a shadow of it, projected by the editing on the consciousness of the spectator.

To sum up: both the visual content of the image and the possibilities of editing mean that the cinema has at its disposal a whole arsenal of devices with which it can impose its own interpretation of a depicted event on the spectator. By the end of the silent era, one can consider this arsenal to have been complete. The Soviet cinema took the theory and practice of editing to their ultimate conclusions, whereas the German expressionist school subjected the plasticity of the image (sets and lighting) to every possible distortion. The German and Soviet cinemas were certainly not the only important schools at the time, and one could hardly claim that in France, Sweden, or America film language lacked the means to say what it had to say. If the essence of cinematic art is to be found in all that plasticity and editing can add to a given reality, then the silent cinema was a complete art. Sound could have played only a subordinate and complementary role, as a counterpoint to the visual image. But this kind of potential enrichment (which at the best of times could only have been minor) would have paled beside the whole range of supplementary reality that was in fact introduced by sound.

What we have done is to suppose that expressionism in the editing and the image is the essential part of film art. It is precisely this generally accepted notion that is implicitly challenged, as early as the silent era, by directors such as Erich von Stroheim, F. W. Murnau, or Robert Flaherty. Editing plays practically no role at all in their films, except in the purely negative sense of eliminating what is superfluous. The camera cannot see everything at once, but at least it tries not to miss anything of what it has chosen to see. For Flaherty, the important thing to show when Nanook is hunting the seal is the relationship between the man and

Nanook hunting a seal in Robert J. Flaherty's *Nanook of the North* (1922).

the animal and the true proportions of Nanook's lying in wait. Editing could have suggested the passage of time; Flaherty is content to *show* the waiting, and the duration of the hunt becomes the very substance and object of the image. In the film this episode consists of a single shot. Can anyone deny that it is in this way much more moving than 'editing by attraction' would have been?

Murnau is less interested in time than in the reality of dramatic space: in neither *Nosferatu* nor *Sunrise* does editing play a decisive part. One might perhaps suppose that the plasticity of Murnau's images has an affinity with a certain kind of expressionism; but this would be a superficial view. The way Murnau composes his images is not at all pictorial, it adds nothing to reality, it does not deform it; rather it strives to bring out the deeper structure of reality, to reveal pre-exist-ent relationships which become the constituents of the drama. Thus, in *Tabu*, the entry of a ship into the left of the screen makes the spectator see it as a metaphor of fate, without Murnau in any way distorting the strict realism of the film, shot entirely on location.

But it was without doubt Stroheim who was the most reluctant to use visual expressionism and editing devices. In his work, reality admits its meaning like a suspect who is being grilled by an indefatigable police inspector. The principle of his direction, a simple one, is to look at the world from so close and with such insistence that it ends up by revealing its cruelty and its ugliness. One can well imagine, in theory, a Stroheim film composed of a single shot, which would be as long and as close up as one liked.

I do not want to limit my case to these three directors. We shall certainly find others, here and there, who reject expressionist elements and do not rely on editing to play a large part. Even Griffith is one of them, for example. But perhaps these examples will suffice to show that in the middle of the silent period there existed a film art that was diametrically opposed to what is normally thought to be true cinema, a language whose syntactic and semantic components are not at all the individual shots: the images are important not for what they add to reality but for what they reveal in it. The silent cinema could only counteract this tendency. Both Stroheim's *Greed* and Dreyer's *La Passion de Jeanne d'Arc* (*The Passion of Joan of Arc*) are virtually sound films. Once editing and visual composition cease to be considered as the very essence of film language, it can be seen that the arrival of sound was not an aesthetic watershed dividing two radically different aspects of the medium. Some people saw that sound was bringing a certain kind of cinema to an end; but this was not at all *the* cinema. The true cleavage plane was elsewhere; it was, and still is, cutting clean across thirty-five years of the history of cinematic expression.

Now that the aesthetic unity of the silent cinema is not as solid as it seemed, caught as it is between two strongly contrasting tendencies, we should perhaps take another look at the history of the last twenty years.

From 1930 to 1940, a certain kinship of expression in the cinema grew up throughout the world, originating in particular from America. Hollywood was riding high with five or six well-tried types of film which gave it overwhelming superiority: the American comedy (*Mr Smith Goes to Washington*, 1939), the burlesque film (the Marx Brothers), the song and dance musical (Fred Astaire and Ginger Rogers, *Ziegfeld Follies*, 1945), the gangster film (*Scarface, 1932, I was a Fugitive from a Chain Gang, 1932, The Informer*, 1935), the psychological and social drama (*Back Street, 1932, Jezebel*, 1938), the horror film (*Dr Jekyll and Mr Hyde, 1931, The Invisible Man, 1933, Frankenstein*, 1931), the Western (*Stagecoach,* 1939). During the same period, the French cinema was undoubtedly the next best after the American: its quality gradually emerged in the trend which might broadly be termed '*noir* realism' or 'poetic realism', and which was dominated by four directors: Jacques Feyder, Renoir, Marcel Carné, and Julien Duvivier. As it is not my purpose to award prizes, there would not be much point in lingering on the Soviet, British, German, and Italian films of this period, which were relatively less important than they were to be during the following ten years. In any case, the American and French films will suffice to demonstrate clearly that the pre-war sound cinema was an art that had visibly reached well-balanced maturity.

A word about content first of all: there were the well-tried genres, governed by carefully worked-out laws, capable of entertaining the largest possible international public, and also of attracting a cultivated elite, as long as these felt no *a priori* hostility towards the cinema.

As for form, the photographic and narrative styles were perfectly clear and they conformed with their subject: a total reconciliation of sound and image. When one re-sees films like William Wyler's *Jezebel,* John Ford's *Stagecoach,* or Carné's *Le Jour se Lève* (*Daybreak*) today, one senses an art that has attained a perfect balance, an ideal form of expression. Conversely, one admires dramatic and moral themes which, although not entirely creations of the cinema, were raised to a certain nobility, to an artistic effectiveness that they would not have achieved without it. In short, these were all characteristics of 'classic' art in full flower.

I am perfectly aware that there is a case for maintaining that the originality of the post-war cinema, compared with that of 1939, lies in the emergence of certain individual countries as film-producers, especially in the dazzling explosion of the Italian cinema and the appearance of a British cinema that was original and free from influences from Hollywood; that the truly important phenomenon of the forties was the infusion of new blood, the opening up of unexplored regions; that the real revolution took place more on the level of subject-matter than of style, and concerned what the cinema had to say to the world rather than the way of saying it.

Jacqueline Laurent in Marcel Carné's *Le Jour se lève* (1939).

Is not Neo-Realism above all a kind of humanism rather than a style of direction? And is not the essential feature of this style self-effacement before reality?

It is certainly not my intention to champion some supposed superiority of form over content. 'Art for art's sake' is just as heretical in the cinema as it is elsewhere, perhaps even more so! But new wine should not be put into old bottles! And one way of understanding better what a film is trying to say is to know how it is saying it.

In 1938 or 1939, then, the sound cinema had, especially in France and America, reached a degree of classical perfection that was based both on the maturity of the dramatic genres that had been developed over ten years or inherited from the silent cinema, and on the stabilisation of technical progress. The thirties saw the arrival of panchromatic film as well as sound. Of course, the studios never stopped trying to improve their equipment, but these improvements were only incidental – none of them opened up radically new possibilities in film direction. Moreover this situation has not changed since 1940, except possibly in the field of photography, thanks to an increase in the sensitivity of film. Panchromatic film upset the balance of values in the image, and ultra-sensitive emulsions allowed modifications to be made in the composition. Now that the director of photography was free to shoot in a studio with a much smaller lens aperture, he could, if necessary, eliminate the blurred backgrounds that used to be the rule. But one can find plenty of examples of depth of focus being employed well before then (by Renoir, for instance); it had always been possible in exteriors and even in the studio with a little ingenuity. It was there to be resorted to if the director so desired. And so what is important here is not so much the technical problem, although the solution of this was considerably facilitated, as the stylistic effect (which I will come back to). In short, ever since the use of panchromatic film and the possibilities offered by the microphone and the crane became general in studios, the technical conditions necessary and sufficient for the creation of film art had been achieved by 1930.

As technical requirements played practically no part in this, the signs and the principles of the evolution in language must be sought elsewhere: in the renewal of subject-matter and, in consequence, of the styles that were needed to express it. In 1939, the sound cinema had reached a point which geographers call the line of equilibrium of a river, i.e. that ideal mathematical curve that is the result of sufficient erosion. Once a river attains its line of equilibrium, it flows effortlessly from its source to its mouth without hollowing out its bed further. But if any geological shift occurs which raises the peneplain or alters the altitude of the source, the water becomes active again, penetrating the underlying land, sinking in, undermining, and hollowing out. Occasionally, if there is a bed of limestone, a whole new network of hollows forms on the plateau; it is scarcely perceptible, but is complex and contorted if one follows the way the water takes.

The Evolution of the Shooting Script Since Sound

In 1938, the way shots were broken down in a shooting script was the same almost everywhere. If, to be conventional, we call the type of silent film based on visual and editing devices 'expressionist' or 'symbolic', we might dub the new form of narrative 'analytic' and 'dramatic'. Suppose, to go back to one of the elements in Kuleshov's experiment, we have a table laden with food and a poor famished beggar. In 1936, the breakdown might have been as follows:

1. General shot taking in both the actor and the table.
2. Tracking shot forward ending in a close-up of his face which expresses a mixture of wonder and desire.
3. A series of close-ups of the food.
4. Back to the character (in medium shot) who walks slowly towards the camera.
5. Slight track back to take in the actor from the knees up, seizing a chicken's wing.

There could be many variations on this breakdown, but they would all still have several things in common:

1. Spatial verisimilitude, whereby the position of the character is always determined, even when a close-up cuts out the decor.
2. The intention and effect of this breakdown are exclusively dramatic or psychological.

In other words, if this scene were acted on stage and seen from a seat in the stalls, it would have exactly the same meaning; the event would still have an objective existence. The change in camera angles does not add anything, it simply presents reality in the most effective manner. First of all by allowing one to see it better, and then by emphasising what needs emphasising.

True, the film director, just like the theatre producer, has a margin of interpretation within which he can inflect the meaning of the action. But this is only a margin, and it cannot modify the formal logic of what takes place. By way of contrast, take the editing of the stone lions in *Battleship Potemkin*; skilfully put together, a series of shots of different pieces of sculpture give the impression that one lion (like the people) is getting to its feet. This admirable editing device was unthinkable after 1932. In *Fury*, Fritz Lang inserted, as late as 1935, a shot of clucking chickens in a farmyard after a series of shots of tittle-tattling women. This was a survival from the age of editing by attraction which brought people up in their seats even at the time and now seems totally out of place in the context of

The stone lions in Grigori Aleksandrov and Sergei Eisenstein's *The Battleship Potemkin* (1925).

the rest of the film. However marked the art of a director like Carné may be, for instance in his enhancement of the scenarios of *Le Quai des brumes* and *Le Jour se lève,* his breakdown of shots remains on the same level as the events it is analysing. It is just a good way of looking at them. This is why we are witnessing the almost complete disappearance of special visual effects, such as superimposition, and even, especially in America, the close-up, which has such a violent physical effect that it makes one aware the director has cut from one shot to another. In the typical American comedy, the director returns as often as he can to a shot of the characters from the knees up (the so-called *plan américain*), which accords best with the spontaneous attentiveness of the spectator – it is a point of natural equilibrium for his mental accommodation.

In fact, this use of editing has its origins in the silent cinema. This is more or less the part it plays in Griffith's work, in *Broken Blossoms* for example; but with *Intolerance,* Griffith was already beginning to introduce the synthetic conception of editing which the Soviet cinema was to take to its ultimate conclusions and which can be found, less exclusively, in several films at the end of the silent period. Besides, it is understandable that the sound image, being much less malleable than the visual image, made editing more realistic again and to an ever-increasing extent eliminated both plastic expressionism and symbolic relationships between images.

And so in about 1938, films were almost always put together according to the same principles. The story was told by a succession of shots, which varied very little in number (around six hundred per film). The characteristic technique of this type of narrative was cross-cutting, which, in a dialogue for instance, consists of alternate shots of either speaker according to the logic of the text. This type of shooting script, which perfectly suited the best films of 1930–39, was strongly challenged by the technique of composition in depth used by Orson Welles and William Wyler.

The reputation of *Citizen Kane* is no exaggeration. Thanks to composition in depth, whole scenes are filmed in a single shot (a device known as the sequence-shot), sometimes even without the camera moving. The dramatic effects which used to depend on the editing are all obtained here by the movements of the actors within a chosen framing. Welles did not of course 'invent' composition in depth, any more than Griffith did the close-up ; all the early pioneers of the cinema used it, and with good reason. The partially blurred image, which came in only with editing, was not simply due to technical subservience resulting from the use of close shots; it was the logical consequence of editing, its plastic equivalent. If at a certain point in the action the director takes for example, as in the imaginary sequence already mentioned, a close-up of a fruit-bowl, it is normal for him also to isolate it in space by the focusing of the lens. A blurred background confirms an editing effect. Whereas it is only an accessory part of the style of photography, it is an essential part of the style of the narrative. Jean Renoir understood this perfectly when he wrote in 1938, i.e. after *La Bête Humaine* and *La Grande Illusion* and before *La Règle du Jeu*: 'The longer I work in my profession, the more I am drawn to *mise-en-scène* in depth in relation to the screen; the more I do that, the more I am able to avoid the confrontation of two actors who stand like good boys in front of the camera as though they were at the photographer's.' And in fact if one looks for a precursor to Orson Welles, it is not Louis Lumière or Zecca but Jean Renoir. In Renoir's work, the tendency to compose the image in depth goes hand in hand with a partial suppression of editing, which is replaced by frequent panning shots and entries into frame. It implies a respect for the continuity of dramatic space and also, of course, for its duration.

Anyone who can use his eyes must realise that Welles's *plans séquence* (sequence-shots) in *The Magnificent Ambersons* are by no means the passive 'recording' of an action photographed within a single frame, but that on the contrary this reluctance to break up an event or analyse its dramatic reverberations within time is a positive technique which produces better results than a classical breakdown of shots could ever have done.

One needs only to compare two stills which are composed in depth, one from a film of 1910, the other from a film by Welles or Wyler, and one will see just from looking at each still, detached from the film, that their functions are diametrically opposed. The 1910 framing more or less takes up the position of the absent fourth wall of a theatre stage or, out of doors anyway, of the best viewpoint of the action, whereas the sets, the camera angle, and the lighting in the second composition have to be looked at with different eyes. Over the surface of the screen, the director and the director of photography have managed to organise a dramatic chessboard from which no detail is excluded. The most obvious, if not the most original, examples of this are to be found in *The Little Foxes,* where the *mise-en-scène* has the precision of a blueprint (with Welles, the baroque overtones make analysis more complicated). The placing of objects in relation to the characters is such that their meaning *cannot* escape the spectator, a meaning which editing would have built up in a series of successive shots.

Take, for instance, a dramatic construction pivoted on three characters in Wyler's *The Best Years of Our Lives* (the scene where Dana Andrews and Teresa Wright break off their engagement). The sequence takes place in a bar. Fredric March has just persuaded his friend to break off with his daughter and urges him to go and telephone her immediately. Dana Andrews gets up and goes towards the call box which is by the door at the far end of the room. March puts his elbows on the piano in the foreground and pretends to be engrossed in the musical exercises of the disabled sergeant who is learning to play with the hooks he has instead of hands. The frame contains the keyboard in close shot, takes in March in close medium shot, includes the whole room, and leaves Dana Andrews quite visible, though small, right at the back in the call box. This shot is clearly governed by two points of dramatic interest and three characters. The action taking place in the foreground is of secondary importance, although interesting and unusual enough to demand our close attention, especially as it occupies a privileged position on the screen and a considerable amount of its surface. The real action, however, the one that at this point constitutes a decisive turning-point in the plot, is taking place almost secretly in a tiny rectangle at the back of the room, i.e. on the very left of the screen.

The link between these two dramatic zones is March, who is the only person, apart from the spectator, to know what is going on in the call box, and who, as is logical in such a situation, is also moved by the prowess of his disabled friend. From time to time, March turns his head slightly, and casts an anxious glance diagonally across the screen at Dana Andrews's gesticulations. The latter finally rings off and without looking round abruptly disappears into the street. If we reduce the real action to its elements, it consists basically of a telephone call made by Dana Andrews. The only thing which interests us at this moment is the telephone conversation. The only actor whose face we want to see in close-up is precisely the one whom we cannot distinguish clearly because he is so far away from the camera and behind the glass window of the call box. His words of course cannot be heard. The real drama is taking place in the distance in a kind of small aquarium which lets us see only the banal and ritual gestures of someone telephoning.

This idea of the call box at the back of the room which forces the spectator to imagine what is going on inside it, i.e. to share March's anxiety, was in itself an excellent brainwave on the part of the director. But Wyler knew very well that alone it would destroy the spatial and temporal equilibrium of the shot. It had to be both counterbalanced and reinforced. Whence the idea of a diverting action *in the foreground,* secondary in itself, but whose visual prominence would be in inverse proportion to its dramatic importance. Although a secondary action, it is not an insignificant one; the spectator is also concerned about what will happen to the disabled sergeant and so is interested in what he is doing. And anyway it is certainly not every day that one sees someone play the piano with hooks! Held in suspense and unable really to see at what point the hero finishes telephoning, spectators are also obliged to divide their attention between the hooks and the call box. In this way, Wyler kills two birds with one stone: the diversion of the piano first of all allows him to hold for as long as necessary a shot which alone would have been interminable and inevitably monotonous, but it is above all the introduction of this pivot of subsidiary action which gives the image its dramatic organisation and quite literally its very construction. The real action is overlaid with the action of the *mise-en-scène* itself, which consists of dividing the attention of spectators

Dana Andrews, Teresa Wright, Myrna Loy, Frederic March, Harold Russell and Cathy O'Donnell in the wedding sequence of William Wyler's *The Best Years of Our Lives* (1946).

against their will, of guiding it in the right direction, and thus of making them participate in their own right in the drama created by the director.

To be more precise, I should point out that this scene is cut twice by a close shot of March looking at the call box. No doubt Wyler was afraid that the spectator would be too fascinated by the piano exercises and might gradually lose interest in the main action, i.e. the dramatic interplay between March and Andrews. The editing probably showed that the two interpolated shots were necessary to recharge the flagging attention of the audience. Such foresight is incidentally very characteristic of Wyler's technique. Welles would have managed to make the call box stand out by its very remoteness and would have held the shot for as long as necessary. For Welles, composition in depth is an aesthetic end in itself; for Wyler, it remains subordinate to the dramatic needs of the *mise-en-scène* and especially the clarity of the narrative. The two interpolated shots have the same effect as bold type or a heavily pencilled line.

Wyler especially likes to construct his *mise-en-scène* around the tension created in a shot by the simultaneity of two actions of disparate importance. This can be clearly seen in the still taken from the final sequence of the film.

The characters grouped on the right, in the middle ground, seem to form the main dramatic point of interest, as everyone has gathered in this room to attend the wedding of the disabled sergeant. In fact, since this action is a foregone conclusion and, in a sense, already over, the spectator's interest is focused on Wright (in white in the background) and Andrews (on the left in the foreground), who are meeting for the first time since they broke off their engagement. Throughout the whole sequence of the wedding, Wyler manipulates his actors with consummate skill so as gradually to bring to the fore the two protagonists, who, the spectator is sure, are continually thinking of each other. The reproduced still shows an intermediate stage. At this point, the two centres of interest, Andrews and Wright, have not yet come together, but the natural though carefully calculated movements of the other actors throw their relationship into clear relief. Wright's white dress, standing out almost in the centre of the frame, makes a kind of dramatic fissure, so that if one were to cut the image in half at the point where the walls meet the action would also be bisected into its two elements. The two lovers are visually and logically thrust into the left part of the frame.

The importance of the direction in which people look should also be noticed in this still. The gaze always forms the skeleton of Wyler's *mise-en-scène*. As well as the actual gaze of the characters, Wyler also excels at getting across to us the virtual gaze of the camera, with which our own eyes identify themselves. Jean Mitry has

Charles Dingle and the steel box in William Wyler's *The Little Foxes* (1941).

drawn attention to the low angle shot in *Jezebel* which places the lens right in line with Bette Davis's gaze as she sees the walking-stick that Henry Fonda has in his hand and intends to use. In this way we can follow the gaze of the characters better than if the camera, as in an ordinary shooting script, showed us the stick from above as if through Bette Davis's own eyes.

There is a variant of the same principles in *The Little Foxes*: in order to make us understand the thoughts of the character who notices the small steel box which used to contain some stolen shares (their absence is going to reveal his theft), Wyler puts the object in the foreground, this time with the camera at the same height as the man, but still symmetrically placed in relation to the actor and to what he is looking at. Our gaze does not meet that of the actor directly through the regarded object, but, as through the interplay of a mirror, the angle of incidence of our own gaze on the box is somehow equivalent to the angle of reflection which leads us to the eyes of the actor. In every case, Wyler guides our mental outlook by means of the strict laws of an invisible dramatic perspective.

The spectator has only to follow the gaze of the characters like a pointing finger and he will have an exact understanding of all the intentions of the director. If these could be made tangible on the image by a pencil line, we would see, as clearly as we see the ghost of a magnet in iron filings, the dramatic forces which are crossing the screen. All Wyler's preparatory work consists of simplifying the mechanics of *mise-en-scène* as far as possible by making it as efficient and as clear as he can. In *The Best Years of Our Lives*, he attains an almost abstract purity. Every point of dramatic articulation is so sensitive that a shift of a few degrees in the angle of somebody's gaze is not only quite obvious to the most obtuse spectator, but is also capable, through a kind of leverage, of turning a whole scene upside-down.

The modern director, in using the *plan séquence* with composition in depth, is not rejecting editing – how could he do so without reverting to a kind of rudimentary gibberish? He is integrating it into his visual style. The narrative of Welles and Wyler is no less explicit than that of Ford, but it has the advantage of not having to forfeit the special effects that can be obtained from the unity of the image in time and space. It matters a great deal (at least in a work that has some style) whether an event is analysed fragment by fragment or shown in its physical unity. It would of course be absurd to deny the marked progress in film language that has been brought about by the use of editing, but it has been gained at the expense of other qualities that are no less specifically cinematic.

This is why composition in depth is not just another cameraman's device, like the use of filters or of a certain type of lighting; it is a vital contribution to *mise-en-scène*: a dialectical advance in the history of film language.

And this advance is not merely a formal one. Composition in depth, well used, is not just a more economical, subtle, and simple way of heightening an event; it affects not only the structure of film language but also the intellectual relationship between the spectator and the image, thus actually modifying the meaning of the film.

It would be beyond the scope of this article to analyse the psychological repercussions of this relationship, let alone its aesthetic consequences, but perhaps it will suffice to make the following general remarks:

1. Composition in depth means that the spectators' relationship with the image is nearer to that which they have with reality. It is then true to say that quite independently of the actual content of the image its structure is more realistic.

2. Consequently, composition in depth demands a more active mental attitude on the part of spectators and even a positive contribution to the direction. Whereas with analytical editing they have only to follow their guide and let their attention focus on whatever the director has chosen for them to see, a certain minimum of personal choice is required here. The fact that the image has a meaning depends partly on their attention and their will.

3. From the two preceding propositions, which are of a psychological nature, there follows a third one which might be defined as metaphysical.

By analysing reality, the very nature of editing assumes the dramatic event to have a unity of meaning. Another analytical process might be possible, but the result would be a different film. In short, the nature and essence of editing is such that it stands in the way of the expression of ambiguity. And it was precisely this that was proved by Kuleshov's *reductio ad absurdum*: each time, an exact meaning was given to the face whose ambiguity made possible these three alternately exclusive interpretations.

Composition in depth, on the other hand, brings ambiguity back into the structure of the image; this is not automatic (Wyler's films are hardly ambiguous at all), but it is certainly a possibility. That is why it is no exaggeration to say that *Citizen Kane* is conceived entirely in terms of composition in depth. One's uncertainty about the spiritual key or interpretation of the film hangs on the very composition of the image.

It is not that Welles purposely refrains from using expressionist editing techniques. In fact, their episodic use, in between sequence-shots with composition in depth, gives them new meaning. Editing had once been the very stuff of cinema, the tissue of a scenario. In *Citizen Kane*, a series of superimpositions stands in contrast to the continuity of a scene taken in a single shot; it is a different, explicitly abstract register of the narrative. Accelerated editing used to distort time and space; Welles's editing, far from attempting to deceive us, offers us a temporal résumé – the equivalent, for example, of the French imperfect tense or the English frequentative. And so 'quick editing', 'editing by attraction', and the superimpositions which the sound cinema had not resorted to for ten years, found a possible use in conjunction with the temporal realism of cinema without editing. I have dwelt on the case of Welles because the date of his appearance in the cinematic firmament marks the beginning of a new period, and also because his case is the most spectacular and significant in its very excesses. But *Citizen Kane* fits into a general movement, into a vast geological shift of strata which, in one way and another, confirms this revolution in expression.

Confirmation along different lines can be found in the Italian cinema. In Roberto Rossellini's *Paisà* and *Germania, anno zero* (Germany, Year Zero) and Vittorio De Sica's *Ladri di biciclette* (*Bicycle Thieves*), Italian Neo-Realism stands in contrast to previous forms of cinematic realism by its elimination of any expressionism and especially by the total absence of effects obtained by editing. Just as in Welles's work (and despite their very different styles), Neo-Realism tends to give a film the feeling of the ambiguity of reality. The way Rossellini looks at the child's face in *Germania, anno zero* is at opposite poles to Kuleshov's attitude to the close-up of Mozhukhin; he wants to preserve its mystery. One should not be put on the wrong track by the fact that the evolution of Neo-Realism does not at first sight seem, as in America, to consist of some revolution in the technique of breaking down shots in a shooting script. There are various means of achieving the same end. Rossellini's and De Sica's are not so very spectacular, but they too aim at eliminating editing and transferring on to the screen the true continuity of reality. It is Cesare Zavattini's dream simply to film ninety consecutive minutes in the life of a man to whom nothing important happens! Luchino Visconti, the 'aesthete' of the neo-realists, revealed just as clearly as Welles the fundamental aim of his art in *La Terra trema,* a film that is almost entirely composed of *plans séquence* where the desire to take in the totality of an event can be seen in the composition in depth and the endless panning shots.

But we could not possibly examine all the films which have contributed to this linguistic evolution since 1940. It is time to draw some conclusions from what I have said. The last ten years have, I think, shown a marked progress in the field of cinematic expression. I deliberately neglected, from 1930 on, the tendency of the silent cinema that was particularly evident in the work of Stroheim, Murnau, Flaherty and Dreyer; but I do not think it died out with the coming of sound. On the contrary, I am sure it was the most fertile aspect of the so-called silent cinema, and the only one which, precisely because the essence of its aesthetic

F. W. Murnau's *Tabu* (1931).

conception was not bound up with editing, called for the realism of sound as its natural extension. But it is true that the sound cinema from 1930 to 1940 owes almost nothing to it, apart from the notable and, in retrospect, prophetic exception of Renoir, the only director who consistently attempted in his films up to *La Règle du jeu* to rise above facile editing effects and seize the secret of a cinematic style which was capable of expressing everything without fragmenting the world, of revealing the hidden meaning of human beings and their environment without destroying their natural unity.

However, it would be out of the question to throw discredit on the cinema of the thirties (in any case, this would not stand up to the evidence of several masterpieces). My purpose is simply to suggest a notion of dialectical progress, the turning-point of which took place in the forties. It is true that the arrival of sound proved fatal to a certain aesthetic approach to film language, but this was an approach that was leading it farthest away from its vocation for realism. The sound cinema did however retain the essential function of editing: discontinuous description and dramatic analysis of an event. It rejected the metaphor and the symbol, and aimed instead at an illusion of objective representation. Expressionist editing almost completely disappeared, but the relative realism of that narrative style which was the general rule in 1937 contained a congenital limitation of which we could not at that time have been aware, so perfectly appropriate to it were the subjects that were treated. This was true in the case of American comedy, which reached perfection within the framework of a narrative where temporal realism played no part. Essentially logical, like vaudeville and punning, perfectly conventional in its moral and sociological content, American comedy had nothing to gain from descriptive and linear precision or from the rhythmic resources of the classical narrative style.

It is above all in the direction taken by Stroheim and Murnau, almost entirely neglected in the thirties, that the cinema has been veering more or less consciously for the last ten years. But directors are not confining themselves to prolonging it, they are deriving from it the secret of a realistic regeneration of the narrative. This narrative is again becoming capable of reintegrating the temporal truth of things, the actual duration of an event which the classical narrative insidiously replaced with intellectual and abstract time. But far from eliminating the achievements of editing once and for all, modern filmmakers are giving them a relativity and a meaning. It is only when related to an increased realism in the image that extra abstraction becomes possible. The stylistic repertory of a director such as Hitchcock, for example, stretches from the powers of the documentary image to superimpositions and extreme close-ups. But Hitchcock's close-ups are not the same as those of Cecil B. De Mille in *The Cheat*. They are just one stylistic device among others. In other words, in the silent era, the editing *evoked* what the director wanted to say, in 1938 the narrative *described*, and today one can say that the director *writes* directly in film. The image – its visual structure and its organisation within time – because it can now draw on greater realism, has more means at its disposal of inflecting and modifying reality from within. The filmmaker is no longer simply the competitor of the painter or the playwright; he is at last the equal of the novelist.

As can be seen from this article (and the preceding one on the *politique des auteurs*), Bazin's approach to the cinema was a profoundly original one. He was not interested in the dry documentation of the film-historian; nor, indeed, did he ever write about a film unless he had some positive point to make (which explains the remarkable fact that he rarely panned a film – he left this to his colleagues). His approach was essentially an aesthetic one, in the original sense of the word: his starting point was what he perceived through his senses. His next step was the analytical formulation of what he instinctively felt while watching a film. Finally, he would attempt to rationalise these feelings. His persuasiveness lies in the fact that instead of baldly stating his theory he takes the reader through all the stages of his thought and gives the impression of having just that moment discovered the truth: a truly creative method of inquiry, the archetype of which is to be found in the *Essais* of Montaigne.

It can be objected that occasionally he split ontological hairs. In his essays on eroticism and death on the screen, one feels that he perhaps allowed his reason to get the upper hand over his emotions. But the fact remains that when he was wrong about a film (which was rarely) his opinion was never the result of prejudice or preconception. He had that quality so rare in film critics: an open mind. And his likes and dislikes have almost all stood the test of time; some of them, such as his admiration of Jean Renoir and Erich von Stroheim, were, in the mid 1940s, pioneering.

His influence on *Cahiers du cinéma* was enormous. But, as often happens, his potentially good influence did not prove in practice to be wholly so. His theories were often complex and bold; those of his disciples were more often pretentious. He was always ruthlessly clear-minded and articulate; they were often indecipherable.

Little in Bazin recommended itself to the critics of *Positif*. Politically on the far left, they despised his 'liberal' middle-of-the-road attitude. But their main difference lay in that conflict which runs right through the history of French culture like a basso ostinato: the clerical versus the anti-clerical. The *Positif* critics never forgave Bazin for being a Catholic. Perhaps they were a little too willing to blame on to him what they detested (and rightly so, I think) in his disciples. To give an idea of the sort of thing *Positif* was reacting against and why, the next section opens with an extract from a very long article by Gérard Gozlan in which, among other things, he formulates a lengthy and detailed critique of Jacques Rivette's *Paris nous appartient*. It is entitled – ironically of course – 'In Praise of André Bazin'.

Peter Graham

5 The Delights of Ambiguity: In Praise of André Bazin

GÉRARD GOZLAN (1962)[*]

A believer in a church, a policeman who is torturing somebody, a crying child, a woman who yields to a man, a frightened soldier – none of these, in spite of their inherent humanity, can ever stand individually as a generalised image of the human condition. Material reality envelops, pervades, and explains their basic behaviour. Reality has more than one level; it is not ambiguous, but complex and deceptive; and any attempt in art to explain or criticise it demands a search, an analysis, a choice, and an organisation. Bazin does admit the need for organisation, but only as a *pis-aller,* for in his opinion the ideal film would consist of only one shot. Since such a film is materially impossible, Bazin distinguishes certain filmmakers who, although remaining faithful to editing, manage to create '*modern* works that are from an aesthetic point of view contemporaneous with the *découpage* of *Citizen Kane, La Règle du jeu, The Little Foxes,* and *Ladri di biciclette.*' Bazin calls this new aesthetic approach *neo-montage,* and defines it as follows: 'the achievement of both physical verisimilitude and logical flexibility in the *découpage*'

La Règle du jeu, for instance, is an admirable attack on the bourgeoisie, but to Bazin it is 'a film that goes beyond the possibilities of editing and seizes the secret of a cinematic style that is capable of expressing everything without fragmenting the world, of revealing the hidden meaning of human beings and their environment without destroying their natural unity.' And Bazin praises Hitchcock (yes, Bazin too!) because he 'excels at suggesting the ambiguity of an event while at the same time breaking it up into a series of close shots'. Ambiguity makes for a 'liberal and democratic' style *par excellence:* 'the director who breaks down the scenario into shots for us makes the choice that we ourselves make in real life. We unconsciously accept his analysis because it conforms with the way we look at a film; but on the other hand it does deprive us of a privilege that has just as strong a psychological basis – and which we give up without realising we are doing so – i.e.

---

* *Positif,* Nos 46 and 47, June and July 1962.

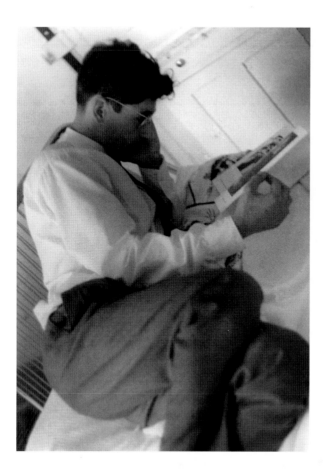

Gérard Gozlan.

the freedom, or virtual freedom anyway, to modify our own system of breaking down reality at any given moment.'

Should one conclude from this mumbo-jumbo that Bazin feels that, when there *is* analysis, spectators are being cheated, and the meaning they get from the film comes to them only via their subconscious? But when no analysis is done for spectators, lo and behold! they actively try to analyse, and actually get close to the truth, as they are 'free to do their own *mise-en-scène*.' The interest and attentiveness of spectators is multiplied ten times: this, one supposes, is psychological freedom. They are given back their independence: this is another kind of freedom, moral freedom. In other words, suppose there are thirty people listening to a lecture; it is quite natural that those who best understand what the lecturer is talking about will be those who are interested in what he or she is saying. But it does not go without saying that they understand better because the lecturer is talking about a subject 'objectively', or without any previously thought out ideas, or without any kind of developed analysis. One may even go so far as to question the validity of a word

Wesley Addy (left) in Robert Aldrich's and Vincent Sherman's *The Garment Jungle* (1957).

such as 'objectivity' in connection with religion. And what if one of the thirty listeners, left free to do his or her own *mise-en-scène,* wants to look at the flies buzzing round the room or at the colour of the walls? Can one then say that that person is nearer the truth than his or her neighbour, who possesses a certain knowledge of what the lecturer is talking about and will have certain 'opinions' about it?

I suppose the answer would be that this is a more moral way of going about things, it is 'democracy'. In analytical editing, writes Bazin, 'spectators simply follow their guide, and let their attention identify itself with that of the director, who choses for them what they should see'; whereas when one enters the realm of the *découpage* passivity is replaced by that 'minimum of personal choice' on the part of the spectator. That is why Bazin praises Wyler in *The Best Years of Our Lives,* because 'an ethical scrupulousness for reality is given an aesthetic transcription in the *mise-en-scène*', and he adds that 'the only way to imitate Wyler would be to espouse the ethics of *mise-en-scène* that have produced their finest results in *The Best Years of Our Lives*'.

I propose to examine a specific example of a shot which is remarkable for the way in which depth of field is used and the *mise-en-scène* organised within a single frame. It occurs in Robert Aldrich's *The Garment Jungle.* The scene takes place in the trade union's headquarters; Renata, the extremist leader, is haranguing his comrades. Suddenly a group of blacklegs in the pay of the employers burst in and break up the meeting. Then comes the following shot: on the far left, in extreme close-up and facing the camera, is the leader of the blacklegs, Renata is in the centre of the frame, and in the background are the union members seated on benches with the blacklegs watching them. This is just the sort of *mise-en-scène* that Bazin likes; for here spectators are not forced by the editing to watch what the director has chosen for them – they are free to look at what they wish: the killer, or Renata, who refuses to give in, or the people in the background, who are immobile or threatening. But we must remember that whatever freedom is given to spectators to do their own little *mise-en-scène*, nothing will be changed in Aldrich's *mise-en-scène*, which is the only one that counts. And Aldrich's *mise-en-scène* in this shot is absolutely inseparable from the context, i.e. what is important for him is the aggressive confrontation of two men, with the mass of union members wavering between them. The spectators' job is not simply to watch what they want to, and say afterwards that they have the right to cuddle up to their girl- or boy-friend, but to perceive the conflict that Aldrich has so remarkably grouped within a single frame: the struggle between a man who represents the workers and a man who has sold himself to the employers.

Does the depth of composition and the organisation of most of the characters within the same frame prove that reality is ambiguous and all on the same level? Not a bit of it. For Aldrich could equally well have given us a succession of shots of the killer, and then of Renata, with reaction shots of the union members – the content would have remained the same, i.e. the ferocious opposition of two men and two classes. Why did Aldrich shoot it as he did? Certainly not in order to give the scene a stylishly modern look, and certainly not because he had been reading Bazin, but simply because the opposition is more striking when shown in this way. The presence in the foreground of the killer's face, which Renata cannot see, makes the latter's position even more fragile and precarious, and suggests the power of the repressive machine. And so depth of composition here does not introduce a new way of conceiving or apprehending reality (editing would have been able to do the same thing too), but simply allows the filmmaker to draw on a greater range of stylistic means to describe reality as he or she feels it. Some of Bazin's disciples would like to suppress cross-cutting entirely, as though it were necessary to attack the very nature of cross-cutting, instead of its unintelligent use. For if, in several of Carné's films, cross-cutting rapidly becomes a tiring device, it is probably because the framing each time gives us no more than a simple shot of each character, so that the *découpage*, instead of enriching the relationship that has already been created between the two characters by dialogue, gestures, and the sets, deprives us of some of this interplay. There is no question of metaphysics or fundamental principles here.

'The spectator's eye can roam freely between the glass in the foreground and the door at the other end of the room, which is opened by Kane' – Orson Welles's *Citizen Kane* (1941).

And yet it is the transition to metaphysics that is important for Bazin. Proof of this is to be found in the way he explains the poisoning scene in *Citizen Kane*. According to Bazin, thanks to the depth of composition, the spectator's eye can roam freely between the glass in the foreground and the door at the other end of the room, which is opened by Kane. The continuity of the spectator's gaze leads, I suppose, straight to the assertion that 'all reality is on the same level'. This again is patently specious thinking, for Bazin leaps from a dramatic meaning that is a specific part of the scene and of the film as a whole to a very general meaning, the most general possible – and also highly debatable. The result is a levelling down of the elements of reality, instead of a demonstration of their organisation, their opposition, and their true relationship. It is no mere coincidence that Bazin's and Wyler's paths crossed: Wyler's style has the same tendency to level down, to iron out differences, while putting the *mise-en-scène* on a level where relationships, conflicts, and contradictions are highly superficial. Nor is it a mere coincidence that Bazin defines Wyler's *mise-en-scène* as an 'attempt to suppress itself', and talks of a 'negative definition' of *mise-en- scène*.

But let's get back to the role of the spectator. Bazin demands that he or she be given 'freedom', i.e. a kind of virginity regained, a completely new purity in the face of the mystery of screen reality. The free person should be something like a mind that has been completely emptied of the farrago it has acquired and learned; it must be ready to re-learn everything from scratch, in that ideal and sacred place, the cinema. The film spectator is a new being, and one should be able to conceive of him or her as being something outside the other elements of reality. Let's take Kuleshov's experiment. It will be agreed that Mozhukhin's face is remarkable for one thing only: it is inexpressive, in so far as expression necessarily implies some sort of content. Why then does Bazin substitute the word 'ambiguous' for the word 'inexpressive'? 'Kuleshov's experiment', writes Bazin, 'gives a precise meaning each time to the face whose ambiguity has made possible these alternately exclusive interpretations.' The fallacy lies in that arbitrary and purely verbal substitution which, for Bazin, but only for Bazin, implies a dubious metaphysical idea, that of ambiguity. The fallacy also lies in a highly debatable belief in the 'passive' role of the spectator. Bazin's whole reasoning pre- supposes that the nature of editing, by tampering with reality, renders the spectator's behaviour completely passive. For it should be said that an actor's expression is suggested to the spectator not so much by the nature of editing as by the spectator's own psychological make-up. I should be very surprised, for example, if a seven-year-old child or a homosexual were to attribute the same passion to Mozhukhin when he 'looks' at the naked woman as would a non-homosexual adult. And since the range of characteristics in any audience is very wide, it is probable that each spectator, according to the interest he or she has in the woman on the screen, will see on Mozhukhin's face a greater or lesser expression of desire. One can see that the famous 'shadow' projected by the nature of editing on the 'spectator's consciousness' is pure invention, since even in this example of schematic editing – Kuleshov's laboratory experiment -the spectator's behaviour must be much richer than Bazin suggests. No one, if one can put it this way, is virgin soil.

Perhaps Bazin was simply naive. Some of those who knew him believe this to be so. It is not difficult to agree with them, on the evidence of this quotation from his book, *De Sica*, published in Italy: 'In order to paint every blade of grass one has to be a Douanier Rousseau.' But when a naive person 'attempts to find in the cinema a substitute for his or her religious faith' (as Claude Brémond puts it in an excellent article in the sociological review *Communications* [No. 1, pp. 211 ff.]), and analyses it so lamentably while remaining skilful enough to avoid talking about realities, how can we distinguish between *naïveté* and mystification? 'Bazin reminds one of pious believers,' Brémond goes on 'who come back from a pilgrimage to the Holy Places without suspecting the trafficking that goes on in the Court of the Temple. One admires their Faith, but not their talents as sociological observers.'

When Bazin invokes 'the metaphysical assertion that all reality exists on the same level,' there is no point in trying seriously to find out what he means by that, or where he unearthed this 'assertion'. Put simply, and less indulgently, it could be said that Bazin's whole system does not begrudge us metaphysical assertions. However many flow glibly from his tongue, there are always others to take their place. One only needs to read a few lines of Bazin to recognise that while some of the ideas are of uncertain origin, others have been all too obviously assimilated from Jules Lachelier, Louis Lavelle, Saint Augustine, and Pierre Teilhard de Chardin. Everything is chucked haphazardly into the melting-pot, in the hope that the essence of that marvellous medium, the cinema, will emerge. We get, as a result, mere jargon rather than vocabulary, linguistic tics and clap-trap rather than solid thought. In almost any connection, he will use religious vocabulary in a foolhardy but revealing manner. Bazin considers the Cannes Film Festival to be 'an order', and talks of 'Holy Places, priesthood, vespers, and matins'. A bullfight is 'the mystic triangle of animal, man, and multitude', accompanied by a 'liturgy and an almost religious feeling'. In Nikolai Ekk's *Road to Life,* rehabilitation is treated as 'purification through trust and love, a conversion which has the instantaneity of divine grace'. For Gerhard Lamprecht's *Emil and the Detectives,* Bazin evokes the 'famous pursuit of the bad man through the streets, which takes on the epic grandeur of a celestial cohort harrying Evil'. The world is characterised by its 'folly'. He talks only of 'cleansing, purifying, washing, and excising' such things as 'obscenity,

Gerhard Lamprecht's *Emil and the Detectives* (1931).

Young woman trying to sell Cahiers du cinéma in Jean-Luc Godard's *À bout de souffle* (1960).

defilement, filth, and decay', and the cinema is entrusted with the not very savoury task of being 'a veronica on the face of human suffering'. Like faith, 'the irrational power of photography carries conviction', realism is a 'regeneration' of the narrative, 'asceticism' triumphs, and 'revelation' too; the director tries to pierce the 'fabric' of the exterior world, and 'administers love and friendship to his creatures'.

There can be no question of leaving André Bazin without making a little pilgrimage to the monthly magazine of which he was one of the pillars. The disciples of Bazin, no less than their master, have emitted, and are still emitting, gigantic blasts of hot air. And so in this part of my article, Luc Moullet, Michel Mourlet, Jean-Luc Godard, Jean Douchet, and many others will be my guests. People will certainly object to the fact that I have not always quoted the directors or the films to which the disciples refer, and will claim that this 'distorts' my inquiry. I have consciously avoided such references in most cases, for when the disciples talk about films and directors, they are such experts at talking about something completely different that what I have done is rather a service to the films and their directors.

The members of the Holy Family (that unparalleled magazine *Cahiers du cinéma*, hereafter abbreviated to *CC*) believe in the 'metaphysical evil' (Rohmer, *CC* No. 61, p. 8) of human creatures which 'agitates a world where night reigns unchallenged' (Douchet, *CC* No. 81, p. 53). By virtue of this 'immediate, eternal and terrifying, conflict between Light and Darkness' (Douchet, *CC* No. 99, p. 46), colour is experienced as an inconvenience or at least as a superfluous element, in a context where black and white directly reveals the essential and does not need to take the iridescent but roundabout way of concrete realism' (Mourlet, *CC* No. 99, p. 22); 'the implacable struggle of white against black, the masses of shadows that criss-cross and collide, streaked with white flashes' (Charles Bitsch, *CC* No. 51, p. 43) swamp Douchet himself, who, having declared that night reigns unchallenged, now states that 'darkness has invaded light', and elsewhere that 'light has totally absorbed darkness, and remains perceptible only as a false glow, a deceptive semblance – woolly, glazed, and glaucous' (*CC* No. 81, p. 53). Jacques Rivette, who also has trouble in seeing clearly, incriminates 'the grimace of the world' (*CC* No., 25, p. 45).

From this first episode, which must have been written during a power strike, you will probably have realised that their point is to make sinners feel that 'humans bear the stigmata of their malediction' and that 'they wander in a world bereft for ever of true light' (Douchet, *CC* No. 81, p. 53). We are all guilty, and pretty big sinners, it is true. The Catholic Alfred Hitchcock likes to illustrate this postulate. However, things always turn out for the better, since *I Confess* 'tells the story of a soul that is invincibly attached to the Light by willpower' (Douchet, *CC* No. 99, p. 46). 'In this struggle, one which materialism might be expected to have won in advance, it is the soul that emerges the victor' (Rohmer, *CC* No. 69, p. 44). Rohmer talks of that 'quality of anguish which *Ordet* makes us experience' (*CC* No. 55, p. 28), of that 'special air we breathe' in Nicholas Ray's *Bigger Than Life,* of 'the faith we can read in the eyes' of the characters, 'faith that is riddled with doubts and yet is ever-present' (*CC* No. 69, p. 44). Henri Agel demands of us 'a *different* kind of attentiveness' (*CC* No. 53, p. 50), and Michel Mardore speaks of 'that poetry of another order which introduces rigour into the secret disposition of a vision of the world that is more esoteric at a secondary level than its superficial commotion allow us to glimpse' (*CC* No. 125, p. 51). Then the Holy Family intones the Midnight Mass: 'It is not so much a *Miserere* as a *De Profundis* in the strict sense of the term ("Out of the depths have I cried unto Thee, O Lord!") that we feel rising during the first part of *Il Bidone,* until it spreads and spurts in our eyes like pus from an abscess' (Agel, *CC* No. 58, p. 34).

In the ideal cinema and in masterpieces, 'the truth is their truth' (Jean-Luc Godard, *CC* No. 85, p. 1). 'Everything here seems to grow from its own base through a perfect spontaneity towards itself and yet in perfect conformity with things exterior' (Claude Beylie, *CC* No. 84, p. 52). And since everything, in this cinema of 'oblation' (Agel, *CC* No. 67, p. 45) is for the best in the best of all possible worlds, we need only to follow 'that irrepressible rising curve towards a certain level of ecstasy' (Rivette, *CC* No. 81, p. 30), or, if you prefer, 'integrate the meanderings of emotion in an infinitely extensible decorative fabric, or better even, freely extract from the plastic totality of the audiovisual field the conducting narrative motif, only to let it plunge back and hear it resound, or finally – and here we are coming back to a refined kind of Neo-Realism – extract from the general human atmosphere the obsessional elements that certainly lurk there' (Beylie, *CC* No. 91, p. 62). Agel goes into raptures about Renoir's *The River,* 'the moving modulation of a voice that says yes, of a soul that consents to the world, that has passed the stage of revolt', and François Truffaut praises these lines, 'the most pertinent that have been written about *The River*' (*CC* No. 45, p. 56). The story that counts is the one 'told by Murnau and Rossellini, about man reaching a state of acquiescence, and through it, oneness' (Philippe Demonsablon, *CC* No. 95, p. 2). And Kenji Mizoguchi, according to Rivette, is representative of an 'art of modulation, whereby everything finally harmonises with this search for a central point where appearances and what is called nature (or shame or death) are reconciled with mankind' (*CC* No. 81, p. 30). Technique is put to the service of this spiritual Oneness: Agel talks of 'the spiritual engagement' that is sustained by tracking shots (admiringly quoted by Truffaut (*CC* No. 45, p. 56)), and Rivette, when discussing Alexandre Astruc, compares 'the movements of the camera to the movements of the soul' and arrives at a 'veritable mystique of the tracking crane shot' (*CC* No. 52, p. 47).

These totally fatuous remarks are strongly reminiscent of the speeches of the princes that govern us. For only someone who assumes that colonial wars are the unhealthy external appearance of French good health will say that 'Ray's films end where Rossellini's begin: with the intuition of a harmony that is to be found beyond the sphere of conflicts and clashes of opinion' (Demonsablon, *CC* No. 95, p. 55). Rivette speaks of 'a bargain that is never broken' (*CC* No. 81, p. 30), and Beylie, using language that could easily be interpreted as pornographic, sings the praises of Renoir's 'exertion, which might be termed encyclopaedic if it did not go hand in hand with a rejection of academicism in a resolutely constructive sense, and which jettisons subsidiary arborescences only to rise more easily, straight up, and full of sap, into the serene sky of aesthetic transcendency' (*CC* No. 80, p. 1).

There is no point in our readers wasting their time wondering about the truth of these assertions, since we are now in the domain of pure beauty, pure spirit, and aesthetic transcendency, where 'the true is as false as the false, and only the ultra-false becomes true' (Moullet, *CC* No. 87, p. 56). Opinions and attitudes shed all materiality: 'To watch Renoir's characters living is to adopt a better point of view about mankind, to live better and to be more oneself, to attain, slowly but surely, a kind of serenity' (Beylie, *CC* No. 80, p. 8). Materiality becomes a 'shimmer', 'an

Marika Green and Martin LaSalle in the final scene of Robert Bresson's *Pickpocket* (1959).

immense and multiple symphony' (Beylie, *CC* No. 80, p. 8), 'a reflection of the divine, a perfect possession of the world and of oneself, a moment like pure water taking the shape of the contours of a vase' (Mourlet, *CC* No. 98, p. 34). 'The soul is the key to the universe' (Douchet, *CC* No. 99, p. 45). Life and the world are conceived henceforth as an 'exchange', 'correspondence', 'secret effluvia that emanate from beings' (Rivette, *CC* No. 52, p. 47). Perhaps that is why when one gets to the last shot of *Pickpocket*, 'although the bars separate the two central characters (the man and the woman), their *souls* have found one another' (Jean Wagner, *CC* No. 104, p. 50). You can lose everything, but you still have heaven.

A woman, just as she was on the first day when God created her, is a woman, i.e. permanently guilty, as the existence of adultery only goes to prove. Michel Dorsday allows us to psychoanalyse the Holy Family when he states: 'In Luis Buñuel's *El*, the man's jealousy is only an exalted form of his purity' (*CC* No. 37, p. 44), a 'purity' which the woman cannot understand, as she is 'by nature incapable of attaining sublimity or responsibility', 'the whole business could have been avoided but for her', and although she may have 'the face of love, she does not have the soul of love'; the woman is the 'symbol of the evil of the world' (*CC* No. 37, p. 44). If a woman takes a lover who is sound in body and soul, she is well and truly sinful in the eyes

Ingrid Bergman in Roberto Rossellini's *Europa '51* (1952).

of the Holy Family, whereas a saintly woman who rejects the temptations of the flesh is innocent: 'In *Europe 51,* the soul (of Ingrid Bergman) fully reveals itself, bathes her body in light, forms it in its own image, and surrounds it with an aura of brightness that makes everything which comes near look dull and pale' (Rohmer, *CC* No. 25, p. 44). Even more innocent is a woman who is decomposing, a woman on her deathbed: 'If she knows how to die, nothing is lost'; on her deathbed, indeed, woman is no longer made up of 'spasms' and 'pleasure', she becomes 'an interior irradiation', and that is sufficient to save an age that is 'trying to redeem itself' (collective introduction to the special *Cahiers du cinéma* issue, No. 30, on 'Woman and the Cinema'). Just as the best Indian is a dead Indian, the best woman is a dead woman.

The governing idea is that great films 'are able to offer and conceal the secret of a world of which they are at once the sole trustee and fascinating reflection' (Godard, *CC* No. 85, p. 1), and they all 'end with the serene joy of someone who has overcome the illusory phenomena of perspectives' (Rivette, *CC* No. 81, p. 30). Do not be surprised that 'loving Renoir is rather the same thing as loving the movements of the stars, the song of the birds, or the beating of a heart in the breast of a woman' (Beylie, *CC* No. 80, p. 8), and you will find all that enclosed in the heart of a film like *Le Carrosse d'or,* which contains the Truth like 'a starfish that opens and closes' (Godard, *CC* No. 85, p. 1). Nothing exists except the cinema, which is the currency of the Absolute: 'There used to be theatre (Griffith), poetry (Murnau), painting (Rossellini), dance (Eisenstein), music (Renoir). But from now on there is cinema. And the cinema is Nicholas Ray' (Godard, *CC* No. 79, p. 44). One can even go so far as to say, with Godard, that *'Bitter Victory,* just as the sun makes you close your eyes, is not cinema, it is more than cinema', 'blind truth' (Godard, *CC* No. 79, p. 45). This approach to films has set off a fashion, and Michel Delahaye begins an article by blinding the reader: 'How can one approach *Elmer Gantry,* a work at once classical and meteoric? The best way is probably the simplest: let's make it quite clear from the start that we are dealing with a work that quite literally *dazzles'* (*CC* No. 121, p. 5i). The atheist and the rationalist are, of course, free *not* to believe, 'everyone has the right to give a non-Catholic view of a Catholic film' (Demonsablon, *CC* No. 58, p. 40), but then he or she must not be surprised to find merely 'the spectacle of a godless world in which the only law is the pure mechanism of cause and effect, a universe of cruelty, horror, banality, and derision' (Rohmer, *CC* No. 25, p. 45).

But follow their advice and 'yield to the facts instead of wanting to shape them' (Rivette, *CC* No. 58, p. 41), 'let yourself be taken over by the order of things' (Mourlet, *CC* No. III, p. 34), do not protest, and 'you will be liberated from everyday cares', sheltered and far from a world which 'if it has not been irremediably condemned, at least seems, in the eyes of Hitchcock, to be increasingly suspect' (Rivette, *CC* No. 58, p. 41). 'All is dust and will return to dust' (Godard, *CC* No. 97, p. 44), the Last Judgment is imminent, and in Hitchcock's *The Trouble With Harry* 'the russet leaves of autumn somehow presage the decay of nature, and almost stand for that decay itself' (Rivette, *CC* No. 58, p. 41). And so what does it matter where 'one chooses to escape from the mesh of circumstances – a prison, an asylum, the maquis, a monastery?' (Beylie, *CC* No. 122, p. 54). 'Directing a film and writing a scenario consists of pointing the eye of the camera on faces and objects long enough to brand them deeply, as the torturer used to brand prisoners, or as a sign from Him marks the chosen one' (Godard, *CC* No. 95, p. 56). In this kind of conception of existence, where everything is put in parentheses so that God can be reached more rapidly, 'it is no longer a question of reality or fiction, but of something completely different, the stars in the sky perhaps, and men who like to gaze at the stars and dream. What are such things as love, fear, contempt, danger, adventure, despair, bitterness, victory? What importance do they have in comparison with the stars?' (Godard, *CC* No. 79, p. 45).

Faced with such self-confidence, we begin to doubt the nonexistence of God. What on earth has happened to Bazin's famous theories about 'ambiguity'. Ambi-

Edmund Gwenn in Alfred Hitchcock's *The Trouble with Harry* (1955).

guity is certainly not what we will find in Cecil B. De Mille, one of the all-time greats according to Godard, and praised because 'the moral of *The Ten Command-ments* is extraordinarily manicheistic – just a straight line, no dialectics: Rameses stands for Mao Tse-tung, and Moses for De Mille himself' (*CC* No. 80, p. 58). Per-haps we will find it in Samuel Fuller then, 'a master of ambiguity' (Jean Domarchi, *CC* No. 57, p. 50). This means, according to Godard, that although Fuller is 'appar-ently a nationalist, a reactionary, a Nixonite', he is too endowed 'with the gift of ambiguity to belong exclusively to any one party' (Moullet, *CC* No. 93, p. 13). 'He is more concerned with fascism as a trait of character than with its political con-sequences' (Moullet, *CC* No. 93, p. 13), which completely fails to explain a film such as *Hell and High Water*, but don't let's press our point…. It is well known that politics do not interest the Holy Family any more than they do Fuller, and Hawks is praised by Godard because *Rio Bravo* simply expresses 'the finest of morals: that a man should earn his daily bread and not care about the rest' (*CC* No. 97, p. 44). The only thing that matters is 'the moral of duty in the work one does, whereby one rejects laziness, inexactitude, and perfunctoriness' (Domarchi, *CC* No. 79, p. 51), in a world 'where a person can happen to be a sheriff just as well as a skilled worker or a ticket-collector' (Moullet, *CC* No. 97, p. 44). 'Rossellini's realism is moral realism' (Domarchi, *CC* No. 123, p. 60). Why tamper with the 'vulnerability' (Agel, *CC* No. 67, p. 45) of these 'simple faces, these gusts of humanity, these furtive expressions, these snatches of life seized almost at random from human beings, this confidence, this "you'll-see-if-it-doesn't-turn-out-all-right" attitude' (Patrice G. Hovald *Italian Neo-Realism*, Éditions du Cerf). The Brasillach branch [Robert Brasillach was a notorious collaborationist during the Second World War; he was executed in 1945] of the Holy Family celebrates Mass in rather a different way: 'If art is basically moral [*sic*], it does not become so by showing the way to abstract equality or freedom, but rather by exalting the exception that is made possible only by the rule, and as it were, however shocking this idea may be, the inequality of every man in the face of his destiny, or rather of his salvation' (Rohmer, *CC* No. 26, p. 18). 'Lang is fascinated only by the exceptional being, who though exceptional is modestly given the humble appearance of a dancing-girl, a female spy, a cop, or a tough cowboy' (Truffaut, *CC* No. 31, p. 52). 'The political ideas of Brasillach were the same as Drieu La Rochelle's; ideas which result in their authors being sentenced to death are necessarily estimable' (Truffaut, *CC* No. 32, p. 59).

I could go on for much longer; *Cahiers du cinéma* is an inexhaustible fund of phraseology and gags. But it will not make our grandchildren laugh; no one laughs nowadays at the complete works of the poet and playwright, Henri Bataille – they are simply not read any more. Well, it is worth pointing out that the man Rohmer sees as the spiritual father of *Cahiers* is none other than Bazin: 'Everything had been said by him, we came too late. Now we are left with the difficult duty of pursuing his task: we shall not fail in this, although we are convinced that he pursued it much further than it will be possible for us to do ourselves…. Only the uncertainty of the future authorises us to hope that we are, if not André Bazin's successors, then at least his disciples, and not too unworthy ones at that' (Rohmer, *CC* 91, p. 45). In this part of my argument, I will say no more. As barristers say, I rest my case.

Since the Nouvelle Vague is itself reluctant to define itself, it is difficult and presumptuous at this point to group certain new filmmakers under a single heading. However, in order to make analysis feasible, it is, I think, possible (partly because of a common background of film criticism which first enabled some kind of definition and because of a catchphrase which they helped to spread) to limit the term Nouvelle Vague to the *Cahiers* group and a few filmmakers whose 'moral and metaphysical outlook' is fairly close to that of the group. But this is only a verbal designation which will make discussion more convenient. For in fact, while we on *Positif* feel that it is not easy as yet to put one's finger on the way in which Jacques Demy, Jacques Doniol-Valcroze, and Claude de Givray resemble, in what they have directed, Godard, Rivette, or Chabrol, we are quite certain that Godard, Riv-

Jean-Claude Brialy (left), Bernadette Lafont (centre) and Gérard Blain (right) in *Le Beau Serge* (1959).

ette, and Chabrol have common preoccupations. But where are we to put Pierre Kast? Astruc? Jacques Rozier? Clearly this can be only a working hypothesis. Once we accept it, then it is quite apparent that Bazin's system has a lot of links with the Nouvelle Vague as defined in this way. And in case anyone doubts the importance of the role Bazin played in the practical training of the Nouvelle Vague, let us confront the latter with some of the governing ideas of the system.

For this confrontation, we could choose any Nouvelle Vague film, or almost any: Chabrol's *Le Beau Serge* (*Bitter Reunion*), in which sacrifice, renunciation, and guilt vie with each other for the chief place, and the communion of human beings is lumped together with Brialy's horrible tubercular cough; Godard's very overrated *À bout de souffle* (*Breathless*), his very odd *Le Petit soldat,* or *La Paresse* (*Sloth*), the episode in *Les Sept péchés capitaux* (*The Seven Deadly Sins*) in which Godard extends the boundaries of nonchalant insignificance and proves once and for all that one should shut up when one has nothing to say; Rohmer's *Le Signe du lion* (*The Sign of Leo*), which bursts at the seams with muddled thinking; Philippe de Broca's *Cartouche*, quite a pleasant film, but marred by an exasperating cult of

Eric Rohmer's *Le Signe du lion* (1959).

the hero. I will not linger over the conclusion of Truffaut's *Jules et Jim* (the ridiculous aspect of our ashes is supposed to prove that our existences are ridiculous too); and the suffocated naturalism of Chabrol's *Les Bonnes femmes*.

We are not of the opinion, however, that everything produced by the Nouvelle Vague has been nasty, stupid, or uninteresting. We do not believe that a large group of directors can all be lumped together or that they should be the objects of constant and unremitting contempt. It is true after all that Chabrol now repudiates the mystic conclusion of *Le Beau Serge*. There is tenderness and humour in Truffaut: *Les Mistons* (*The Brats*) is a pleasant first film and *Tirez sur le pianiste* (*Shoot the Pianist*) is good Marcel Aymé. There are one or two good ideas in *À bout de souffle,* and some charming digressions in *Une femme est une femme* (*A Woman is a Woman*), a film that consists entirely of digression. No one can deny that the striking and morbid sensibility revealed by *Le Signe du lion* and *Paris nous appartient* (*Paris Belongs to Us*) produces some fine moments. It is even possible that the Nouvelle Vague will one day produce masterpieces. But I would like to make one point: these masterpieces may well turn up eventually, but the Nouvelle Vague will produce them only by going against the drift of what it is trying to produce at the moment. In order to try and clarify this point, I have decided to take a close look

The party at the Neuilly flat in Jacques Rivette's *Paris nous appartient* (1960).

at *Paris nous appartient*. More than any of the others quoted above, Rivette's film is the one I feel best represents the most ambitious side of the Nouvelle Vague: the desire to bear witness to our age.

As far as I have been able to fathom its extremely involved plot, which has certainly been affected by several successive versions of the script and re-editings which cut down its length, *Paris nous appartient* is a cryptic film full of bizarre characters. A certain De Georges, a doctor like Mabuse or Cordelier, seems to be rather powerful and to have few scruples. Pierre (François Maistre) does some rather shady work for him – at least that is what we are left to suppose, as he does not dare to talk about it to his nice, naive younger sister, Anne (Betty Schneider). Others perhaps stand for 'the left'. At three one morning, for instance, in a flat in Neuilly, we get to know some individuals who are inspired by some subversive and anarchist spirit. They include: an anti-McCarthyist who has been expelled from the USA, Philip Kaufman (Daniel Crohem); Terry (Françoise Prévost), a woman of means who supports needy artists; a nasty piece of work, Bernard (André Thorent), who has a rather uncharitable way of kicking Philip out and is able to parry awkward questions about the death of Vladimir Mayakovsky. We should not overlook the charming young women who just talk, a couple of proud-looking Spaniards who recall 'their defeat', Rivette himself talking about 'crushed revolutions', finally the unspeakable Chabrol, who talks a lot of stuff and nonsense, which, although left-wing rubbish, is none the less rubbish. The individuals at this select gathering, drunk and rude, simply glare at each other and exchange insults to a point where it gets embarrassing for them and the Revolution they are supposed to stand for. I say they represent the Revolution because they talk about it in hurried snatches, with facial expressions that are heavy with significance; but to tell the truth, we are here entering unknown country, and this lack of definition is part of the film's intended meaning. How did these people gathered together here first meet? What is their ideology? What are their tactics, their policy? When do they discuss? When do they act? What are their resources? Who assists them, what are their financial means? We never know, just as we never know anything about De Georges, except that he may be supposed to stand for the Forces of Money, that he likes *ingénues,* and that he is as enigmatic as Evil itself.

And so the situation described in *Paris nous appartient* can be taken as you want to take it; let's call it a 'fable', which aims, through its abstraction, to give a synthetic account of most of all possible generalities. This is a method used extensively by Bazin. In fact, this 'possibly left-wing' get-together, of which we are given a general description, reminds one of nothing so much as the 'definitely right-wing' get-together which is so preposterously portrayed in *Les Cousins* (*The Cousins*). In the latter film, there may be less talk of politics, more loot and more chicks; the obsessions of the character played by Brialy are Nazi-like, but Bernard's hypocrisy is just as repulsive. Just as much is drunk, and what a good idea to make the characters of *Paris nous appartient* exclaim from time to time, as though illuminated by the Grace of God: 'We are all fools!', or else 'The whole world is in exile!' For it has to be drummed into people's heads that all is in all and vice versa. 'My film,' says Rivette, 'will be a film in which the strongest characters will behave in rather a cowardly way, the most intelligent will talk the most rubbish, and the most lucid will completely delude themselves' (interview in *Radio-Cinéma-TV*). This duality, which leads to a synthetic conception of the universe, is reconstituted by Rivette as follows:

I have deeply experienced this search for truth via error which constitutes the main theme of the film. What do we see for more than two hours? People who want to be able to explain the world to themselves through a single idea (the idea of a fascist organisation and conspiracy), who can't help deluding themselves and getting into terrible trouble. This doesn't mean that fascism doesn't exist; far from it, I would say that to a certain extent it stands for the Forces of Evil. What this does mean is that it is too easy to explain the world through a single idea. An idea can only exist because of a contrary idea, there must be a dialectic, etc.' (interview in *Les Lettres françaises,* No. 905, December 1961).

The guilty then are those who are taken in by 'the fascination of the oversimplification of a single solution. There lies the danger' (*ibid*). And Terry, who lets herself be taken in and shoots Pierre whom she mistakenly holds responsible for the death of Gérard[1] is clearly Rivette's mouthpiece when she learns the lesson from her mistake: 'It's so convenient to envelop everything, including one's inertia and cowardice, in a single idea. Evil has more than one face – that would be too easy.'

Of course it *may* be that Rivette wants to depict as thoroughly as possible an age in which the problems of living and understanding life have yet to be clearly defined – don't let's be ashamed to admit it. It *may* be that Rivette intended to allude to problems that would give us food for thought: on the one hand, the intelligent and stubborn resistance of capitalist and reactionary forces that are often still immature; and on the other hand, the problems faced by Communist parties since the death of Lenin. The solution of these problems has led not only to the victory of socialism in one part of the world, but also to the tragic mistakes which we may legitimately suppose not to have been inherent in a revolutionary state.

But then we want to see the goods. Well, *Paris nous appartient* does not keep its promises about problems of this type that we would have liked to have seen treated. If Rivette found himself unable to solve them, he might at least have made an effort to pose them properly. But just look at Rivette's strange conception of fascism: 'To a certain extent it stands for the Forces of Evil.' We realise that the system of Bazin the master, and the embellishments contributed by his disciples, are rich in metaphysical *a priori* statements and journeys to the Heaven of pure religious Ideas. But that simply will not do. It was not a bad idea of Rivette's to try to denounce the dangers of oversimplification, but the trouble with *Paris nous appartient* is that it is a film that is both extremely schematic and extremely confused. After all, a search for the truth via the false, if one's aim is *practical* truth, must consist of something meatier than all that rushing about, 'doors being opened and closed, people going up and down stairs, actions that turn out to be useless, a long effort in a labyrinth in order to depict the process of the truth' (*ibid*). This assimilation of a search for the truth with a Journey to the centre of the earth clearly results in a curious conception of dialectics: 'the lack of a single solution', or, if you like, an ambiguity that renders the contradictory richness of reality, without our really being able to find out what this richness, this contradiction, or this reality consists of. For two hours, we follow the comings and goings of Anne Goupil. For Rivette, who follows her 'lovingly', she must, like Marina in *Pericles,* be the sign of Innocence metaphysically ensnared in the toils of society and politics, and buffeted on high seas by an unfavourable wind, a malicious wind, a crafty wind that the Holy Family is always breathing down our necks. Bazin and Bresson make no bones about saying that 'it blows where it will'. That crafty old fox, the drama critic Jean-Jacques Gautier, was not all that far from

Paris nous appartient (1960): Betty Schneider (right) tries to comfort her sobbing neighbour.

the truth as Rivette conceives of it when he saw in Anne 'all that can remain of traditional purity and innocence, all that can be salvaged of eternal childhood in this "creature"' (*Le Figaro,* November 1960). Anne shares with the great Saints the ability to safeguard all that is 'eternal' in each of us, in our troubled times where everything is going wrong, in a world where shadows spend their time running after each other: as total blackness is as significant as total whiteness, the total realism of the black screen is here offered us – it is, of course, not just any old realism, but one that is nourished by the shadows and half-shadows of reality, being in consequence the most realistic realism that exists.... . Thus, like Groucho Marx, who 'worked [himself] up from nothing to a state of extreme poverty', *Paris nous appartient* starts out from nothing and ends up with *all,* or *nothing,* as you will. Jean-François Revel has put it in a nutshell: 'This film has deliberately been placed under the sign of ambiguity. Mystery dominates the film. It is at once a documentary on Paris, a gangster film, a spy film, and a horror film, a Greek tragedy, a Shakespeare play, a psychiatric study, a metaphysical meditation, an application of Einsteinian relativity, and an indictment of fascism. And so Rivette's world is both subject and object of one of the richest *Weltanschauungen* that has ever been brought to the screen. As such, it concerns us all.' And, a week later, replying to letters: 'Let's get things straight: *Paris nous appartient* is a nonentity' (*France-observateur,* No. 608, December 1961).

From the very start we feel at sea, and we feel this is what the director deliberately intended. Anne, whose attention is caught by a strange groaning sound, comes out of her tiny bedsitter and finds, in another little room on the same landing, a young woman sobbing, who assures her that 'the hour is nigh', that 'waiting is difficult', and speaks of Hiroshima as though the destruction of the world were to be found in Nostradamus or in that eternal guiding myth, the Bible. Anne charitably tries to console her. 'Leave me alone,' says the woman, 'I can't go on. In any case, it doesn't matter, no one can do anything more for me.' And just to hammer the last nail in the coffin, she adds that 'no one will escape the common lot', and that 'the world is threatened'. And so we suppose that we poor shadows are well on the way to being totally removed from the face of the earth, because there exist ferocious and terrifying organisations which swoop down on people and destroy them. This at least is what Philip Kaufman declares, but when Anne wants to know more he answers back: 'I am certain of nothing.' So things get more and more obscure: 'If it is necessary to retain obscurity in order not to distort reality, let's keep it. Anyway, reality itself is often obscure' (interview in *Clarté,* No. 41, February 1962). Especially as 'the biggest fool is the person who thinks he has the truth. Philip is half crazy, it's significant' (*ibid.*). This is probably the profound reason why the walls of Philip's flat are covered with little objects that look like monsters, skeletons, or shrunken heads: it allows the human beings to be surrounded by a decor of Anguish, Suffering, and Approaching Death, and convinces us that Philip is hysterical. *Paris nous appartient* ends with Gérard's suicide and another of Philip's crises: we are doubtless supposed to realise that we are still at sea, that this absurd world does not easily yield the truth, which should be looked for – why not? – among epileptics! As far as the last shot is concerned, it is remarkable for its blurred listlessness: there are the gloomy waters of the Lac d'Ermenonville, gloomy birds, a gloomy sky, and faces as long as death; it is not at all difficult to recognise here the entire condition of contemporary mankind.

Before she got to know Gérard, Terry had a Spanish guitarist, Juan, as a lover. It seems he was very talented, and when he died he left some recorded guitar music somewhere or other. Gérard insists on trying to find this record in order to use it for his production of *Pericles*. Rivette's brainwave was to have made this record a symbol of the Truth that is being sought throughout the film: Anne tries to find Juan's will out of love for Gérard and his play. *Kiss Me Deadly* tried using the same device, but it is significant that here a work of art should replace the catastrophic Pandora's Box. It may be that the twentieth century is doomed to destruction, but people of quality, who, being sensitive and emotional, are secretly hostile to all kinds of forced political commitment, know just how exquisitely fragile Man-

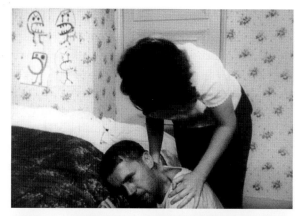

Paris nous appartient (1960): Philip's flat: Daniel Crohem and Betty Schneider.

Paris nous appartient (1960): the gloomy waters of the lake.

kind is, and persist in protesting in its name. Poets, Beacons, Witnesses, Guides, Seers, Lights, Wise Men, Mountebanks, anyone you like, they all talk, in their Messages, of the imminence of the Apocalypse and of the oppression of slaves crushed beneath the weight of the social order.

Fritz Lang (quoted in the film with an extract from *Metropolis*) is one of these. It is no coincidence that Rivette made Gérard an artist, and it is not merely an autobiographical need; Rivette, like Bazin, believes in Art as a total demystification of society. It would have been vulgar to have made Gérard a skilled worker or a hairdresser. In order to bear witness to the anguish of his age, he has to be a stage producer. The hero of *Le Signe du lion* is an artist too: a composer and violinist. The pianist of *Tirez sur le pianiste* is thrice smitten by Destiny, but he still has his piano. The *petits bourgeois* love to imagine that art is not a job but a vocation, a priesthood, and that the only hope left to man in this 'rotten' world is Creation in the form of completely purified Work. After Gérard's suicide, Jean-Val, his ex-assistant, takes over the rehearsals of *Pericles* without trying to find out where exactly the truth is to be found, and whether somebody was killed, and if so, by whom: 'The theatre,' said Gérard, 'is not an illusion but a reality.' Truffaut goes one better and says that 'the only thing left is the struggle to make the purity of the theatrical vocation triumph' (*Arts,* August 6, 1958). In the context of a politically apathetic civilisation that has been deformed by 'specialists', the artist will henceforth regard his work as an outlet, and by making himself a specialist too he will hoist himself out of the rut of everyday life. Presumably the main fault of a man working in a car factory is that he is not an artist, for if he were he would not adopt the cause of a party or a union or any system of any kind (except of capitalist exploitation of course), and as he would not be a union member he would not be bashed on the head by blacklegs in the pay of the employers.

The best sequences of the film are not the most ambitious ones. They are those that describe the life and work of actors in Paris. Perhaps they are acted a little listlessly at times, but they are admirably conceived and directed. The explanation is simple: these scenes are the only ones which give a little life to a particular concrete and topical problem – that of the actor in present-day France. Apart from them, *Paris nous appartient* is a *thin* film. The idea that underlies it is a hollow kernel: the characters, the images, the details, and the situations do not exist, and this should not surprise us. A film is a good film only when the situation depicted reveals the reasons which make it necessarily as it is. This presupposes a culture, an aim, experience, and organisation. Then and only then is there a chance that the spectator, too, will discover the amazing organisation of reality. That is why it can be said that the idea arises in the spectator from an organised spectacle and that the meaning of a film emerges from its temporal form instead of preceding it. Bertolt Brecht's art, at least, is based on this idea.

But if someone comes along and says that *Paris nous appartient* portrays the uncertainty, the confusion, the 'equivocality' of our existence and our age, then I say 'Long live Bazin! But leave Brecht out of it.' I mean by this that Rivette is making a fool of us and of himself when he sees himself already evolving towards a Brechtian manner: 'I'd like to follow the example of Brecht: *Paris nous appartient* would be *Drums in the Night*; and the trilogy I am planning set in the eighteenth century, more or less an adaptation of *The Life of Edward II of England*' (*Clarté,* No. 41, February 1962). The Brechtian spectacle defines the how and why of the situation it describes; it is an effort to reveal the true organisation of society and expose its contradictions. It requires a demonstration, a 'dismantling', to make the spectator grasp this. Its purpose is radically different from that of Rivette: Brecht is never ambiguous. That is why not only conservatives but 'liberals' hate him.

On the contrary, in *Paris nous appartient,* Terry, as dawn approaches, tells Philip to get into her car: 'Where are we going?' asks Philip, who has not yet got

Paris nous appartient (1960): 'Where are we going?'; Daniel Crohem and Françoise Prévost.

over his crisis. 'Oh, we'll see,' replies Terry. This is not methodical doubt, nor is it a decision to ask real questions; it is the country priest's sermon, it is a wreath of mist that is gingerly wafted across the scene. I feel that *Paris nous appartient* is fairly representative of the Nouvelle Vague, and offers a rather accurate definition of the present state of the *bourgeoisie,* which, in order to get out of a class struggle which is anything but avoidable, has chosen scepticism as its motto: 'I shall probably never make socially or politically committed films, for in this field, the field of problems, it is no longer sufficient to leave question-marks. One has to contribute constructive ideas, assertions, perhaps even solutions. My doubts, my scepticism, my deep conviction that everyone has their reasons [Renoir again] would only add to the confusion.' '*Le Petits soldat* is political to the extent that the developments of the plot are due to political motives, but it can also be said that the film is not political because I don't take sides with anybody and because the subject is not orientated as it is in Russian films' (interview with Godard in *Le Monde,* September 13, 1960). One can understand that some people are reluctant to classify *Paris nous appartient* as a left- or right-wing film: it is clearly an 'anti-political' or, as Rivette puts it, an 'anti-thesis' film. Rivette sees in Terry's cold-blooded murder of Pierre the decisive proof that innocent people will always get themselves killed, by left-wing fanatics as well as by right-wing fanatics, for, at the same moment, we learn that Juan did not commit suicide but was liquidated by the Falangists. The Left and the Right have the same vices.

We should not allow ourselves to be hoodwinked into believing that *Paris nous appartient* really portrays some kind of revolt of Eternal Mankind against the Bureaucrats and Commissars of every country, or of Human Dignity against *all* kinds of fascism. All one can say is that the portrayal is dull and insipid. *Paris nous appartient* does not truly deal with the atomic peril or with people's general political attitudes or with the behaviour of our contemporaries; and Rivette is no new Plato, or if he is he can only serve us up with flimsy *idées reçues*. Can you really see the Truth in a fight between blacks in a tunnel? Indeed, I don't believe any Nouvelle Vague film has tried harder to put up smoke-screens and brick walls for the spectators and actors to bash their heads against (walls, Kafka, Plato's cave, get it?), so that someone who has not understood a thing should come out of the cinema saying: it is the work of a genius, it's just what I felt without being able to express it.

We on *Positif* feel there is nothing for us to understand in a slipshod hotchpotch such as this, however subtle it may be, and that, using realism and 'up-to-dateness' as a pretext, the artist has no right to give us a chaotic portrayal of a chaotic period – he or she should try rather to fathom it; we are not ashamed to state and state again that *Paris nous appartient,* like *À bout de souffle,* lures fools into taking it seriously. At a time when various forces throughout the world are fighting each other and are winning or being defeated according to a pattern of history, Rivette has made one of the most 'obscurantist' films of the Nouvelle Vague. And so one can perhaps consider Rivette as a kind of Eugène Ionesco of the Champs-Elysées. The seductiveness of fascism has not affected him as it once did the author of *The Bald primadonna,* who has since changed his tune a bit, but the 'religious roots' (metaphysical, as they say) are always present. Under the pretext of defending Mankind, the idea is to attack the governing systems and committed individuals who create and uphold them: 'Those people,' says Terry, 'who want to destroy everything and who start by destroying themselves.' The main purpose is to safeguard eternal (or traditional, if you like) values by pretending to believe that they are perpetually present behind the appearances of the modern world. In this, the Nouvelle Vague has fulfilled its role. It has shuffled the cards, it has made sloppiness a prime virtue, it has distorted the critical aspect of scepticism and jettisoned its valuable side. The Nouvelle Vague directors have not turned carefreeness and humour into liberating elements, but instead nice discreet digs at a Fate that could not care a damn, which is taken by them to be classical tragedy one day and romantic poetry the next.

Without realising how silly he is being, Chabrol replies to the critic Georges Sadoul's inquiry into 'Neo-romanticism in the Nouvelle Vague' as follows: 'Yes,

I am a neo-romantic because we are living in a romantic period.' The central character of *À bout de souffle* protests against the inability of human beings to communicate with each other (what, again?) and tries to live out a frenzied individuality which proves to be less individual than the behaviour of Jean Seberg; he calls himself Laszlo Kovacs just to show that he is disowning his origins, just as the central character of *Le Signe du lion* has no homeland: 'I am a bit of everything – Austrian, American, Swiss.' *Paris nous appartient* teems with exiles and misfits: the man deported from the United States is the brother of the émigré from Budapest (who lives in the same hotel as he does) and of the Spaniard we met in the drawing-room in Neuilly; and, in the very first shots of the film, we see sweet Anne being bored to death by her English lessons, which only goes to show that she too is a misfit. A great primordial nobility, a marked thirst for purity, an elevation of the feelings – all characterise these individuals: 'The central character of *Le Petit soldat* is right-wing, and at the same time he is left-wing because he is sentimental' (*ibid.*). Someone in *Le Signe du lion* says of the film's central character: 'He is a weak but good man.' How curious *Le Signe du lion* is: Rohmer wanted to show the omnipresence of Fate by following a violinist who wanders round Paris and becomes a tramp because it never crosses Rohmer's mind to make him earn a living. This is, of course, supposed to emphasise 'the essential loneliness' of Man.

For Rohmer, then, the walk along the banks of the Seine becomes the purgatory of a lonely man who is hounded by the idiotic immanence of civilisation and the indifference of nature: water, stone, crowds. Compare Joris Ivens's Seine, in *La Seine a rencontré Paris,* the product of human labour, which channels and orders nature. And what would be the point of making Pierre, the central character of the film, work anyway? For at the very moment when he sinks to the bottom of the abyss, he is saved by an inheritance and made a rich man. The camera confirms the miracle: it pans up from the base of the church of Saint-Germain-des-Près to the top of its spire and into Universal Night. 'I believe profoundly,' says Truffaut elsewhere, 'in original sin and in the metaphysical aspect of life.'

This is classicism if you like, but it is withered classicism. It is romanticism if you like, but it is meagre romanticism. There is however a tremendous ambition: to portray individual dramas and set them against the background of collective dramas – to be the Honoré de Balzac of our time. The Balzac or the Resnais? The place has already been filled, well and truly filled. *Hiroshima mon amour* is the perfect illustration of the dreams of the Nouvelle Vague; but Resnais alone is capable of realising them because he never poses the problem in the jumbled form of a 'film-discussion on life, liberty, death, and anguish'. (interview in *Clarté,* No. 41, February 1962). As far as Rivette is concerned, the definition needed is: *petit bourgeois* romanticism in the manner of Jean Sarment – and who reads Jean Sarment

Emmanuelle Riva (left) in Alain Resnais's *Hiroshima mon amour* (1959).

nowadays? – as opposed to the very different romanticism of the *bourgeois* Victor Hugo or the *bourgeois* Maurice Barrès, as opposed to the masterly and virile fantasy of *Kiss Me Deadly* and Resnais' powerful conceptions. It is the *petit bourgeois* romanticism of a cry-baby who is afraid of both past and future. 'In the last 30 years,' says Philip, 'methods have changed.... All those who refuse to yield to Efficiency, the Establishment, Technique, are simply crushed.' There can be no doubt that Philip is here speaking for the director. And yet methods of oppression have always existed and have always been brutal: the Romans crucified Spartacus, the Inquisition burnt heretics, the Yankees shot the Indians, colonialists burnt down black Africans' villages, and policemen beat up strikers. Why the restrictive 'In the last 30 years'? Probably for the same reasons Godard puts forward when he says he would be incapable of making a film about the Resistance: 'There was a way of talking and feeling that has no connection with our present-day behaviour" (interview with Godard in *Le Monde,* September 13, 1960). *Petits bourgeois* not only fear the future (and consequently do not even try to conceive of it) but they are also afraid of looking too closely at the History they have mastered. They would find there the image of their own shabbiness and the sources of a romanticism they believe they originated – in fact their own is the sign of a total inability to come to grips effectively with a historical movement that is certainly bloody but none the less alive. André Bazin would, I think, have liked *Paris nous appartient*.

From a booklet devoted to the Nouvelle Vague by Raymond Borde, I quote the following portrait of the new type of hero given to us by the films of Roger Vadim, which could also serve as the portrait of many Nouvelle Vague central characters: 'He says little, and puts on an air of controlled suffering. He is both a priest *manqué* and an aristocrat. He is the incarnation of the young introverted right-wing that has lost the picturesque quality that the royalists of *Action française* had. He is supposed to hint at some kind of metaphysical torment; he looks elegantly pained; in short, he is striking an attitude. He is a misogynist... . He keeps his distance, dreams perhaps of the Old Régime and goes along with the new one. What strikes me most about him is the lack of any sign of being "anti"' (*Premier plan,* No. 10, p. 12).

Philip Esnault is also to the point: 'The profound anaemia of the young filmmakers can be explained by the situation of a generation that does not know what to do with itself and by the very real confusion of the *bourgeoise élite* from which they issue, by the intellectual and moral suffocation that is caused by a certain Parisian way of life. Nothing is more difficult to express than a mentality of refusal, a spirit of affectation, an attitude of escapism. Nothing is easier than to clutch on to myths and masters. Will our filmmakers of tomorrow be anything more than mere disciples? Their social scepticism camouflages their great respect for money as a liberator, and their scepticism in sex camouflages a romantic belief in shared happiness. The theme of failure immediately shows through, since salvation through love is made impossible by other people. But it is clear that this loneliness is more metaphysical than social. We may have the nasty feeling that, when reference is made to the celebrated "interior realism" or when pure statement is used as a pretext, all that is being hidden is a shunning of responsibilities ...' (*Les Lettres Françaises,* March–April 1960).

In this study, I have approached only a few of the questions raised by André Bazin. His system and its development remain to be studied in depth: its connections with the philosophy of Teilhard de Chardin, Lachelier, or the 'naive beliefs' of Daniel Rops, and its practical application by critics on daily, weekly, or monthly journals. There are other aspects too which I have not had the time or the energy to approach. However, the system can be summed up as follows: its starting-point is the ontology of the cinema, its essence, and for convenience's sake it brushes aside such aspects as History, Economics, Politics, Technique, Society, etc.

At the end of this inquiry, one is naturally prompted to ask a fundamental question: what happened to French criticism which, between 1945 and 1958, gave such confused and implicitly reactionary conceptions as those of Bazin the freedom of the city, and allowed them to become part of our daily lives? It is natural that right-wing critics should welcome a critical system that lies at the crossroads of so many traditions – *bourgeois,* idealist, liberal, religious, and social democrat. It is natural that right-wing critics should not scorn a 'dialectic' that cleverly combines the prestige of rationalism and the irrational powers of the image, borrowing the linguistic charms from the former, and the guiles of faith from the latter. It is natural that right-wing critics should agree with a system which rejects the notion of 'committedness' and gives pride of place to 'psychological' or 'moral' criteria. It is less natural that such left-wing critics as Sadoul and Albert Cervoni should consider Bazin to be respectively 'the best French critic' and 'a remarkable dialectician' (*Positif,* 'Inquiry into left-wing criticism', No. 36, November 1960). One's only answer can be that Marxist criticism in France has revealed its lack of seriousness, its lack of criteria, at the very time it most needed to be lucid.

It seems to me that Cervoni's summing-up of Bazin holds one of the keys to the problem: 'Bazin, a left-wing critic, was neither Marxist nor even materialist.' That, in black and white, means that the old Marxist and materialist notions must be revised, since a spiritual and non-Marxist system is here considered enough to make a 'left-wing critic'. Which means that without needing to analyse a situation portrayed in a film from a Marxist, or even materialist, standpoint, one can still end up with good concrete results, with a 'criticism' and a 'demystification' of *bourgeois* values and the *bourgeois* order. Or else, if left-wing criticism can be conceived of outside the sphere of a radical attack on the *bourgeois* system and ideology, one is supposed to accept the specious arguments of reformist criticism. 'I would say,' Cervoni goes on, 'that an entirely honest critic is pretty close to becoming a left-wing critic, if he has not already become one.' This is the stunt of the 'ray of sunlight', of the resolutely *optimistic* critic. There is clearly no longer any need to be a Marxist, let alone a materialist, in order to become a left-wing critic. You just need to be honest, to be quite simply a human being, to exist. The notions of revolt, analysis, and effectiveness are lost in the darkness of time. And probably because the French public is on the whole less receptive today to a Marxist approach and method of analysis, Marxism is left, with its accomplice, materialism, in the cloakroom. This makes the public happy. But through wanting to reconcile opposites, the Left is losing ground every day without realising it. It is caught between two stools: on the one side, it is stubborn on a strictly political level (for instance, in the argument between *Humanité-dimanche* and Bazin in February 1956 about censorship, the Church, and Catholic criticism; or else in the violent dispute which pitted Sadoul against Bazin on the question of Bazin's brilliant and remarkable article on 'The myth of Stalin in the Soviet cinema' (*Esprit,* August 1950); and on the other side, the Left respects social-democratic ideology so as not to cut itself off from possible allies; in fact, this ideology is sometimes even adopted, adapted, and imbibed. Should such tactics be considered a sign of 'increasing carelessness and unbridled eclecticism' (Roland Barthes), of 'complacent slavery' (Borde), of

Edith Scob in Georges Franju's *Les Yeux sans visage* (1960).

simple mimicry, or the result of supremely adroit conduct? One cannot answer at the moment except by looking at the evidence as it comes in. The results are not very brilliant. Marcel Martin is well aware of this, when he regrets that no one denounced, if not 'André Bazin man of the Left", at least 'his uprooted aestheticism which is an indisputable feature of right-wing criticism' (*Positif,* 'Inquiry into left-wing criticism', No. 36).

In fact, a lot of damage has been done. It is easy to poke fun at the hazy distinguishing marks of Bazin's system, but there can be no doubt that Bazin, although he did not create his disciples (they would have existed without him), helped to cement fallacious theories and give them that appearance of solidity which permits even the most insubstantial of ideas to keep out of danger. Bazin was somebody who united what should have been disrupted. His heir today is Sadoul. Sadoul, too, tries to put everything on the same level, instead of looking for contradictions and creating oppositions. Not only does he attempt to link the new French cinema with the generations that have preceded it (for example, Jacques Demy's *Lola* with the tradition of 'poetic realism'), but he also puts widely differing directors into the same basket by talking of a 'Paris school', a '1960 generation', a 'neo-romanticism', and the list, alas, has not been completed. On the contrary, some films should have been criticised and others defended, in order to encourage what was good in the

French cinema. A new cinema which has been able within the last few years to offer us such films as *Hiroshima mon amour, L'Année dernière à Marienbad, Une vie, Moi un noir, Zazie dans le métro, Cuba si!, L'Enclos, Les Yeux sans visage,* and *Marines* (to quote only a few films without going back too far) does not need to be defended *en bloc*; but it does demand that the grain be separated very carefully from the chaff. Is there a new French cinema? Yes, as long as two mistakes are avoided: opposing it to the old, *en bloc,* and linking it with the old, *en bloc.*

There can be no doubt that Bazin was a man of taste and a scrupulous critic. None of his articles is botched, and that in itself is a recommendation. Sometimes even, when he managed to tear himself away from his beloved ambiguities and went into the attack, he could produce good strong stuff: articles such as 'The myth of Stalin in the Soviet cinema' and 'La politique des auteurs' are more than ever relevant. This good side of Bazin remains to be studied. But Bazin did have to be put in his proper place, and not left in a false situation that was a little too reminiscent of De Gaulle at the helm of the Ship of State, or of Pope John XXIII blessing Italian Christians and socialists just before his 'opening towards the Left': 'They are all my little children.'

Notes

1. I have not introduced Gérard yet. He is the young theatre producer who wants very much to put on Shakespeare's Pericles; but as he has no backers he has to take his actors as they come. He is supported by Terry, which visibly is not very much to his liking. One day he is asked to put Pericles on in a big Paris theatre: Terry has slept with an influential impresario. But in the end Gérard refuses to compromise. He stagnates for a time, then commits suicide, acting partly on a whim, but much more in protest against his failure in the theatre.

It may of course be argued that one can prove almost anything when one quotes out of context. But I think Gozlan's procedure is legitimate. Where I have checked the reviews he quotes from, none of them has been deformed. This is because Gozlan's aim is less to prove a case or to move from point to logical point than to evoke the atmosphere and tone of *Cahiers* during a certain period.

However, it would be only fair, I think, to quote here a couple of the texts in their entirety. The first, Claude Chabrol's notorious plea for 'little themes', contains a lot of hard common sense. But it is marred by Chabrol's j'm'en-foutiste ('couldn't-care-less') attitude and conscious prejudice against the ambitious theme per se. A similar, and equally persuasive, article could be written, containing just as great a proportion of truth and falsehood, championing the big, as against the little, theme.

The second article, Jean-Luc Godard's review of Alexandre Astruc's *Une vie*, is remarkable for a number of reasons. Not only is its tone, blustering, halting, pretentious and full of paradoxes, very close to that of the films he was later to make; but Godard, who sees the universe in his own very personal terms, spots in Astruc's film (or more likely reads into it) some of the characteristics of his own work: abrupt changes of tone, gratuitousness, gestures and acts seen out of context, almost abstractly.

Peter Graham

6 Little Themes

CLAUDE CHABROL (1959)[*]

irectors who want to make a film on a theme of their own choosing have two solutions open to them. Depending on their aspirations they can describe the French Revolution or a quarrel with the next-door neighbours, the apocalypse of our time or the barmaid who gets herself pregnant, the final hours of a hero of the Resistance or an inquiry into the murder of a prostitute. It is a question of personality: the important thing, surely, is that the film should be good, that it should be well directed and well constructed, that it should be good cinema. The only distinction one can make between the apocalypse and the prostitute, the revolution and the barmaid, the hero and the quarrelling neighbours is on the level of the ambitiousness of the theme. For there *are,* of course, big and little themes. Anyone who doesn't agree should put up their hand.

From here on, it's child's play: it is easy to tell which film deserves one's attention and which one does not. I take two sheets of paper, and on one I write the following synopsis:

The Apocalypse of Our Time. Scenario: After a total atomic war, life has disappeared from the face of the earth. The sole survivor is a black, who is all alone in New York. He organises his life as best he can, but suffers from loneliness. After a couple of months he realises that another human being, a white woman, has survived the catastrophe. He meets her. Soon he falls in love with her, but his racial complexes make happiness impossible for him. Two months later, a white man appears in a dinghy. He too wants the woman. At first the black acts self-effacingly, then he reacts and challenges the other man. The white man decides on a duel to the death, and in the deserted city, in front of the United Nations building, the two last men on earth throw themselves into the final struggle. For it is, of course, war, man's folly, that is 'the apocalypse of our time'.

---

* *Cahiers du cinema* No. 100, October 1959.

Claude Chabrol.

On the other sheet of paper I write this:

The Quarrel between Neighbours. Scenario: In an isolated part of the Causses, a poor farmer lives alone. He has organised his life as best he can, but he suffers from loneliness. One day, another human being, a woman from the city, appears. Her car has broken down. She yields to the charms of the countryside. The farmer does her the honours of the house and shows her his primitive life on the land. He soon falls in love with her, but his peasant status, compared with her status as a city-dweller, makes happiness impossible for him. A little later, a former farmer, who has lived in the city for some time, decides to return to the land. He settles down on the neighbouring farm, and soon he too wants the woman. To start with, the first farmer acts self-effacingly; then he reacts and challenges the other man, who thereupon decides on a duel to the death. In the desolate windswept Causses, in the shadow of the wild Cévennes mountains, the two men fight. For it is, of course, true that farmers enjoy a 'good quarrel with their neighbour'.

I compare the two sheets of paper, get my friends to read them, submit them to producers. There's no doubt about it: *The Apocalypse of Our Time* is a big theme, and *The Quarrel between Neighbours* a banal and worthless story. I shoot *The Apocalypse,* and the result is the biggest load of tripe for years. Everyone is amazed, and no one more than I. However, some people are gullible enough to be taken in: maybe the film is imperfect, but the subject is of such importance that everyone should be interested in it. They proclaim: '*The Apocalypse of Our Time* is interesting for several reasons.' But although I may be a sucker, I can recognise a good film when I see one, and I realise that my life's work is indeed of little worth.

Sidney Poitier and Tony Curtis in Stanley Kramer's *The Defiant Ones* (1958): a Big Human Theme.

In a flash of clear-sightedness, I have another look at *The Quarrel between Neighbours* and I realise the subject is the same; I also realise that it doesn't hold water. Once shorn of its apocalyptic setting and brought down to earth, *The Apocalypse of Our Time* doesn't belong to our time or to any other. As *The Quarrel between Neighbours* proves, it does not point to a social, psychological, or even metaphysical truth of any kind. *The Apocalypse* was rubbish, as was *The Quarrel between Neighbours,* and for the same reasons.

This is what I am getting at: quite apart from any cinematic considerations, which are irrelevant here, a big theme is no more valid than a little one. It is a decoy which from time to time becomes a booby-trap.

To take my argument a little further, it wasn't at all the theme that was big in the story of the Apocalypse, for the same sequence of events can result in the most inept of peasant dramas. The setting is a camouflage: a deserted city does not offer any greater cinematic possibilities than the Causses – on the contrary – but the cretin who has seen neither of them is impressed.

Look, cretin, here are the traps into which you fall: the big themes.

An *exhaustive* list of big themes:

(a) Big Historical Themes:

Adam and Eve (especially if they are not shown naked). Certain allegories are allowed on condition the names of the characters are explicit: Eve or Eva, with Adam as a surname. The serpent is of course the seducer.

Joan of Arc, and by extension: saintliness, the big-hearted or heroic prostitute (Nurse Marthe Richard is on duty, a Resistance fighter, she sleeps with Hitler to steal some documents from him, a victim of the cold war), children, mothers, and a general.

The French Revolution, and the one which is still continuing throughout the world, the class struggle, strikes, suffragettes, equal rights for women.

Wars, which everyone hates, but which do produce heroes, good causes, and bad ones too. Joan of Arc can easily be included under this heading.

The atomic bomb, the apocalypse of our time.

(b) Big Human Themes:

Love, characterised by the problem of the couple (without the intervention of the serpent): brief encounters, subtle changes of heart.

The Brotherhood of Man: I am my brother's keeper, and I take heed lest he fall.

Mine Own Executioner: sunk to the bottom of the abyss, and now a man, he finds the strength to climb up again.

The Green Paradise: the mysteries of childhood and life, the conflict between innocence and the adult world.

Death: he looks back over his life and dies of shame. He was too cold, he didn't love his fellow men.

God: I leave the Church, thou leavest the Church, he leaves the Church. Why are we all leaving the Church?

That's all.

In my opinion, there's no such thing as a big theme and a little theme, because the smaller the theme is, the more one can give it a big treatment. The truth is, truth is all that matters.

7 Elsewhere
(Alexandre Astruc's *Une vie*)

JEAN-LUC GODARD (1958)[*]

I couldn't care less about the merry-go-round, with its Walt Disney-type deco-ration, the lunch on the grass with its plastic imitation table-cloths, the ball of wool that is the colour of chewing-gum. I couldn't care less about all the lapses in taste that Astruc, Claude Renoir, and Mayo have committed. And as for Roman Vlad's saxophone. … Actually, he plays rather well. But in any case the beauty of *Une vie* lies elsewhere.

It lies in the yellow dress of Pascale Petit as she shivers amidst the Velazquez-grey dunes of Normandy. 'That's not true, they aren't Velázquez-grey! Nor Delacroix-grey for that matter,' the 'connoisseurs' will squawk.

But in vain. Already Christian Marquand is leaning over the end of the jetty and holding out his hand to Maria Schell. The 'connoisseurs' are foxed by a film that moves so quickly it seems almost to be running on the spot. It is well known that the fastest racing cars are those that have the best brakes: so it is with *Une vie*. One thought one knew Astruc; one started building up theories, without noticing that the sequence was over and that the film had gone off in another aesthetic or moral direction. One talked of Velázquez without noticing that Pascale Petit's dress was Baudelaire-yellow and Maria Schell's eyes Ramuz-blue. Why Ramuz? Because behind Guy de Maupassant's cardboard characters, behind Jeanne and Julien, it is the face of 'Aline' or of 'Jean-Luc Persécuté' that Astruc is filming. There is nothing surprising in this, for it is well known that Astruc has long admired the author of *Les Signes parmi nous*. And why did I also mention the author of *The Albatross* just now? Because the first shot of *Une vie* gives the whole film a Baude-lairean stamp. Because Schell runs down to the sea as fast as her legs will carry her and Petit's dress echoes the most famous line of the poet, who said to Manet: 'You are the foremost in the decadence of your art.' One could also mention Thomas Hardy, William Faulkner too, and the Charlotte Rittenmayer of *Wild Palms*, who can be seen here transposed in the character played by Marquand; but Astruc him-

* *Cahiers du cinéma,* No. 89, November 1958, pp. 50–3

Jean-Luc Godard (left) and Raoul Coutard.

self said so much about this (perhaps too much) that the admirers of *Le Rideau cramoisi* have started frantically searching for something which they have been surprised not to find. What does all this prove? Simply that I was talking about painting without realising that *Une vie* is the film of a novelist, and about taste without realising that it is the film of an uncouth director.

Well there we are, I have defended the film against those who admire it for the wrong reasons. As for the others, my task is easier; *Une vie* is almost the opposite of the typical Astruc film, in so far as we had confined Astruc to a prefabricated aesthetic system which he has now broken out of.

Who cares if the version now being shown in cinemas bears little or no resemblance to the one intended by the scenario? Who cares if each scene is systematically cut short just at its climax by the editing? *Une vie* must be admired as it stands. And, as it stands, *Une vie* doesn't look very much like an inspired film. Madness behind realism, Astruc has said in an interview. But he has been misun-

Maria Schell and
Christian Marquand
in Alexandre
Astruc's *Une vie*
(1958).

derstood. Julien was mad to have married Jeanne, and Jeanne mad to have married Julien. And that's that. The idea was not to show *La Folie du Docteur Tube,* but to show how silly it was for a man of the open air to fall in love with a domesticated woman. As a matter of fact, *Une vie* worries Astruc's most enthusiastic admirers, just as *Le Plaisir* worried those who thought they knew their Maupassant. People expected Astruc to be lyrical, whereas what they got was Astruc the architect.

Une vie is a superbly constructed film. So may I, in order to illustrate my point, use terms borrowed from classical geometry? A film may be compared to a *geometrical locus,* i.e. a group of points that possess the same property in relation to a fixed element. This group of points is, if you like, the *mise-en-scène*; and that single property common to every moment of the *mise-en-scène* is the scenario, or, if you prefer, the dramatic outline. All that's left is the fixed element (which may possibly even be mobile): the subject. Well, what happens is this: with most filmmakers, the geometrical locus of the subjects they claim to treat never extends beyond the place of shooting. What I mean is that the action of their film may very well take place over an enormous area, but most filmmakers never *conceive* their *mise-en-scène* in terms which extend beyond the limits of the set. Astruc, on the other hand, gives one the feeling he has conceived his film over the whole area demanded by the scenario, no more no less. We see only three or four Normandy landscapes in *Une vie*. And yet the film gives one the uncanny feeling it has been *thought out on the true scale of Normandy,* just as *Tabu* was on the scale of the Pacific and *Que Viva Mexico!* on that of Mexico. Perhaps I am over-interpreting the evidence; but the evidence is there. The fact is too remarkable to leave unmentioned. And all the more so as Astruc and Laudenbach did not make things easier for themselves by showing, as I said, only three or four aspects of the woods of Normandy. For the difficulty was not to show the forest, but to show a drawing-room which one *knew* was only a few yards away from the forest. What was even more difficult was not to show the sea, but to show a bedroom which one *knew* was only half a mile from the sea. Most films are constructed on the few square metres of décor that are visible through the viewfinder. *Une vie* has been conceived, written, and directed over two hectares.

Astruc has set up his dramatic and visual coordinates over this vast invisible area. Between the abscissa and the ordinate there is no curve that might reveal some secret progression in the film. The only curve is either the abscissa or the ordinate – which in fact adds up to two kinds of progression, one horizontal, the other vertical. The whole *mise-en-scène* of *Une vie* has this basic principle as its axis. Schell and Petit's dash down to the shore is horizontal. Marquand bending down to help his partner on to the jetty of the port is vertical. The exit of the married couple after the wedding feast is horizontal. The stroke of the knife that rips open the bodice is vertical. Again, the movement of Jeanne and Julien rolling in the corn is horizontal; that of Marquand's hand seizing Antonella Lualdi's wrist is vertical. And so on. For Astruc, the *mise-en-scène* of *Une vie* lay quite simply in emphasising one of these two movements, horizontal or vertical, in every scene or shot that had its own dramatic unity, and in doing so in an *abrupt* way, so that all that did not form part of this abrupt movement sank into the background before or after it.

In *Les Mauvaises rencontres,* Astruc was still using this kind of effect, this carefully thought-out recourse to violence, in the manner of Juan Antonio Bardem: on a cut, on a door that opens, a glass that breaks, a face that turns away. In *Une vie,* on the other hand, he uses it in mid-shot, extending the technique of Richard Brooks and particularly Nicholas Ray so far that *the effect becomes almost the cause.* What is beautiful is not so much Marquand dragging Schell out of the château as the suddenness of the gestures that give the suspense of the film a new lease of life every few minutes. This discontinuity that is latent in continuity might be called the tell-tale heart of *Une vie* – if only to show how close is the link between this supposedly cold film and the true master of mystery, Edgar Allan Poe, the most abstract author of all.

Just like *Bitter Victory, Une vie* is a wonderfully simple film. But simplification does not mean stylisation. Astruc is here very different from Luchino Visconti, and it would be pointless to compare the two directors. In *Le Notti bianche,* Maria

Schell was certainly more efficiently used. But in *Une vie* she is used in a better, more profound way. In his own time, Maupassant was, I suppose, a modern writer. Paradoxically, then, the best way to capture a genuine 19th-century atmosphere was to give the whole film an undisguisedly 1958 tone. Astruc and Laudenbach have succeeded magnificently. The only proof I need is the admirable answer that the admirable Marquand gives to the woman who has offered him her dowry and her chateau: 'Because of you, I have ruined my life.' And another example: Marquand's bearing as he carries Schell in his arms seems just as modern as Jean-Claude Pascal's similar handling of Anouk Aimée seemed old fashioned in *Les Mauvaises rencontres*.

When one has heaped all the praise one can on Petit (Astruc went to work on her in just as phenomenal a way as Renoir did on Françoise Arnoul in *French Cancan*), who slides through the undergrowth as easily as a slow-worm and hides beneath the sheets better than Roger Vadim's girls, all will not have been said. The title of *Une vie* might well have been 'On the Threshold of the Unknown', with all its overtones of science fiction. For *Une vie* forces the cinema to turn its gaze in another direction.

'Le Roi est nu' ('The Emperor Has No Clothes') is the typically colourful title of an article on the Nouvelle Vague in general by Robert Benayoun which is in its own way almost a manifesto. *Positif* was put in a difficult position at the time of the Nouvelle Vague. Its violent attack on the films of the *Cahiers* directors was interpreted by some, not least by *Cahiers*, as sour grapes. This was unfair in the light of the evidence. It was hardly likely that *Positif* would adore the films of those whose criticism they had been reacting against only a year previously. What they objected to was the fact that *Cahiers* gave the impression that they alone were the Nouvelle Vague. What about Alain Resnais, Georges Franju, Alexandre Astruc, Louis Malle, Jacques Demy, Philippe de Broca, Jacques Rozier, Agnès Varda and the rest of them? asked *Positif*. Benayoun's article, aggressive and virulent though it is, is not merely destructive; it is a call for the kind of cinema that *Positif* believes in.

Peter Graham

8 The Emperor Has No Clothes

ROBERT BENAYOUN (1962)[*]

'To measure a circle, you can begin anywhere.'

Charles Fort

'If the cinema looks in upon itself too much, it will be in danger of ending up as a kind of subculture, consisting of approximations, pale reflections, quotations, and hazy reminiscences; it will be as though it were shut up in a furnished flat whose walls were covered with photographs of furniture, whose books were only about furnishing.'

Robert Benayoun: 'Against the Cinema of Furnishing.'

Have you been abroad recently? There are two things which make foreign countries jealous of us: De Gaulle and the Nouvelle Vague. And I'm not saying that just to be clever: observations from afar tend to synthesise, and the two subjects I have mentioned are not as unconnected as one might think at first sight. French propaganda abroad uses the Nouvelle Vague (just as it does the liner *France,* or the oil-wells of Hassi-Messaoud) in order to prove that France is not, as has been suggested, a country of old men. It is only natural that use should be made, for this purpose, of such very young old men as the leaders of the Nouvelle Vague, who, like the government itself, are haunted by the touching desire to make a career and to *last.*[1]

The Gaullist régime, like the Nouvelle Vague, still keeps up the illusion abroad with an unruffled display of contradictions, combined with shilly-shallying, hollow catchphrases, patriotic jingles, and a breezy use of clichés. It is characterised, as is the Nouvelle Vague, by an avowed determination to maintain confusion in order to stand its ground, by an unholy fear of intervention or rivalry from outside, and by a

---

* *Positif,* No. 47, July 1962

Robert Benayoun.

manifest propensity to amalgamate contradictory theses. Finally, De Gaulle (like the Nouvelle Vague) is trying to keep permanently at bay that moment when it will become clear, as in the Hans Christian Andersen fairy-tale, that the king is naked.

Plenty of other comparisons will come to mind in the course of this article: it is quite clear that Gaullist France, with its raucous demagogy and its blindness to realities, was ideal ground for a school of *ultra-bourgeois* expression, based on entertainment, compromise, and other feeble characteristics inherited from their elders.

I will be taken to task at once for the tone of this article. Why did I not opt for the stiff objectivity of the historian and cast over a movement that is five years old the veil that is usually destined for the millennia that sandwich Christ? I must admit that I would have been incapable of doing so. To the very young people of the Nickelodéon and Cinéquanon cine-clubs, the year 1957 must have an aura of antediluvian legend, reminding them of the time when, with their voices hardly broken, they were refused entry to horror films; but in the bound volumes of the important trade paper, *La Cinématographie française*, the Nouvelle Vague does not take up very much room. The films were more often phantasmal than palpable. And those who have not seen Jean-Daniel Pollet's *La Ligne de mire* might be tempted to think that, because it is to be found in the Cinémathèque of Babel, it is a work by Herbert Quain.

And so I'm going to be unfair. I may even go a bit too far and make a summary judgement of a film which might deserve a longer analysis. But the pamphleteer has the privilege of being able to lacerate something he does not completely abhor simply in order to clear the ground; he can point out the most obvious faults, and leave the filmologists to pick their way through the haystack. The lenience of film-lovers is notorious: put them in their leather seat in a darkened cinema and they will set off in search of that famous quarter of an hour which can redeem the most incompetent, but alluringly titled, film. And I'm not going to go into any detailed discussion of the shots or sequences which, in this or that Nouvelle Vague film, soothed my regrets at wasting time.

Let me put it bluntly: the catchphrase 'Nouvelle Vague', which arose as everyone knows from an investigation into youth by Françoise Giroud which appeared in *L'Express,* was first applied by that same weekly to a film by Marcel Carné called *Les Tricheurs.* The film was extraordinarily vulgar, redolent of the immediate post-war period. It was nevertheless well received, and the catch-phrase made a hit. It was used again for Claude Chabrol's *Les Cousins* and was, as we know, successful. And I would not fall into the bad habit of certain columnists who denigrate a film on the strength of its publicity handout, had not those responsible for *Cahiers du*

The party scene in Claude Chabrol's *Les Cousins* (1959).

cinéma, who pontificate glibly in the manner of Martin Heidegger, André Malraux or Alfred Korzybsky, themselves taken such enormous delight in the most unpleasant demands of this activity.

From 1958 onwards, a new kind of production was the done thing: a low budget, no stars, a small camera crew, a sensational subject, and some explosive publicity. The national Press was most co-operative. The members of the Nouvelle Vague had no difficulty in finding a mouthpiece, and they began to rewrite history. To quote Godard, that master-purveyor of hot air: 'I purposely shot the film at great speed, it was an improvised rough job. ... People had never shot a film like that before.'[2] And elsewhere: 'Studio sets are never constructed with a ceiling to them... . The walls were painted white, something that's never done in film-making.'[3] French newsreels were astonished that anyone dared, *for the first time,* to camouflage a camera in the middle of a street in order to film passers-by. True, the Italians had never filmed the Champs-Élysées or the Place Clichy in this way. It became almost obligatory to include in every Nouvelle Vague film one or more long promenades on foot or in a taxi, so that Paris could be discovered 'for the first time'. The new cinema was indubitably fond of *flânerie*, and had one quality in common with the tourists one sees in travelogues: the ability to *see* everything without *looking* at anything.

The leaders of the Nouvelle Vague had the avowed desired to appropriate the true talents of the French cinema, so they did a bit of hijacking: 'The Nouvelle Vague was born at Cannes the year that *Hiroshima mon amour, Les Cousins, Orfeu Negro,* and *Les Quatre cents coups* were shown,' François Truffaut categorically declared to the journalists of America.[4] All at once, the press hastened to rope into the Nouvelle Vague filmmakers who had long preceded it, contradicted it, or had no connection with it at all, namely Alain Resnais, Agnès Varda, Chris Marker, Jean Rouch, Jacques Baratier, Armand Gatti, Marcel Hanoun, and so on.

Amidst all this carefully built-up chaos, what innovations did the Nouvelle Vague really make, apart from introducing new production conditions and a network of limited but effective mutual aid on the level of public relations? It would be easier to ask: what innovations *could* it have made? A random re-reading of *Cahiers du cinéma* is very revealing. That over-estimated magazine, whose chief merit has been to exist longer than its rivals (and regularly publish excellent interviews with directors), has been swamped by three or four successive waves of callow and blustering prophets. Truffaut stated in black and white what a poor opinion he had of Jacques Doniol-Valcroze, only to find himself proved wrong one day by some arrogant successor. In the pages of *Cahiers,* the predominant ethos has always been 'make way for me', and this was also the driving force behind the Nouvelle Vague. As generation after generation went its way, the idols were shuffled: those who once worshipped Orson Welles, John Huston, and Roberto Rossellini were ousted by the champions of Robert Aldrich, Howard Hawks, and Anthony Mann, and then by those of Samuel Fuller, Fritz Lang, and Joseph Losey. Today, all this has been swept away by a new brood of *cinéphiles* who are blithely ignorant of any films that are more than five years old, and new gods have been installed: Edgar G. Ulmer, Raoul Walsh, and Vittorio Cottafavi. The *politique des auteurs* is, as can be seen, a dialectic of hormonal rejuvenation sustained by the criterion of rediscovery on virgin ground. This ability to refocus at will on this or that decade of film history incidentally throws light on another, less obvious, ability: that of denying the true origins of the movement when these origins might be embarrassing. So it is that the Nouvelle Vague officially recognises Jean-Pierre Melville, Alexandre Astruc, and Roger Vadim as its involuntary begetters, whereas it displays the greatest contempt for René Clément or Alberto Lattuada. And yet one can find the whole of Godard in certain scenes of *Monsieur Ripois* (*Knave of Hearts*) or the *Gli Italiani si voltano* episode in *Amore in città* (*Love in the City*).

But let us not talk of intellectual rigour. *Cahiers du cinéma* has, from one generation to the next, exalted such perishable goods as Albert Lamorisse's *Crin Blanc: le cheval sauvage* (*White Mane*), Sacha Guitry's *Si Versailles m'était conté* (*Royal Affairs in Versailles*), Joseph Mankiewicz's *All About Eve*, Jacques Becker's *Touchez pas au grisbi*, Jean Cocteau's *Le Testament d'Orphée*, Nicholas Ray's *Hot Blood*, or Jean Renoir's *Le Déjeuner sur l'herbe*. They have never followed the slightest critical line that one can clearly discern, published the slightest aesthetic manifesto to define common standpoints, or elaborated the slightest theoretical system worth taking seriously, apart from an incredibly senile attempt by Eric Rohmer, that Robinson Crusoe of obscurantism.[5]

The *politique des auteurs,* a kind of gimmicky bottle-opener, was always finding that the wine had turned bad: the revelation of Stanley Donen at Gene Kelly's expense, the downfall of Aldrich and Ray, Alfred Hitchcock's sardonic two-timing of an English interviewer,[6] the unexpected triumph of Michelangelo Antonioni, the decline of Renoir, and so on. Cinematic specificity, which allowed Fereydoun Hoveyda to admire Ray's *Party Girl* simply *because* he found the plot particularly silly, was held up to ridicule by Richard Roud in *Sight and Sound*: 'Unfortunately, when a critic has to quote Hegel and Kant in reviewing a film by Minnelli, it is not because, as Hoveyda maintains, the cinema is at least as important as literature, painting and the drama. It is because somehow the critic feels he must dignify his liking of the film by the most impeccable intellectual references. It is a curious paradox that those French critics who delight in non-intellectual, irrational films always feel called upon to discuss them in the most pedantic and academic way possible. The trouble, one feels, is that they like the second-rate but daren't admit it.'[7]

Louis Malle's *Zazie dans le métro* (1960).

In place of the aesthetic, political, moral, and sociological attitudes of Neo-Realism, the filmmakers from *Cahiers* set up a régime of blatant amateurism, of wilful
paradoxicality which led them to adopt, through pure whim, certain techniques
which the Italians had acquired through necessity. Improvisation which, in Italy,
had been an ascetic hardship became for them a sinecure. *À bout de souffle* set the
fashion for any old thing done in any old way; and although this fashion certainly
arose from a deep dissatisfaction with traditional filmic language, it could never
raise its convulsions above the level of untidiness. It was, in the full sense of the
term, 'rough-draft cinema'.[8]

Of course, this bias towards glaring negligence was one way of taking the bull
by the horns. The Nouvelle Vague is a school of critics who dare each other actually to try their hand at film-making. It is *film-making to see if one is capable of
film-making*. It is a mystery how the directors of the Nouvelle Vague, in their criticism, have thrown discredit upon Huston, whom they call an amateur. For the
movies they produced themselves are amateurish: films in which incompetence, if
not the rule, is adopted as a feature of style.[9]

In comparison with everyday, technically over-slick productions, these slapdash films momentarily took the public by surprise – they saw in them, and rightly

so, a certain quality of freshness. But it was the freshness of the first attempt; the Nouvelle Vague was important only so long as there were plenty of first attempts. Once incompetence had been overcome (probably reluctantly) and replaced by virtuosity, one pretty quickly noticed in someone like Chabrol an irrevocable decline in sincerity. Once a Nouvelle Vague director learns his profession properly, his breeziness misfires and becomes grotesque. Godard, at the present stage of his career, is no longer creating cinema; moreover, he is trying very hard not to look too much as though he is.

For ten years film criticism has had to put up with the lenient annotations of the two great mahatmas of double-talk: Georges Sadoul and André Bazin. And so the last five years have quite naturally been marked by the conviction that it is more worthwhile to make films than to talk about them. The French Cinémathèque was stormed by voracious young men who, to satisfy their secret dream of becoming directors one day, set about wolfing masterpieces by the dozen.

The first result of this was that their films were filled with undigested cinema.

There were quotation films, in which such and such a scene from Hitchcock, coupled with another one from Luis Buñuel, leads up to a long Jean Vigo sequence, shot in a Roberto Rossellini manner but rejuvenated by Paddy Chayefsky techniques. This more or less bulimic assimilation incidentally reflected a real fascination with the act of nutrition. Those who so admired the *pâté de foie* sequence in one of Becker's films lingered long in their own films over breakfasts, snacks, and banquets.[10] But when the act of creation is replaced by the act of consumption, there arises a phenomenon well known in all cannibals: the eater thinks he has invented what he has eaten.[11]

The cinema, when continually rehashed in this way, inevitably ends up by becoming insipid. The Nouvelle Vague film will give us an imitation, round a bistro table, of some fleeting gesture glimpsed in the third reel of the 1955 remake, in 'Scope, of an old B Western. The height of subtlety consists of making one film in order to say one would like to have made another: 'I would like to dance as they do in Minnelli musicals,' declares Madame Karina, who fails precisely to do so.

The myth of specificity has caused a filmic gold-rush. Paris, already full of young people who possess a painting technique but do not do anything with it, has suddenly found itself invaded by thousands of *cinéphiles* for whom the mere process of direction has taken the place of an act of creation. Their only desire is to make films without even asking themselves what they are going to say in them. By giving the simple fact of self-expression a quotient of value, by substituting the *way* of saying something for any kind of motivation of expression, the champions of the Nouvelle Vague sound as ridiculous as De Gaulle when he reduces his speeches to the formula, so well described by Jean-François Revel: 'You are there, I

'I would like to dance as they do in Minnelli musicals': Anna Karina in Jean-Luc Godard's *Une femme est une femme* (1961).

am here, everything is fine since I am talking to you.' Charles Bitsch's stupid witticism: 'Antonioni has nothing to say and he says it badly' suggests that, in contrast to the latter director, who indissolubly fuses form and content, the Nouvelle Vague is secretly proud of having nothing to say, but of saying it well. This being the case, it is hardly surprising if one has the impression that Godard's films reflect the state of mind of certain manic depressives who spend a lot of time listening to themselves talk without knowing what they are talking about.

Their declared aim is to make great strides forward without worrying too much about an itinerary. And in order to make great strides, the idea is to go as quickly as possible. There is a deceptive creed prevalent among *cinéphiles* which holds that by making many films, of any kind, one will end up one day by finding out what one wants to say, and in that very way one will say it. This delusion is surely just as dangerous as an overlong period as assistant director. In so far as automatic writing cannot be achieved by several people together, there is a fundamental improbability that mere professional activity will strike a creative spark out of a subject. Such an attitude, if not discouraged, would threaten the cinema with an invasion far more catastrophic and depressing than the 'cinema of furnishing'. One might as well build, in great haste and without an architect's plan, a host of houses in the hope that one of them, by some fluke, will be more beautiful than the others.

The Nouvelle Vague has given birth to a mystique of trial and error that enshrines the act of scribbling and glorifies the unfinished. We are supposed to believe that something can be created simply because the author indulges before our very eyes in a bumbling search for a means of expression. It is Henri-Georges Clouzot's *Le Mystère Picasso* (*The Mystery of Picasso*) with, instead of Picasso, someone who is learning to paint. We are supposed to admire the fact that a person is learning to paint, and if we remain by his or her side for a few years we will (perhaps) witness the birth of a painting. Faced with the virtuality of a work that cannot be discussed since it does not yet exist, we are supposed to find the greatest beauty in the greatest flop. Under the pretext of the immediacy of fashion, the highbrow spectator is asked to make out a blank cheque for a future that is all the more promising for remaining distant. It even gets to the point where directors attach a special importance to every slip of speech made by the actors, edit together two versions of the same pout, rave about the chance wobble of the camera, the disastrous shadow of a cloud, the unforeseeable deterioration of the film stock. A Nouvelle Vague film ends up by becoming the resultant of its own shortcomings. And the director ecstatically mucks the whole thing up, in the hope of prompting increasingly admirative derision on the part of the public. If the watchword of Neo-Realism was: '*Facciamo un film; un uomo cerca lavoro*' ('Let's make a film; a man looks for work'), that of the Nouvelle Vague might well be: 'I am shooting a film; just look how badly made it is!'

The irony of this is that specificity, which grew from an attempt to make film language autonomous, dooms the latter to systematic deterioration. It encourages a tendency to unmotivated expression, lacking in any deeply felt necessity, and results in a whole string of mannerisms that are destined to die a quick death. The filmmakers of the Nouvelle Vague have not caught up with the literature that they so despise. If they devote to the sound-track the assiduous care they deny their dialogue, it is because they have no roots in the intellectual realities of their time. If they turn their nose up at what they call 'big themes', it is because they are still clinging to the ataxia of pubescent mental defectives, and see themselves threatened by the spectre of culture as though by some omniscient father figure, at once a philosopher and a poet. As far as thought is concerned, their films are thirty years out of date. They are the exact equivalent of those insignificant novels that Gallimard has been publishing every year since 1930 just for form's sake, and which the publicity men tart up to make them seem modern.

It should be mentioned at this point that the theory of specificity is influential now only in the field of criticism; the filmmakers themselves have long since sacrificed it on the altar of demand. Not only is the Nouvelle Vague now undertaking a fair number of literary adaptations, but it soon gave up the criterion of the 'complete *auteur*' which was the rage in 1950 and which, for my part, I continue to uphold. Messrs. François Truffaut, Claude Chabrol, and Philippe de Broca have set up new teams of scriptwriters, with Marcel Moussy, Paul Gégauff, and Daniel Boulanger, who have quite simply replaced the old teams, Charles Spaak, Michel Audiard, and Henri Jeanson. Godard, if I am to believe what I read in the newspapers, is adapting his next film from Alberto Moravia, as many have done before him. The time when it was a question of all or nothing is past, they are now all doing their little bit in the *film à sketches, Les Sept péchés capitaux* (The Seven Deadly Sins). One can see that in *Jules et Jim* Truffaut has ended up shooting just the kind of film he would once have attacked: the very principle of a commentary lifted straight from the book (by Henri-Pierre Roché) and read, quite simply, on the sound-track contradicts all that he was foolish enough one day to write. By this I mean that Truffaut, whose lack of culture has always astonished me, had a lot of luck to come across a good book, and to have liked and understood it.

If I keep harping on this idea of specificity, it is because it has acted as a decoy to the young cinema. All cinematographic culture needs to be sublimated, to be confronted with the important ideas of the moment, with the very latest developments in art, science, and poetry. A film is a conflict between rhythm, visuals, thought, and language. Any filmmaker who claims to say something without having a precise idea of what the creative act implies remains a mere technician possessed by a functional frenzy. The cinema cannot be reduced to a syntax of repeatable devices, nor can Cinemascope and the zoom lens play the part of a linguistic manifesto. André Bazin was reluctant to analyse anything on the basis of editing, and yet he was not able to convince us of the intrinsic, almost animistic virtues he saw in the sequence shot. The same is true of art, where the use of materials has been unable to alter the major directions of modern painting as practised by Jackson Pollock or Arshile Gorky.

The childish mistake of the Nouvelle Vague directors has been to have made the cinema a god as it was in Dziga Vertov's time, to have encouraged a professional freemasonry with pretensions to autonomy, and to have attributed to technique the illusory role of an emancipator. Their attitude to literature displays as much old-fashioned isolationism as William Jennings Bryan did before the First World War. They substitute the mirage of narrative style for thought and encourage intellectual indifference in young people.

When the indescribable Luc Moullet writes: 'Ethics is a question of tracking shots', it is only to admire 'the gratuitousness, fortunately total, of the camera movements' in the work of Samuel Fuller.[12] The beauty of his tracking shots, if I have understood aright, exempts Fuller from any moral concern, or, better even, authorises him to transcend the world in an orgasm of lateral and circular movements which some see as the very trademark of political uncommittedness. Well, it so happens that every camera movement reveals a movement of thought (an inverse, parallel, or asymptotic movement), even more than the use of the adjective or the third person singular by a writer. The use of violence in *mise-en-scène*, so admired by critics of the extreme right, cannot simply be ascribed to aestheticism, for every style has its moral attitude. Edouard Molinaro, who draws his inspiration from one of the most praiseworthy departments of the American cinema, the film noir, cannot help unconsciously inserting, when transposing the techniques of directors like Robert Wise and Aldrich, a morbidity of impact, a taste for physical bruising and a contempt for human fibre which show him up as the repressed policeman of his short film, *Appelez le 17*. Just as Louis-Ferdinand Céline's torrential sentences betray his anxious fanaticism and his phobia of logical argument, so Fuller's insidious tracking shots contain the hysteria of intellectual rape. 'He has a fine uncouth style,' Moullet sums up admiringly. No, such alibis of externalisation simply won't do. What the contemporary French cinema lacks is a philosophical and aesthetic training which could distinguish between creation and mere *mise-en-scène*. The jazz pianist Oscar Peterson, speaking as a teacher of modern music, once declared: 'I don't teach my pupils style, I teach them how to think. A musician needs above all to have a sense of direction, and a kind of honesty in his invention.' It is quite obvious that the majority of Nouvelle Vague films are *badly thought out*, except for the more literary among them – *Lola*, *Le Farceur* (*The Joker*), and especially *Paris nous appartient* (*Paris Belongs to Us*).

The way the filmmakers of the Nouvelle Vague shy off the important theme is extremely revealing. They refuse to commit themselves, they escape into formalism. There is, they claim, no subject that cannot be transcended, enlarged, or contradicted by the director. One can make an anti-racist film with a racist script, a film for all the family set a few hours before the end of the world, a social film on the falling of a rose petal, a cosmic epic on the passing of the hour at the Greenwich meridian. But it is the moral attitude of directors towards their subject that justifies their role. Chabrol has said that there are no big themes. He has certainly never plucked up the courage to 'shrink' one, as one shrinks a head; he prefers to magnify microscopic truths. You can fiddle around with the sound-track or the

Anouk Aimée in Jacques Demy's *Lola* (1961).

Jean-Pierre Cassel (centre) in Philippe de Broca's *Le Farceur* (1961).

photography, hustle actors and jostle the camera. But certain basic concepts cannot take that kind of treatment.

The Nouvelle Vague directors' fear of a theme gives itself away in their febrile attempt to amuse. The minute anything important or serious is touched upon, they take refuge in the insipid or the banal. Every point is made by means of gags in the *mise-en-scène*; a sly remark about intellectual treason is treated facetiously. We often get a reassuring wink; we are often informed that none of what is being said is of any consequence. And the mental vacuum is camouflaged by a monologue which makes random mention of a few book titles, or treats us to a quotation from Maxim Gorky which, as a joke, is attributed to Lenin.

At this stage, the argument about content inevitably runs into political considerations. I always mistrust those who display complete indifference to anything in the sphere of ideology. An inquiry in *Cahiers du cinéma* imagined that the difference between right-wing and left-wing criticism could be removed; it would be done by 'the removal of ethics to the advantage of aesthetics'. I would like to stress that those 'artists', Truffaut and Godard, who, in the name of aesthetics, categorically refuse to be put on either side, agree in their basic credo: 'It amuses me,' says Godard, 'to shuffle the cards.'[13] 'What interests me,' says Truffaut, 'is to contradict myself.... I like anything which is confused.'[14] It goes without saying that these are activities that no one denies them. Truffaut, who rebuked me in 1956 for ranking

Alain Resnais's *L'Année dernière à Marienbad* (1961).

him with the young Turks of right-wing criticism, recently gave an interview to the magazine, *Clarté*, which allows us to form a more accurate judgement of his political evolution – which is considerable, as one can judge for oneself:

> 'A man must vote, but not an artist. He cannot. He needs to try to discover what is interesting in the other person's point of view.... . There are communist directors in France, and it is they who should be asked to make films about the workers.... . I refuse to put love at an opposite pole to the bourgeoisie or the police. Policemen fall in love too.'[15]

Elsewhere, in a outburst of ingenuousness, he admits: 'I knew nothing about politics. I would not have been able to tell you what the FLN [the National Liberation Front in pre-independence Algeria] was, and then all of a sudden, thanks to TV, I became interested in current affairs.'[16]

This conception of art, which values equivocation and deliberate mystification, this marked taste for everything that blurs one's vision or makes comprehension difficult, represents in all likelihood what Godard, in a brief moment of illumination, put down to a kind of 'right-wing anarchism'. Here is a typical argument: 'In *Le Petit Soldat*, I thought the honest thing was to show friends, I mean people for whom I would go and fight if necessary, and even if I don't exactly sympathise with

The torture scene in Jean-Luc Godard's *Le Petit soldat* (1963).

their cause, the Algerians I mean, to *show* them torturing. I thought that torture could be more persuasively condemned if one saw one's own friend practising it.'[17] A remark that does not exactly tally with the following one: 'As I am sentimental, I suppose I am left-wing. Especially compared with my best friends – they are distinctly right-wing.' Here is another quotation in the same vein: 'To me, an artist cannot help being left-wing. Even Drieu La Rochelle was left-wing. Similarly Nikita Khrushchev and John F. Kennedy are right-wing, they are totalitarian.' And to conclude: 'On the one hand I am against the police; on the other, I am for them – in the Balzacian sense, in so far as it is mysterious.'[18]

Of course, one has to take into consideration the degree of provocation that informs this faintly preposterous series of statements – their main purpose is to flabbergast the interviewer, easy in this case as it is Michèle Manceaux.[19] But even when one has done so, one quickly realises that Godard attaches no importance to anything he says. The weight of the spoken word does not worry him, he says anything that comes into his head, just as he films anything that comes into his head, no doubt because 'remorse perhaps results in freedom'.[20] Such self-confidence of course allows him to revere the Establishment, by abstention. Under the guise of anarchy, what we have is a catatonic wait-and-see attitude, a kind of mental hibernation.

Some readers may well have found the thread of this article a trifle sibylline. But I did not impose on myself the rather thankless task of quoting just for fun: I think there is an almost inevitable similarity between the above-quoted remarks and the kind of cinema which they underlie. It is of no great importance to know whether those who made the remarks were unconsciously summing-up their moral conception of aesthetics, or whether, on the contrary, the practice of film-making as an intellectual diversion ensured that sooner or later they would reveal their true political colours. This would involve descending to a personal level; what concerns us here is their films.

And it is here that the Nouvelle Vague directors' bias in favour of formalism turns against them. As they have no notion of the elementary processes of the unconscious in artistic creation, they think themselves rid of all that they repress, and adduce a lack of interest in politics which is contradicted by their continual defiance when they deny their bias. However, their epigoni are less cautious: 'Fascism is beautiful,' declares Moullet, who writes a little later: 'The only opinion of Fascism that is worthy of consideration is that of somebody who has been tempted by it.'[21] Marc C. Bernard, who considers that 'every historical subject should be conceived and treated as though it were the subject of a gangster film', states that 'brutality is one way of doing things, and an honest one too'.[22] It goes without saying, as his mentor Michel Mourlet points out, that only 'brutality of expression and of photography' is meant by this.[23] We had got the distinction. Mourlet, in an article entitled 'In Defence of Violence', explained it well: 'The work of Walsh is an illustration of Zarathustra's aphorism: 'Man is made for war, woman for the warrior's rest, and what remains is folly'.[24] We can find in these wild admirers of Jacques Laurent, 'the writer who has written the finest and frankest sentences about girls' muscles,'[25] the traditional aesthetic alibis of the extreme right and the cowardice of all those who admire and adore gangsterish ideas and brutal language, while at the same time shrilly denying their inevitable context.

To put it bluntly, this is the kind of furtive hide-and-seek that eventually reveals the most treacherous characteristics of right-wing thinking. There are not many intellectuals nowadays who avouch reactionary ideology. But the subtle talkers who are deaf to their own words, the over-zealous champions of form as opposed to content, and the passionate devotees of mental chaos – i.e. the freedom to say anything that comes into their head – all unfailingly reveal a nostalgia for arbitrary power.

And so the argument about content is to me the chemical element which *precipitates* the environment and separates the molecules. Contrary to what one might expect, defining left-wing cinema in relation to right-wing cinema is not the same thing as gauging a work's degree of political effectiveness. On the contrary, I think the left-wing cinema can be defined by its faults. An unsuccessful left-wing film is always top-heavy with content, it is often awkwardly sincere, and it covers too many problems at once because it is too keen to convince. It tends to be too explicit and to simplify the forms of exposition. To go from there and exhort left-wing filmmakers to include more deliberate indifference, carelessness, and blurred impressionism on the pretext that they are in fashion would be absurd. On the other hand, one might ask them to have recourse more frequently to Hegelian dialectic, to give themselves more distance from their subject, to use analogy more frequently, to be more unbridled in their lyricism, and to employ a technique of surprise which would counter the current tenets of sloth; these are all qualities that one finds in directors such as Valerio Zurlini, Alexander Singer, and Alain Cavalier.

Positif is now at what might be called a turning-point in its existence. It will attempt to rid the *French cinema of bourgeois ideas*. The Nouvelle Vague, compared with other post-war movements in the cinema, represents a palliative regression, a misuse of analytical and critical activities which tends to limit or discredit the genuine attempts at renewal which film language is undergoing; the real contribution of these attempts will be assessed by *Positif* and will be compared with that of the Nouvelle Vague. Our aim in demolishing these *bourgeois* attitudes is above all to attack excessive chauvinism. What is happening every day in Poland and Italy, what is still happening in the prodigious melting-pots of America pours ridicule on the dilatory experiments of our playboys. We shall stand up for the principle of internationalism, which destroys outdated concepts of schools and throws into relief the significant and constant values of the moment.

What we write will be aimed in particular at the younger generation. They have been conditioned by the Algerian War, and their frequently brutal collision with political and social realities means that they are hardly likely to find sustenance in the deification of technique or in the demagogy of form which results in bread being replaced by its image, the image by its reflection, and the word by its echo.

The normal process of professional training (film school, assistantship) should not necessarily be championed in place of the dilettante formulae of the Nouvelle Vague. The future surely lies in the hands of a generation of filmmakers who are above all preoccupied with their own ideological emancipation and are already making, as best they can, militant films that bear witness to modern society – and on the side are learning how to use a camera. This generation is using its ingenuity not to devise systems of self-publicity, but to overcome, in the secrecy that circumstances demand, the material difficulties that their convictions impose upon them.

We shall treat the cinema as *one* of several means of expression, neither inferior nor superior to the others, and we shall submit films to criteria which do not subordinate moral and sociological considerations to aesthetic ones. We shall be careful not to confuse the mere practice of a profession with the creative act, or communal activity with the elaboration of a work of art. We shall ask that filmmakers be allowed to mature their works, instead of being forced to do slapdash jobs simply because the industry demands two films a year from them. We shall allocate to each film as much time as is needed for any important work, literary or philosophical, to be generated. We shall not indulge in the unbelievable glibness of talking about the cinema solely in technical terms, we shall refuse to set any limit on our imagination, and we shall subject films to all kinds of analogy. We shall base our appreciation of cinema on the identification of the intellectual content with its external envelope, and we shall make a sharp distinction between personal style and the mannerisms of the day. We shall go back to the fundamental idea of a 'personal universe' that was established by the review *L'Age du cinéma*. We shall answer any attempts to confuse by applying unruffled analysis which, while completely impervious to notions of fashion, will not exclude the wildest interpretations.

It goes without saying that such a standpoint is situated at opposite poles to the ideal of *improvised cinema*. If it still holds that 'true art cannot help being revolutionary', we shall always refuse to put a limit on the number of themes or subjects that it may be permitted to treat. We are here in full agreement with the manifesto that André Breton and Leon Trotsky drew up in 1938, *Towards a Free Revolutionary Art*, the terms of which remain indisputable:

> To those who try to persuade us that art should be subjected to a discipline which we consider to be radically incompatible with its means, our refusal will be categorical. It is our deliberate will to keep to the formula: *any licence in art*. (...) In defending freedom of creation, we intend in no way to justify political indifference. It is far from our purpose to wish to resuscitate the concept of so-called 'pure' art, which usually serves the far from pure aims of reactionary ideas. It is more worth while to trust in the gift of prefiguration which is the prerogative of all authentic artists, which implies the beginning of a (virtual) solution to the most serious contradictions of their age and orientates the thinking of their contemporaries towards the urgent need to establish a new order.

Notes

All notes by author Robert Benayoun

1. France can boast nothing less youthful than the group of filmmakers who have emerged from *Cahiers du cinéma*. They possess none of the normal qualities of youth: *naïveté*, idealism, humour, hatred of tradition, erotomania, a sense of injustice. François Truffaut is as old as Maurice Cloche or Léonide Moguy, Claude Chabrol as old as Julien Duvivier, Jean-Luc Godard as old as Curzio Malaparte. Only Jacques Rozier, an outsider, seems to be the same age as his central characters.

2. *L'Express*, July 27, 1961.

3. *L'Express*, January 12, 1961.

4. R.M. Franci and Marshall Lewis, 'A Conversation with François Truffaut,' in *New York Film Bulletin*, No.s 12, 13 and 14, 1961.

5. See Eric Rohmer's article, 'Le celluloïd et le marbre' ('Celluloid and marble'), in *Cahiers du cinéma*, No. 44, February 1955: 'Can the greatest of painters be so bold as to claim that the face he has painted is truer than the one we see on the screen?' Rohmer, because he wants to prove that the cinema is far superior to all other disciplines, awkwardly camouflages his meaning with a smokescreen of precious overblown language and displays a gigantic ignorance of the latest trends in the arts he claims to disparage. It is true that Rohmer is neither a musician like Charles Chaplin, nor a painter like Douglas Sirk or Vincente Minnelli, nor a poet like Luis Buñuel, nor an architect like Michelangelo Antonioni, nor a man of the theatre like Orson Welles, nor a choreographer like Stanley Donen. According to the latest reports (of *Le Signe du lion* [The Sign of Leo]), he is no filmmaker either.

6. Richard Roud, 'The French Line', *Sight and Sound*, autumn 1960.

7. Richard Roud, op. cit.

8. The same dissatisfaction, expressed by that isolated precursor, Louis Malle, resulted in *Zazie dans le métro*, an adult, articulate and unusually audacious experiment. The seed of ten Nouvelles Vagues is contained in that towering achievement. Malle is an indefatigable searcher, one of those who work for the progress of others; his perpetual dissatisfaction means that his explorations are hazardous, but we are always the richer for them.

9. In George Cukor's view, Orson Welles is also an amateur.

10. It is well known that the theatre director, Roger Blin, will only put on plays in which something is eaten. They alone contain a modicum of reality, he says.

11. The whole of the beginning of *Jules et Jim*, Truffaut's best film, is marred by a string of utterly parasitical private jokes and borrowings which make the whole thing look like a preamble designed to be 'in the Nouvelle Vague style'.

12. Luc Moullet, 'Sam Fuller sur les brisées de Marlowe' ('Sam Fuller In Marlowe's footsteps'), *Cahiers du cinéma*, No. 93, March 1959.

13. *L'Express*, July 27, 1961. Quoted by Michèle Manceaux.

14. *Clarté*, No. 42, Interview with Truffaut.

15. Ibid.

16. *Télé-7 jours*, January 1962.

17. *L'Express*, July 27, 1961.

18. Ibid.

19. I shall not quote here the long interview with Godard on the subject of torture, which is an utter disgrace. It was however quoted, without comment, in *L'Express* (June 16, 1960). It is worth noting that *L'Express* is Godard's official mouthpiece. What's more, each member of the Nouvelle Vague has queued up for his little interview in *Clarté*. That includes even Jacques Rivette and Chabrol, who was involved in a lengthy confrontation with the Soviet director, Grigori Chukhrai, during the Week of Marxist Thought (*La Nouvelle Critique*, No. 133, February 1962.

20. *Le Monde*, September 13, 1960.

21. Luc Moullet, op. cit.

22. *Présence du cinéma*, No. 13, May 1962.

23. *Présence du cinéma*, No. 14, June 1962.

24. *Cahiers du cinéma*, No. 107, May 1960.

25. Marc C. Bernard, *Présence du cinéma*, No. 14, June 1962.

In this 1962 interview, a much-mellowed Truffaut, the most engaging and modest of the *Cahiers* directors, takes stock of the Nouvelle Vague phenomenon, discusses the problem of moving on from being a critic to becoming a director, suggests why certain Nouvelle Vague films failed, and talks about the influence of the American cinema on the Nouvelle Vague.

Peter Graham

9 Interview with François Truffaut

CAHIERS DU CINÉMA (Jean Collet, Michel Delaye, Jean-André Fieschi, André S. Labarthe, Bertrand Tavernier) (1962)*

Where, in your opinion, does the Nouvelle Vague stand today?

It varies from day to day. At the moment, things are not looking as rosy as all that. But one should not forget that when things were going well, our wildest hopes were surpassed. At the end of 1959, there was a kind of euphoric ease in production that would have been unthinkable a couple of years earlier. I remember, for instance, an article by Marguerite Duras in which she described working on *Hiroshima mon amour* with Alain Resnais. Resnais told her that they would have to work on the principle that it would be a wonderful thing if they could manage to get the film a commercial release. Compared with these modest intentions at the start, the international success of *Hiroshima* is, I think, very significant.

We all had roughly the same experience. When I was shooting *Les Quatre cents coups* (*The 400 Blows*) I was horrified to see that my budget – about £20,000 – had gone up to £25,000. I got into a panic, and felt I had involved myself in something that would not easily make a profit. But once it was finished, the film more than paid for itself, what with the Cannes Film Festival and sales abroad. In the USA alone, it was bought for £35,000.

We were euphoric. In 1959, the situation was abnormally favourable and predictably this led to some wild dreams. Certain producers believed the secret to success lay solely in youth, novelty, and so on; and they lost no time in prospecting for new talent.

A brief history of the New Wave

But a lot has been said about this. One thing is perhaps worth remembering: the first failures were the result of compromises. Say a producer was launching a director who had never made a film before. He would say to himself: all he needs

---

* *Cahiers du cinéma*, No. 138, December 1962, pp. 41–59

is a first-class lighting cameraman. Well, it can be a very great mistake to give a beginner a cameraman whose style is classical. The end-product will be a formless hybrid. Such cameramen cannot help young directors in the way that, say, Henri Decae or Raoul Coutard can, or a cameraman used to semi-professional conditions (e.g. Melville's cinema). What's more, they cannot make a director turn out a classical, traditionally made film either.

People made the same mistake in other ways, by imposing traditional scriptwriters or stars on films that were not suitable for them. We too were led astray by mistaken ideas about how we ought to approach the cinema. When we began to want to make films, Rivette was the most active among us. At that time, only Alexandre Astruc could really consider himself a film director. And whereas the rest of us just thought about the cinema without quite daring to formulate our ideas, Rivette was the first to propose a concrete solution. He made us get together, he put forward suggestions such as the idea of associated filmmakers, of groups of directors, and other similar ideas. I remember we approached Resnais, and asked him if he was interested in participating in our group. On paper, it looked wonderfully simple: Astruc would make a film with Resnais as assistant, Resnais would make a film with Jacques Rivette as assistant, Rivette would make a film with myself as assistant, and so on with Charles Bitsch and Claude Chabrol. We discussed the budget – and we went into it quite thoroughly – and saw that we could make each film comfortably for £18,000. We then had the further idea of approaching such and such a producer, and saying: 'You make a film for £75,000 without knowing whether you'll get your money back or not. We'll make you four films for the same price, and one of them is damn well bound to be a success.'

Resnais was interested, so was Astruc, but he was already a professional, with thousands of appointments and heaps of fat scenarios lying around. So we went to see people like Robert Dorfmann and Henri Bérard, with a script that had been written by Rivette, Chabrol, Bitsch, and myself, and which Rivette was to direct, called *Les Quatre jeudis*. It was a script which was based on a real event and was greatly influenced by the American cinema (of the Nicholas Ray school). I think the film would have had the same qualities and defects as a film like Alain Cavalier's *Le Combat dans l'île* (*Fire and Ice*). It would have been torn between French realism and American oversimplification. As far as I can remember, Roger Leenhardt made some pretty tough but justified criticisms of it. Anyway, we submitted the script, but no one was enthusiastic about it and that was the end of that.

It turned out that we were mistaken in thinking that producers were interested in producing low budget films. We did not know the old rule of French cinema, whereby the producer is not the man with the money but the one who finds it, and that his only certain profit comes from his percentage on the film's budget, which itself includes his salary on the one side, and the cost of the film plus unforeseen expenses on the other. The higher the budget of the film, the higher his or her percentage. That's why people make films for £200,000 and more when they could cost half as much, and why the last thing they care about is how the film does at the box-office. Of course, to a certain extent they *do* care about this, but as far as big budget films are concerned, whatever happens they end up with a fair salary – which makes them practically speaking employees.

That's why it did not work. The author of the film would also have to be its producer, so that the interests involved in the film affected one and the same person, instead of conflicting.

It's commonly said that the present crisis is a crisis of young directors.

True, but old directors are also affected. And the Nouvelle Vague is certainly not finished. The two most Nouvelle Vague producers in Paris, Pierre Braunberger and Georges de Beauregard, are still in business, whereas there are rumours that Jean-Paul Guibert, the producer of all Jean Gabin's films, is losing heart. When Guibert loses £100,000 or more on Denys de La Patellière's *Le Bateau d'Emile* (*Emile's Boat*),

New Wave directors at a colloquium in La Napoule, May 1959. From left to right: (front row), François Truffaut, Raymond Vogel, Louis Félix, Edmond Séchan; (second row) Edouard Molinaro, Jacques Baratier, Jean Valère; (third row) François Reichenbach, Robert Hossein, Jean-Daniel Pollet, Roger Vadim, Marcel Camus; (back row) Claude Chabrol, Jacques Doniol-Valcroze, Jean-Luc Godard, Jacques Rozier it's the equivalent of what Beauregard will lose on three or four of his films which have not done well. What's unfair is that one never sees articles in the national press about the failure of certain films such as Henri Verneuil's *Le Président* (*The President*), *Le Bateau d'Emile,* or Verneuil's *Un Singe en hiver* (*It's Hot in Hell*). Far from it. A careful publicity campaign gives the impression that they are successes. The same was true of Jean Dréville's *La Fayette* (*Lafayette*), which was one of the biggest flops of recent years. It lost almost £500,000, about half its total budget.

Doesn't this mean that the public has changed?

Why did *Le Bateau d'Emile* fail when, in spite of a high budget, it seemed pretty certain of breaking even? Because the film offers the public nothing it cannot see on television. It's a realistic film in the French tradition. The snag is that there are two or three programmes a week on television which are of exactly the same type. And although the actors in them are not well-known stars, they do hold their public.

Roughly speaking, in a large French town of 200,000 or 300,000 inhabitants there are some 15,000 students. When *Vivre sa vie* is showing at a cinema, they go to see it. The critics have been enthusiastic about it, and this naturally intrigues them. At least 10,000 of them take the trouble to go and see it. That is far more than can be bothered to go and see *Le Bateau d'Emile*. There's hope for us here.

Justified success

Isn't the system of distribution badly organised? It was designed for films that are now out of date.

That's true. But I'm temperamentally opposed to any kind of discrimination, and would not like to see the creation of a cinema circuit specialising in Nouvelle Vague films, parallel to a larger more general circuit. I don't think a film should address a limited audience; this seems to me to contradict its function. We are in show business, and all films should have the same distribution. This of course does not mean that cinema managers should not use their heads. If people are used to seeing Westerns and Jacques Demy's *Lola* is suddenly put on, obviously wavelengths are going to get muddled up and all three – the manager, the public, and the film – will suffer. Ideally, of course, people who go to see Westerns should also go to see *Lola*, and vice versa, but this certainly would not be the best way to go about it.

Similarly, distributors should know certain things which unfortunately they do not. If it so happens that distributors can be almost certain that their film is going to be torn to pieces by the critics, they would perhaps be better advised to release it in the provinces first; whereas if it looks as though the critics will be favourable, Paris should get the first look.

And what about those films which, rightly or wrongly, are labelled as 'unreleasable'?

All those films have ended up by being released, one after the other. The success of 1959 went to people's heads, and some of them went a bit too far. I don't think a film should try to be new in every aspect. Perhaps a film by a new director needs something which keeps it anchored to the traditional cinema – a simple or strong subject, the presence of a star, or something like that. One feels that a lot of people have made their films without a thought in their head. In those of them which didn't do well, there is visibly too great a gulf between the director's ambitions and the result.

In 1955, I wrote an article in *Arts* in which I said that the crisis in the French cinema (which was very real at the time) boiled down to a crisis of aspirations. I wrote: there are seven directors in France who aim to make a good film (which could, for example, be in line for the Prix Louis Delluc); twenty don't really give a damn; thirty-five only think of money but do a more or less honest job; and lastly, there are fifty who are utterly deplorable. How could ambition be stimulated? There had to be greater competition between films. And this is what happened in the end, beyond all one's expectations.

Let's take a look at some of the Nouvelle Vague films which have not been a success. There are those that are excellent but which go completely over people's heads; those that are no more than interesting; and then there are the failures. As far as the latter category is concerned, there's only one thing to be done, which is pan them. That's normal enough. The problem comes when one tackles the films which are interesting but not well made. They all have one point in common: the scenario does not mean the same thing to the director as it does to the public. In this case, the faults probably arise from excessive self-confidence on the part of the director; or it may be that he or she has adapted a type of theme which requires something more than mere sincerity. Some themes permit one to speak from the heart; what one has to say is so simple that no one can fail to understand. There are no problems here. Other themes, however, pose problems which need think-ing out. Problems of construction, for example. The camera has to shift from one character to another, it moves around, and that's where craftsmanship comes in. When one is in a particular place, one must be able to recognise it. The director is sometimes quite certain the audience can recognise the flat which the characters left half an hour previously, whereas the audience may well not recognise it at all. That side of film-making is important too.

For the sake of argument, let's divide films into two categories: those that are completely personal and reflect the state of mind of the artist when he or she shot it (*À bout de souffle/Breathless*, for instance, which in my opinion is above all a kind of cry); and those that are shot in a cool and calculated manner, that are man-ufactured objects and should therefore be manufactured as well as possible. For example, all films of the detective-story type have to be well constructed. There are several ways of going about them. I feel that Paul Paviot's *Portrait-robot,* Jacques Doniol-Valcroze's *La Dénonciation (The Immoral Moment),* and Chabrol's *L'Oeil du malin (The Third Lover),* would all have gained from being discussed before shooting, perhaps in collaboration with somebody like Pierre Kast, who has a clear logical mind, or with a scriptwriter like Marcel Moussy. There can be no doubt that although all three of them are interesting films, the audience does not grasp exactly what the director wanted to say.

All in all, I don't think all that many films have been given an unfair deal. As far as I'm concerned, I have had only one misunderstanding with the public, *Tirez sur le pianiste (Shoot the Pianist),* and I consider myself entirely responsible. And that, quite apart from the fact that the film was released in a manner that didn't correspond very well with its type.

You just mentioned one of your articles. How do you see your former position as a critic now?

My line in *Arts* was the same as it was in *Cahiers du cinéma.* Especially at the start, for later I went in a rather more personal direction, as I had to discuss films which did not interest *Cahiers.* I also learnt to comply with certain requirements. In *Cahiers,* one doesn't have to tell the story of a film, but in a weekly paper one has to and this was a good exercise for me. Before then, I hardly even saw the films. I was so intoxicated by the cinema that I saw only movement and rhythm. Well, I had to force myself to consult a synopsis (at the beginning anyway), as I found it rather difficult to sum up a story. That brought home to me all the faults of cer-tain scenarios, certain conventional narrative principles and techniques. This rich period was the equivalent for me, I suppose, of the training of a scriptwriter. It led me to see more clearly and evolve my tastes, my predilections, my biases. I came to dissect films so much that during my last year on *Arts* I was no longer writing criticism proper, I was speaking as a director. I used to get worked up only about what resembled what I wanted to do myself, and often I got too carried away and too nasty. Conversely, I still have something of the attitude of a critic. So when I finish a script, I feel I know, well perhaps not its faults, but at least what risks there are of being conventional and cliché-ridden. This guides me and gives me a kind of protection against this danger during shooting.

Each film presents different pitfalls. In *Les Quatre cents coups* it was the poetry of childhood; in *Tirez sur le pianiste,* the attractiveness of someone who always proves other people wrong; in *Jules et Jim,* the character of the woman, who could

Jean-Pierre Léaud (right) and Patrick Auffray in François Truffaut's *Les Quatre cents coups* (1959).

have become a first-class self-willed bitch. It so happens that by striving to avoid these pitfalls I made all three films sadder than I had planned. If you read the original script of *Les Quatre cents coups,* you will be surprised to find the framework of a comedy. In *Tirez sur le pianiste,* where the danger was having a character who was too moving, I emphasised the egotistical side of the artist, his desire to cut himself off from the world, and his cowardice, so much so that he ends up being rather unattractive, a very hard and almost antipathetic man. That may even be one of the reasons why the film failed. The same thing nearly happened with *Jules et Jim*; I didn't want the character played by Jeanne Moreau to be entirely sympathetic and I made her a little too hard.

My articles and my films

When you made Les Quatre cents coups, did you worry a lot about this sort of problem?

I made the film in a very instinctive way. The subject predominated. Such and such a scene had to be seen through the eyes of the boy, and so had to be shot in a certain way. Moreover, the film had a documentary side to it, and that required a good deal of neutrality. In fact, the people who were disappointed by *Les Quatre cents coups* were the *cinéphiles*. Over and above what a film expresses, they feel the need to find a *form* which arouses them like a stimulant. Well, the film had no such form, it was neutral; the direction was purely moral, self-effacing. When I see it again now, I also find it rather awkward, but the required effects were often very simple ones and it's a film which makes me feel very nostalgic. I get the feeling I'll never again find such a direct subject. There were things in it about which I felt so deeply that I had no choice, there was only one way to shoot them. What's more, now that I tend to produce more refined work (I am not using the word in a flattering sense, in fact I don't find it a step forward), I yearn for simple effects which are able to move everyone at the same time – I am very sensitive to the collective spectacle.

As for *mise-en-scène*, I first became really conscious of it from *Tirez sur le pianiste* onwards. At the same time I wished I hadn't chosen such a flimsy story, so I tried to enjoy myself a bit.

Basically, there was the same principle in my criticism as there is in my direction. People say my films have nothing to do with what I used to write. Nothing could be further from the truth. I have the reputation of shortening my films a lot just before they come out, and then shortening them again between their first run

Charles Aznavour (left) in François Truffaut's *Tirez sur le pianiste* (1960).

Jean Riveyre (left) and Claude Laydu in Robert Bresson's *Le Journal d'un curé de campagne* (1951).

and their general release. When I wrote an article, I often cut a third of it before taking it along to *Arts* as I was haunted by the idea of being a bore. I sometimes went so far as to replace long words by short ones. First of all I wrote rapidly, in a flurry, then I cut every third sentence to make it flowing and readable.

I always thought of the director while writing my article. I wanted to influence him (but when I attacked him, my way of influencing him could become very offensive). Above all, I wanted to convince him. I used to say to myself: 'This word will convince him more than that one.' That's also why my last year on *Arts* was less valuable. I would forget about the script the director had filmed and end up by suggesting the one he *ought* to have filmed.

But my tastes have not changed very much since then. I read recently: 'By having constant recourse to a voice-over commentary, Truffaut the director is betraying his theories, etc.' In fact, I adored *Le Journal d'un curé de campagne* (*Diary of a Country Priest*), *Les Enfants terribles* (*The Strange Ones*), and *Le Plaisir* (*House of Pleasure*), and my criticism of Jean Aurenche and Pierre Bost's adaptations was precisely that they were bad theatre, whereas it would have been more worthwhile to read a text out loud. This solution has always seemed better to me, when the interest of a book lies in its prose.

Now that you're a filmmaker, don't you look at things differently?

I certainly don't make judgments in the same way. If I had to go back to film criticism, I would produce something different, but for another reason. The kind of
cinema I used to champion is now with us. And now I can see its drawbacks (for
it was inevitable that there would be some). Often people quote at me some of the
things I wrote and that embarrasses me a lot. In *Arts,* I wrote, during a festival
and without quite having recovered from the euphoria of *Et Dieu…créa la femme*
(*And God Created Woman*).: 'From now on, films no longer need to tell stories, it
is enough to describe one's first love-affair, to take one's camera on to the beach',
and so on. All that has become such cliché nowadays that it pains me a lot when
what I wrote is quoted in connection with the cinema of today. On the contrary,
scriptwriting has been so maltreated since then that I now feel like seeing some
well-told stories. Of course, one shouldn't come to the conclusion that we ought at
all costs to revert to the good old days of cinema.

I made *Jules et Jim* almost as a reaction against slipshod scenarios. I was told, for
example, that I ought to have transposed the period of the book and brought it up to
date. Everything could have fitted very nicely into the context of the Second World
War. But as I was tackling the problems of women and love, I didn't want my film

Christian Marquand and Brigitte Bardot in Roger Vadim's *Et Dieu … créa la femme*
(1956).

to fall into that category of film which is so prevalent nowadays, with a sports car (I would have needed one for the bridge sequence), whisky for the rendezvous, and, of course, the gramophone for a bit of music. I would have churned out a perfect piece of 'new cinema'. Through the solution I adopted – faithfulness to the book – I hoped to give *Jules et Jim* the atmosphere of one of those little films that MGM used to produce twenty or twenty-five years ago: Tay Garnett's *Mrs Parkington*, Victor Saville's *The Green Years,* etc., films whose only fault was that they were conventional, but which *did* give the impression of a fat 800-page book, with the years rolling by and people's hair going grey. I didn't want to follow a fashion, even a fashion that has resulted in films I like, such as Kast's, for instance.

From *Les Quatre cents coups* to *Tirez sur le pianiste*

Are you someone who likes to make films for their own sake, without thinking of your audience?

No, I could never summon up enough enthusiasm to make films just for myself. I wouldn't make films if they weren't going to be seen. I have to feel I am producing a piece of entertainment. I could never write a novel, it's too abstract for me. I would prefer to advise singers on how to present their songs, to direct them, or else quite simply to put on a music-hall show. When I do a job, I prefer it to be collective, and I must feel that the public is there to judge it. I have been asked to produce a radio play. This interests me, as the problem of voices is fascinating. But I shall try something that hasn't been done very often before: while the actors are performing, there will be thirty people in the studio who will act as an audience. I hope their reactions will help the actors.

Nor could I make a film if I knew it was automatically bound to be a success. My films are gambles. For me, shooting a film is like laying a bet. People took a strong dislike to the script of *Jules et Jim*. Distributors said: the woman is a tart; the husband will be grotesque, and so on. The gamble, for me, was to make the woman moving (without being melodramatic) and not a tart, and to prevent the husband from seeming ridiculous. I like to try to obtain something which isn't obvious at first sight. The same was true of *Les Quatre cents coups*. But there the problem was a false one, as the bet was won in advance. Only, I didn't realise this, and began the film more ingenuously than one could imagine. The gamble was to make people accept a boy who does a bit of thieving every five minutes. I was told: 'But you're mad. The boy will be antipathetic. Audiences won't stand for it.' During the shooting, people were particularly surprised to see a kid pinching things left, right and centre. It looked as though I was doing a documentary on juvenile delinquents. I did take some notice of these warnings, and now wish I hadn't. In fact, neither myself nor my friends knew that an audience will forgive a child anything and that it's always the parents who get the blame. I was wrong in thinking I was striking a balance. I was very naïve, but the film turned out to be naïvely rather subtle. Now, four years later, I can see that it's Hitchcockian. Why? Because from the first shot to the last, one identifies with the boy. At the time it was made, a lot of praise was heaped upon a silly film by Robert Montgomery, *Lady in the Lake,* in which the whole film is seen through the eyes of one person. But a subjective camera is the negation of subjective cinema. When it replaces a character, one cannot identify oneself with him or her. The cinema becomes subjective when the actor's gaze meets that of the audience. And so if the audience feels the need to identify (even in a film where the director has no such intention), it automatically does so with the face whose gaze it meets most frequently during the film, with the actor who is most often shot full on and in close-up. This is what happened with Jean-Pierre Léaud in *Les Quatre cents coups.* I thought I was being objective, doing a documentary on him. But the

Charles Aznavour and Marie Dubois in François Truffaut's *Tirez sur le pianiste* (1960).

more I shot him from the front, the more he gained in presence and the more the audience *became* him. I realised this when watching the film in public: I heard people scream (the sort of reaction they have when watching a film by Hitchcock) as soon as the mother appeared behind the window-panes of the classroom. It's true that as the scene was a difficult one I gave it a lot of preparation, instead of improvising as I often did on set; but the anxiety arises from the fact that the spectators sense that the child is particularly concerned (and all the more so as they feel very sympathetic towards him when he says his mother is dead). So it was a totally naïve film, which I shot without knowing the first thing about the rules of film-making. At the same time, it was unwittingly subtle, much more than what I have made since.

In a sense, I made *Tirez sur le pianiste* as a reaction against *Les Quatre cents coups*. For with the success of the latter film came the sudden realisation of its unevenness; and this worried me so much that I told myself to be careful never to play down to my audience. But I don't quite realise what happened with *Tirez sur le pianiste*. It must have been that I was too faithful to the book. I was also too sure of myself because *Les Quatre cents coups* had been such a success. But I also feel that as a general rule one's second film is worse than one's first. For instance, *Une femme est une femme (A Woman is a Woman)* – as *Le Petit Soldat* was banned, I consider it to be Godard's second film – was made under the euphoric influence of *À bout de souffle*. *Vivre sa vie (My Life to Live)* marked Godard's regaining of control.

For one's first film, one takes the plunge: 'What the hell! I'm risking everything. Perhaps I'll never make films again, but while I can I want to see what I can do.' People's reaction to one's first film is very important. If it is a success one is always surprised. This affects one's second film. Alain Resnais' *L'Année dernière à Marienbad (Last Year in Marienbad)* reveals great self-confidence, which arose from the unexpected success of *Hiroshima mon amour*. All these second films I mentioned have one thing in common: they are less complete than the first ones, where there was a whole beginning of life to express, where one wanted to say everything one had to say. One's second film is voluntarily less ambitious in intent. The third one is the most interesting; it is a reflection of the first two and marks the start of a career.

When one thinks about *Tirez sur le pianiste*, one can see that the scenario does not stand up to analysis. It clearly lacks the kind of guiding line one can find in my other two films. In *Les Quatre cents coups*, the idea was to show, as simply as possible, a boy being driven by certain moral prejudices. The same was true of *Jules et Jim*: done one way it would have been pornographic, another way coarse, another way conventional, and so I had to do it completely differently. The trouble with *Tirez sur le pianiste* was that one could do it any way one wanted, there was a content which didn't require a particular form. Charles Aznavour has a great comic talent, and I could have made a very funny film out of it. He also possesses great authority; I could have made a very imposing character out of him. At the start I had no particular ideas about this, I simply wanted madly to use Aznavour after his performance in Georges Franju's *La Tête contre les murs* (*The Keepers*); but it would have been better if I had known him longer. What was courageous about *Tirez sur le pianiste* was that I used flashbacks, while knowing very well that they can never go down well. I said to Braunberger: 'Do you remember Alexandre Astruc's *Les Mauvaises rencontres*? And Max Ophüls's *Lola Montès* (*The Fall of Lola Montes*)? And Joseph Mankiewicz's *The Barefoot Contessa*? They did not work out because of the flashbacks.' That's why the whole thing was ruined.

It is a rule: one should not mix things. One cannot be plumb in the middle of one story and plumb in the middle of another one too. With a bit of thought I certainly could have given *Tirez sur le pianiste* a chronological narrative line. It just needed a bit of work. The film has *something*. But no one could say: 'It's the best that's been done on such and such a theme.' There is no theme.

Unless perhaps, it's this one: a man is caught up in a mechanism, tries to reject it, but ends up by resigning himself to it. Courage, cowardice …

But even then there are superfluous things in it. And what about the director who resigned himself to being caught up in the mechanism of the *film noir*? I had never thought about it before, but as I was shooting *Tirez sur le pianiste* I realised I hated *films noirs*. I would never now write articles praising Jules Dassin's *Du rififi chez les hommes (Rififi)*. I feel there is no point in making gangsters moving, in showing crooks weeping and pitting goodies against baddies. The film that results has all the *bourgeois* conventions simply transposed into the world of gangsters. That's why I suddenly decided to make my gangsters funny. It was the only solution if I was not to lapse into conventionalism. I rather made fun of them. To compensate for this, I also had to make them rather frightening, which I did through the kidnapping of the boy and the death of Marie Dubois. That brought people up with a start – they might otherwise have thought they were watching British cardboard characters. The only thing is, it is dangerous to change course during a film. One should have one idea at the beginning and reinforce it during the film, as I did in my other two films whose themes were originally expressed rather weakly in the scenario. If I'd known, beforehand, that Aznavour and Nicole Berger would make a wonderful couple (the others did not go together so well), I would have made a film about those two.

One thing which must have worried the public in Tirez sur le pianiste was the change of tone. This is a characteristic of several films which have not done well – including Une femme est une femme – and it is something the French public doesn't seem to be able to accept.

Yes, that's the most difficult thing to make them swallow. Incidentally, in the USA they understood *Tirez sur le pianiste,* but in a different way: they didn't stop laughing once, even during the most dramatic sequences. The first song was funny, so they laughed all through the second one, which wasn't supposed to be.

Anyway, say what you like, I'm still convinced that *Tirez sur le pianiste* needed another month's work. Slap together two or three reels of film that appeal to you, and you won't necessarily make a film that appeals to other people, even if what's in them is good. It's also true that a change of tone is a thing which has to be carefully worked out; it's a gamble worth trying occasionally. Jean Renoir has brought it off.

Lessons from a failure

But his La Règle du jeu (The Rules of the Game) was a failure with the public.

Yes, but *La Règle du jeu* is one of the rare cases of a film which went completely over the heads of the public. In his *Une partie de campagne (A Day in the Country),* on the other hand, there are some false changes of tone. The characters are very schematic. There is the fat lady who makes people laugh, and the two little fops from Paris … why, it's pure Maupassant! There is an element of cautiousness about the film. The only reason the story does not become improper or smutty is because one isn't shown everything. Just suppose one really saw Jacques Brunius lying on top of Jane Marken, or imagine them getting dressed afterwards. The film consists of a selection, in a double love-story, of the moments which people are willing to see. It is true that sometimes an audience should be given a good shaking-up. I really think it's very important to please the public, but I also think that one should start out with the intention of premeditated assault. One should force people to watch something they are bound not to like, force them to approve of a character whom they hate or refuse to watch.

Roughly speaking, there is the belief that there are directors who think of their audience and there are those who don't. That's not quite true. There are those who think of their films as an entity which the audience is part of, and those who think only of that part of the spectacle which is the film. What does the cinema a lot of harm is the kind of idea people have of a person like Resnais. Resnais would never say: I think of my audience. Nor does he do so, strictly speaking. But he *does* consider his film as a spectacle, and I am quite sure that when he made *Marienbad* he thought of his audience's emotional reaction, of

Jacques B. Brunius and Jane Marken in Jean Renoir's *Une partie de campagne* (1936).

the line of his scenario, of its balance – for otherwise there would have been no reason for not making *Marienbad* last eight hours. Resnais is not Erich von Stroheim, his films last an hour and a half, and they are composed in a very studied fashion.

Well, some young people see Resnais' films as an example of courage instead of an example of skill. It all began with *Hiroshima*. They said: 'Resnais is wonderful, he has proved that anything is possible.' Not at all. All that's proved is that anything is possible for *Resnais*. At first sight, in *Hiroshima,* there was everything there should not have been: the combination of adultery and the atomic bomb, of a general problem and a very particular one, of a social and a political problem, and within its political aspect, the mixture of a big problem – the bomb – with a smaller one, the scandal of reprisals after the Liberation. That was like mixing oil and water. And so it was an extraordinary achievement to have got it across. But it doesn't mean one should try to repeat what only Resnais could bring off.

A lot of films were made by people who admired the artistic freedom of *Hiroshima.* It was thought that there was no need for a subject any more, no need to think of the public. But Resnais *did* think of them. He knew very well that by making Riva do this or that he would generate a particular emotion in the cinema. The naïve filmmaker is encouraged instead of discouraged by *Hiroshima*. I don't mean that *Hiroshima* should necessarily act as a discouragement, but that one should realise the skill of the man who managed to bring it off, and not think: 'That's fine, I can do that too.' I think Resnais would help people if he emphasised the difficulties he encountered, instead of giving them the impression that they should make anything that comes into their head.

It remains to be seen why it was that certain films, such as *Une femme est une femme,* didn't get across to the public. As far as this film is concerned, I would say that one can reach one's audience in almost any conceivable way, but not by assaulting their basic peace of mind. If one plays around with the sound-track and the images in too unusual a way, people start objecting – it is a normal reaction. They ripped up the seats in Nice because they thought the projection room was not properly equipped. Of course one could explain things to people through articles, but in those cinemas where the film was put on, audiences were taken by surprise. Godard went too far for them in the sound-mixing. When the girl comes out of the café, there's suddenly no sound, just complete silence. People immediately think the projector has broken down. Although, of course, those spectators in Nice were not civilised – one simply does not knife cinema seats.

A similar case was *Lola Montès*. This film offered a striking paradox: it was an *avant-garde* film shot within the framework of the commercial cinema. Moreover, when one re-sees *La Ronde* in the light of *Lola Montès*, one can see that Ophüls came very close to disaster – *La Ronde* was very coolly received at its premiere at

Jean-Claude Brialy (left), Jean-Paul Belmondo and Anna Karina in Jean-Luc Godard's *Une femme est une femme* (1961).

the Opéra: there was no story, and one could sense an enormous gulf between the author and his characters. At that time, people expected Ophüls to produce something of the Christian-Jaque type.

Another factor involved in *Une femme est une femme* is the originality of the film: it breaks all the rules of its genre. People expected to see a nice little classical story: a girl and two men in Paris. ... The very story line, in fact, that one expects to be told in a classical way. They were flabbergasted. Just imagine *Marienbad* with the same sound-mixing. No one would have batted an eyelid. Whereas here people expected to see one thing, and they were given something else. This didn't make them at all happy. What was needed was the kind of label *Marienbad* got, to the effect that it was a strange film that didn't fit into any category.

In *Une vie (End of Desire)*, one would have thought there was plenty to please the public: Guy de Maupassant, colour, Maria Schell, and so on. But the story didn't correspond to the title, and the film was subtly turned against Maria Schell, whereas people came with the expectation of liking her. There too, what they were led to expect and what they got were two entirely different things.

I have also wondered about this problem in relation to my own films. I thought the title of *Les Quatre cents coups* suggested a lot of things which were not all in the film, and people were going to feel cheated. But they didn't, perhaps because the scenes were short and there were a lot of them. As for *Jules et Jim,* I thought that two men's names as the title of a film chiefly about a woman sounded a bit funny. But they accepted it.

Chabrol's *Les Bonnes femmes (The Good Time Girls)* seems to me to have failed for the same reasons as *Lola Montès*: it comes too close to the theatre of derision. That was Beckett's influence. There is a good theme to be found in girls who are destined to die, but when one shows working-class people such as shop-girls, the audience expects something realistic, dramaic, or psychological – in fact, anything but what they got.

The success of the 'unusual' Nouvelle Vague films was due to the fact that they were totally unusual and were labelled as such; people came to see them as curiosities. Resnais, who is considered a specialist in all that is unusual and, so to speak, holds the patent for it (that doesn't make me think any the less of him), has the right to do this sort of thing. But if one day he agreed to make a 'normal' film, there would be serious consequences for him.

As for Demy's *Lola,* it probably failed because of the post-synchronisation. I know Rivette doesn't agree with me, and has told me in no uncertain terms that he feels it was just what was needed and that Demy wanted to make the voices tend towards song. Okay, but in *La Baie des Anges (Bay of Angels)* at any rate, Demy took a hell of a lot of trouble over the direct sound-track.

People don't mind a realistic story becoming melodramatic, but they do mind a film that starts as melodrama and ends up by going beyond it.

That's probably true, but it's just what Demy likes to produce: over-melodramatic melodrama. This is perhaps the result of his almost perverse sense of refinement. All the same, I was moved, and I think the general public was too.

There's one phenomenon especially which is making things difficult at the moment. The attitude of the Parisian critics and *cinéphiles* is openly hostile to the difficult film. When films used to be vulgar and play down to their audiences, they said what a disgrace it was to treat people like fools. It would now seem that the critics, and even the audiences of premieres, are concerned most of all with whether a film is going to make a profit. For a film to run the risk of losing money is shameful in their eyes. This attitude is especially noticeable in the critics of the dailies. The idea of helping a film's career used to appeal to them, but now they think that out of date. The paradoxical result of this is that the initiated and educated public, as well as the critics, have become more hostile to difficult films than the industry is. At the premiere of *Eve*, Losey was blamed most of all for having made a film which courted disaster at the box-office. What happened was that everyone expected things to change, and now that they have, everyone is irritated if the product is too specialised. Nowadays, people have even turned their spite on Antonioni (whom, by the way, I don't like). There was delirium about two of his films, and now people are giving him a good working over. This had happened to Bergman and is now happening to Losey. It all starts in Paris, but everyone else follows suit. It's all the more unfortunate for Bergman, as his last film, *The Silence,* is a good deal better than the preceding ones.

What amuses me is the way people get hot under the collar about private jokes or winks at the audience. It's quite simple: when we started we were so happy to be making films, and films before then had been such solemn affairs, that it seemed wonderful to be able to make a few jokes. I found it was an amusing way of personalising a product which up to then had been awfully impersonal. In fact, this didn't irritate our friends, nor those who weren't aware of what was going on, but simply the friends of our friends. The critic Charensol said to himself: 'I saw eight private jokes in that film, so there must have been at least fifteen,' and he got annoyed at the idea of the seven he had failed to catch. If a private joke replaced something important, then of course someone who couldn't understand would feel out of it, and it would be a stupid device. But when it's added after everything else, why should anyone worry? Say one has a character called Tartempion; one might as well call him Delannoy or Domarchi, if that gives it a double meaning. But this is where the initiated public starts objecting, for they decide to identify themselves with the general provincial public. Whereas the latter doesn't mind at all, and with good reason.

One shouldn't let the audiences of first-run cinemas lay down the law. In the last account, they are a public neither of film-lovers nor of ordinary people. Film-enthusiasts love *Marienbad,* popular audiences love *Ben Hur.* The audiences of first-run cinemas yawn during both of them and don't even know why.

There's another new element. Nowadays, everyone talks in figures. So-and-so says such and such a film had 167,273 admissions. What the hell has that got to do with it? When I was on *Cahiers,* I would never have mentioned such figures in an article. I think the fashion for statistics came in with the Nouvelle Vague. People tried to make comparisons: did *Les Cousins* do better than one of Clément's films, etc. If one is going to talk figures, one should be thorough about it. Then one can see that many films which don't do very well in France more than make up for it abroad. On the other hand, films scripted by Audiard hardly ever leave French-speaking countries. There's the difficulty of dubbing dialogue which, once translated, no longer stands up to examination. What's more, Gabin doesn't mean very much abroad. Whence the desperate device of *Un Singe en Hiver,* where Belmondo was stuck in with Gabin so that the film could be sold abroad.

But don't let's lose our heads. We must persevere. Okay, we are living in a capitalist system, so let's use the weapons at our disposal, let's shuffle the cards. Look at the case of Godard. In one sense, he is marginal to the general body of the film industry; and yet he could, if he wanted to, find a way of integrating himself into the system. His is a case apart. He's interested in making a mixture of everything: the moment his story becomes fictional, he becomes Rouch-like, and then he suddenly goes off in another direction. But his career has been very logical. Look at the articles he wrote in *Cahiers.* From the beginning, he always displayed a kind of disdain for total fiction. He always liked films in which the subject was destroyed. But his temperament is so strong that one cannot question what he does. He does it in a certain way and he's right.

Let's imitate Hitchcock

What does the American cinema mean for you, now that you're a director?

In comparison with American directors, I think we are all intellectuals – even myself, who am less so than the others. One shouldn't cheat; one shouldn't pretend to be unsophisticated or ingenuous when one's thinking about a script or putting the final touches to it. One shouldn't force oneself. That's probably where Melville is wrong, in imitating the brutality and uncouthness of the Americans. But as long as one considers the cinema as a popular art – and we all do as we were brought up on the American cinema – then we can go off on another tack: we can discipline our work so that it becomes complex and has more than one layer of meaning. It's the same principle as the three films superimposed on each other that Hitchcock produces. He is one of the few filmmakers who appeals to everyone, so he's a good example to follow. I believe that we can apply his principle. To be more precise, this is only worthwhile when one works a film out carefully. Resnais elaborates a lot. I don't think you will find *effective* devices or emotions in *Marienbad* which cannot also be found in *Vertigo*. I maintain that Resnais was absolutely right to make *Marienbad*. But if one is not Resnais, if one doesn't possess that extraordinary control which he has over what he is working on, one will do better to be less ambitious. Not that one should limit one's ambitions; one should simply be modest in the way one achieves them, one should make films whose appearance is unpretentious. I don't think the world needs my films, I don't think the world needs me; I feel rather that I must get myself accepted by it, and that the way to do this is by my work.

Nowadays it's said that people no longer go to the cinema in a haphazard manner, they go to see what they have heard about. We should honestly find out if this selective public is large enough to render a film that costs £50,000 profit-earning, and whether it might not be advisable also to reckon on those who are not selective. Such a film, in order to break even, must make at least £250,000 at the box-office. One should work out how many admissions that means at 3s 6d per seat. One would have to include people who come in by chance or through habit. Can one afford to forget about them? And so the inevitable conclusion is that *Les Bonnes femmes,* for instance, needs to be seen by people who are exactly like the characters of the film: shop-girls, who have come to the cinema instead of going dancing. Well, people who see themselves in a film can't see themselves in perspective; they can't understand the film – its intention is abstract and, what's more, partly based on a derisive attitude. It transcends mere derision, it's more profound than that, that's why I like it – but people can't grasp that.

It's at this point that one might imagine another way of making the film than the one Chabrol adopted, which was almost too pure and confidential. The same film, saying the same things, could have had a second story: the story of the murder, that of Weidmann. Instead of coming as a finale, the crime could have acted as a kind of suspense which would have gripped everybody while still allowing Chabrol to say what he wanted to say. What if we tried for a moment to imagine how Hitchcock would go about a film like *Les Bonnes femmes*. First of all, he would choose an extremely simple title, something like *The Shop-girl Vanishes*. The film begins. One fine morning, the first shop-girl doesn't turn up at the shop; she is not

Clotilde Joano (left), Stéphane Audran (centre) and Bernadette Lafont in Claude Chabrol's *Les Bonnes femmes* (1960).

at home either, she has simply disappeared into thin air. Surprise. When Hitchcock gets to the second girl, he will own up and show us the young woman being strangled by the motor-cyclist. Horror. As for the third girl, there would be pure suspense; the audience *knows* that the motor-cyclist is a killer, but the girl does not. A short lovers' walk through the forest, a bit of love-making in idyllic surroundings; then the works. Finally we get to the fourth girl who, of course, will be saved just in time, by her fiancé probably, and the criminal will end up nicely mangled by his own motor-bike.

Don't tell me it would be inferior or vulgar done that way. Just think of *Shadow of a Doubt* and Uncle Charlie's thoughts: the world is a pigsty, and honest people like bankers and widows detest the purity of virgins. It's all there, but inserted into a framework which keeps you on the edge of your seat. *Les Bonnes femmes* is a calculated, well thought out, cerebral film. So why not make the extra effort which would have consisted of telling the story in entertainment terms, then superimpose on to this basic layer of the film a second and even a third layer? Even so, it remains, for me, Chabrol's best film.

Mario David and
Clotilde Joano in
Les Bonnes femmes
(1960).

I think above all in entertainment terms – music-hall, variety – but I also have preoccupations which are not shared by the majority of my audience. The problem of *Jules et Jim,* for instance, doesn't interest all that many people. What's more, nine out of every ten people who see the film consider divorce shocking. To ask these people to sympathise with a couple of layabouts who never do an honest day's work and live with the same woman is tantamount to an insult. So I have to give them something instead, emotion for example, as when the characters push themselves to their very limits; I am thinking of the weeping scene (which was improvised) between Werner and Jeanne Moreau. I don't want people to come out of the cinema saying 'This is scandalous.' I would be the first to be pained by this. Of course, it's impossible to satisfy everyone, but it *is* possible not to ruin their evening entirely. If they come out saying 'Luckily there was that song', or 'Luckily there were some nice shots of the countryside', or 'Luckily there were some war newsreels', well, that's something, and it's better than nothing.

One has to know exactly what one wants to obtain, and, above all, one shouldn't try to obtain more than one thing at a time. The idea is to create emotions. So, before each film, each scene, each shot, we pause a moment and ask ourselves how we are going to create this emotion. Everything that comes into the film, the scene, or the shot, which doesn't answer this question becomes a parasitic element which should be rejected. We are working in a medium that is both literary, musical, and visual; everything must always be simplified as much as possible. A film is a boat which is always on the point of sinking – it always tends to break up as you go along and drag you under with it. And if one pays no attention to this fact, then one's had it. In our job, one should never consider oneself indispensable. In one respect, the Americans are infuriating: if a good film has been a failure at the box-office, they are ashamed of it. That's going too far. In another respect, they do have a healthy 'show business' side to them. One doesn't come across people in Hollywood who think that all is due to them and say it's a disgrace they didn't receive such and such a prize or subsidy. The French attitude is that all films should be subsidised, whatever they eventually turn out to be like. In short, people want the advantages of both the capitalist and socialist systems.

The massive arrival of the Nouvelle Vague directors has created a lot of competition and has made the system tend to become more like that of Hollywood. It has become more difficult to escape from a given category, or to recover from a failure. As things stand at the moment, it's better to have made no films at all rather than to have just made one which was a flop.

Orson Welles, who has never been commercial, commands such respect and admiration, and has such prestige, that every four years or so he manages to make something like *The Trial*. Someone puts their faith in him and the fifteen greatest actors in Europe are delighted to shoot with him. That's all very fine. Perhaps Resnais will reach the same position one day. In the long run, there is a kind of justice. People said to Raoul Lévy: 'Why don't you take Orson Welles to direct *Marco Polo*?' 'Who? Welles? Why, he's through, he's no good any more.' And now Raoul Lévy is beseeching him to agree to finish off the *Marco Polo* which Christian-Jaque started.

Cinema is complicated

You mentioned a kind of justice. Aren't you taking for granted that there are producers willing to accept risks?

Yes, but the mistake producers made was to take too long to get used to the idea that it's the director who *makes* a film, and that a film will never be worth more than its director. Once they had got this into their heads, they should never, of course, have given a difficult film to a director who had been used to commercial filmmaking, nor vice versa. The results can be absurd. A balance must be struck. The Hollywood system was balanced. And it's amazing to watch the terrible way

Oskar Werner and Julie Christie in François Truffaut's *Fahrenheit 451* (1966).

Hollywood declined as soon as the traditional structure broke up. Everything went well when films were the result of a production line, when the director had no say in the matter, when scriptwriters were paid a yearly salary, when films were edited by specialists who had no contact with the director, and so on. The moment the chains were loosened, the whole thing collapsed. In another domain, there's nothing worse than half-baked Hollywood cinema. For instance, things are going badly in Germany at the moment. There is Madame Kubachewsky who gives strict orders about the way a good film must be made: there must be nice characters, flocks and pastures, children's choirs, fine clothes, and a happy ending 'even if it's completely unexpected'. When people swallow all this advice, the result is the 'Sissi' series, which has managed to prove itself, but whose posters look as though they were advertising Camembert rather than a film. And now even Madame Kubachewsky is having trouble.

The Americans had one inimitable quality: in every department they knew how to give life to what they were working on. And the scripts were often admirable pieces of work. I have just received a scenario by Philip Yordan. Everything is there, including the humour; there's no need to change a line, one could just go out and shoot it. Basically the American cinema consisted of the best and the worst. It was usually happier when dealing with traditional subjects, but as long as it did so the results were brilliant.

Lastly, not everybody deserves to be given total freedom. A lot of new film-makers aren't mature enough and they really do make too many blunders. Most of the films I see are poorly edited. Because of self-satisfaction, lack of critical acumen, and laziness, their directors are unwilling to make cuts. Once upon a time I laughed at Becker when he said: 'The cinema is very complicated.' Tempera-mentally, I was on the side of those who said it was simple. But it's a luxury to say that, and not everyone can afford to. There are some very plucky people who produce their own films, and do everything themselves, even though this means getting over a mountain of difficulties. But in the last account, it's not in their inter-est to do everything themselves; it ceases to be a question of courage, but becomes ignorance or carelessness.

When one has a good look round, one can see that there's no really good pro-ducer or scriptwriter in France. And so one finds oneself terribly alone to face one's responsibilities, much more alone than an American director. We have to have some of the qualities which go to make both a good director and a good scriptwriter, as there is no room in the French system for the film director pure and simple.

One should also begin to think about television as a new vehicle. It's a medium of expression which has advantages as well as shortcomings. The other evening there was a play which was badly directed but very well acted by three elderly actresses. In the cinema, it would have been a total disaster. No one would have gone out of their way to see it. And yet it has been one of the better programmes on television this year. When one comes across a subject of that kind and one wants very much to direct it, one should shoot it on a very low budget for television, I feel.

In another respect, television uses a lot of long-held shots, and almost never comes off when cross-cutting is used. And so as a reaction it's a good idea in the cinema to revert to a classical breakdown of shots and chop them up a lot. Five years ago, when I was a critic, I found all French films ugly. That is why the first films of Vadim and Malle were important, simply because they displayed a basic minimum of taste; nowadays, everyone has taste, and films are tidier on the whole. So one should aim at something higher, at something beautiful, intelligent, clear, moving, interesting. In other words, as Ingmar Bergman put it, we should make very one of our films 'as though it were our last', we should force ourselves to make progress.

Finally, to illustrate further the virulence of the critical debates of the time, here are three pieces that look at Jean-Luc Godard's *À bout de souffle* from different standpoints. First, there are extracts from Luc Moullet's "Jean-Luc Godard", a typical example of *Cahiers* hagiographical writing at its worst: bristling with paradoxes, impenetrable and confused, with occasional flashes of insight. Then there is an extract from a chapter entitled *Cinéma français d'aujourd'hui*, Raymond Borde's contribution to the Premier Plan volume on the *Nouvelle Vague*. Borde was a regular contributor to *Positif* before becoming head of the Cinémathèque de Toulouse, and this piece is characteristically vitriolic against a film directed by one of the *Cahiers du cinéma* critics-turned-filmmakers. Finally, there is a piece by Georges Sadoul, who was from an older generation (he was born in 1904); he was a communist critic and film historian, best-known for his *Histoire du cinéma mondial* and various film dictionaries. His review of *À bout de souffle* is a balanced one, indicating how he changed his own mind on the film and skilfully combining enthusiasm with reservations.

Peter Graham

10 CASE STUDY

CONTRASTING VIEWS OF
À BOUT DE SOUFFLE

Jean-Luc Godard
LUC MOULLET (1960)*

During the four months leading to the official premiere of *À bout de souffle* on 16 March 1960, Jean-Luc Godard and his entourage acquired unprecedented notoriety before the film was even released – this was due to the award of the Jean Vigo prize, the release of a record (by Columbia), of a novel (published by Seghers) loosely and inaccurately based on the film, and especially to the press reviews which displayed an unusual and equally passionate penchant for praise and demolition.

Of all the films shot by the French cinema's new directors, *À bout de souffle* (*Breathless*) is not the best, since it does not quite equal *Les Quatre cents coups* (*The 400 Blows*); nor is it the most powerful: there is *Hiroshima mon amour*. But it is the most representative.

À bout de souffle's typicality has meant it has been a much greater box-office success than other movies by young directors. It is the first of them to have been released in a chain of cinemas patronised chiefly by the 'right kind of audiences', an 'average public' untainted by snobbery. It has succeeded in the ambition which for the past 10 ten years has been closest to the hearts of the up-and-coming generation: the ability to make films not just aimed at art-house audiences, but capable of having successful runs in such legendary Paris cinemas as the Gaumont-Palace, the Midi-Minuit, the Normandie, the Balzac, the Helder, the Scala, the Vivienne

---

* *Cahiers du cinéma*, No. 106, April 1960, pp. 25–6.

Jean-Paul Belmondo and Jean Seberg in Jean-Luc Godard's *À bout de souffle* (1960).

or the Radio-Cité. *À bout de souffle* is not dedicated to Joseph Burstyn, or even to Warner Bros or 20th Century-Fox, but to Monogram Pictures, formerly Allied Artists. In other words, it pays tribute to the most commercial form of American cinema, as we shall see.

[…]

A masterpiece is always esoteric

It is notable that the form of *À bout de souffle* entirely reflects the behaviour of its male central character, and indeed that of its female central character. More than that, it justifies such behaviour. Michel (Jean-Paul Belmondo) and, even more so, Patricia (Jean Seberg) are disconcerted by the disorder of our times and by the constant moral and physical accretions and changes that are totally specific to the age we live in. They are victims of that disorder, and the film accordingly offers a point of view on both internal and external disorder, just like *Hiroshima mon amour* and *Les Quatre cents coups*, and represents a more or less successful effort to overcome it – less rather than more, in fact, for if it were truly successful, disorder would not exist any more. Shooting a film about disorder without the structure of the work being impregnated by it would seem to me to be the most cogent reason for condemning such a film. What I admire about *Les Quatre cents coups* is the fact that disorder is resolved throughout the film thanks to Truffaut's detachment, and above all, in the final sequence, through a visual solution that imposes order, and the fact that Truffaut is here both a youngster and a 70-year-old man. But in so doing he evinces a little more natural mischievousness than frankness, since an artist is only one person when he or she makes a film, and any evolution within the work is necessarily feigned, either in its source or in its conclusion. Godard's superiority over Truffaut resides in the fact that whereas Truffaut, through diligent effort, strives to squeeze the civilisation of our time into a classical mould, the more honest Godard seeks justification for the age we live in within itself.

Some claim that in art value is order and non-value disorder; I do not believe that, since the distinctive feature of art is that it obeys no law; even respect for the public is a myth that deserves to be denounced on occasion. *Mise-en-scène* recreates that impression of disorder via two distinct channels, as always with Godard: first through naturalness, freedom and a randomness of invention. Godard takes from life everything he perceives without making a choice. Or more precisely he chooses everything he sees, and sees only what he wants to see. He omits nothing, and merely tries to reveal the meaning of everything he sees or everything that

Jean Seberg in *À bout de souffle* (1960).

occurs to him. Constant and natural changes of tone create an impression of dis-order. In other words, one should not be shocked by the fact that in the course of a love scene we suddenly switch from William Faulkner to Jean de Létraz. Similarly, when Godard makes a pun, it is either a good or a very bad pun, in which case its deliberate mediocrity makes us laugh. What Godard shows us is the profound unity that emerges from that disorder, from that permanent and external diversity. It has been argued that the film has no construction and does not evolve any more than its characters do, except during the final quarter of an hour, and then only slightly. But that is because Godard is against the idea of evolving, just like Alain Resnais, who reaches the same conclusion through the totally different channel of a highly constructed film. This notion, then, is part of our *Zeitgeist*: the camera is a mirror that is taken along a path, but there is no longer any path. Like *Hiroshima mon amour*, *À bout de souffle* could have a running time of two hours, as indeed it did after its first cut. Joseph Losey's highly remarkable *Time without Pity* (1957) has a very precise construction and a constant development, but both of them are highly arbitrary! Godard conforms to a higher order, that of nature, the order in which things come before his eyes or into his mind. As he says in *Charlotte et son Jules*: 'The mere fact that I utter a sentence means there is necessarily a connection with the sentence that precedes it.'

À bout de souffle is a series of sketches, of interludes which at first sight have no connection with each other, like the interview with the writer Parvulesco. But through their mere existence, these episodes have a strong connection with each other, like all life's phenomena. The interview with Parvulesco clearly sets out the main problems that the two lovers have to face. Like Sir Philip Sidney's *Astrophel and Stella* (1591, *À bout de souffle* consists of isolated little circles which, at the end of the sequence or the sonnet, end up being linked by an identical cone to a common point – Stella in Sidney's poem, and Patricia or something else in Godard's film.

So the type of effect produced matters little, as long as there is an effect within a shot. That is realism. Hence the proliferation of little ideas and gags. Godard has been criticised for including a succession of private jokes that only cinephiles or Parisians can understand. Members of the general public will not understand them, but will not worry about not understanding them because, with very few exceptions, they will not even spot them. It is true that they will accordingly miss much of the point. But it so happens that a high proportion of great works are naturally esoteric, and none more so than those by Aristophanes, which cannot be read without notes. A work has all the more chances of becoming eternal if it describes precisely and exhaustively a single time and a single space. Even film classics such as those by D. W. Griffith and Claude Autant-Lara overdid the private jokes, which we mostly fail to spot because they are no longer our contemporaries.

When Michel looks at Patricia through a rolled-up poster and kisses her, it is a tribute to a never released movie by a minor American filmmaker [Samuel Fuller's *Forty Guns*]. There is no need to be aware of that in order to enjoy the effect, which does not however work as well as it does in the original.

Godard could be more justifiably criticised for some of his little ideas that do not come off. The turning on of the street lamps along the Champs-Elysées does not add anything.

Is there any point in the subtitling that highlights the glaring differences between the French and American languages? Or in the reference to a film by Guillaume Apollinaire with dialogue by Bud Boetticher? Or in the lack of any credit titles? Original and amusing ideas, maybe, but no more than that.

None of all this matters very much, since one detail comes hot on the heels of the previous one, and we do not have time to realise how ineffectual one of them might be.

On the other hand, in the films of Jacques Doniol-Valcroze or Claude Chabrol – *À bout de souffle* is incidentally the greatest contribution that the man with horn-rimmed glasses has made to the cinema – such effects are less frequent and not as good, which means they stick out more.

Why the constant criticism?

What I have just said is wrong, and I apologise for that. What is peculiar to Godard is that whatever is said about him will always be true (at the same time as he does what he says he will, he obeys his principle of 'always doing the opposite of what I say I will', he confessed to Michel Leblanc in *L'Etrave*, December 1959). Criticism of Godard must always be right, but it always accumulates untruths by omission, for which Godard has reproached me violently. For, like life itself, cinematographic truth is ambiguous, unlike verbal truth. In *L'Express* (23 December 1959), Godard says: 'I have to admit I have a certain difficulty in writing. I wrote: 'The weather is fine. The train enters the station.' I then spent hours wondering why I could not just as well have written the opposite: 'The train enters the station. The weather is fine,' or 'It is raining'. Things are more straightforward in the cinema. The weather is fine and the train enters the station at the same time. There is an inevitability about it. You have to take the plunge.'

This explains Godard's liking and repulsion for criticism, which enables him to clarify the disorder he observes. Periods of disorder and progress, such as the 18th and 20th centuries, as opposed to periods of great stability and creation, such as the 17th and 19th centuries, which produced a number of geniuses, marked a triumph of self-reflection and of attempts at synthesis (hence the many pictorial, cinematographic and literary references in *À bout de souffle*). Those periods were chiefly marked by the work of critics (neither Racine nor Molière produced any true criticism, unlike Voltaire and Diderot, who broadly speaking did nothing but that), who were naturally gifted exponents of synthesis. And when it comes to synthesis, editing has an important role to play. So today we have an abundance of creators-cum-critics and editors who never clearly outstrip their fellows. No single member of the new generation stands out from the rest of the field. If *À bout de souffle* is better than *Hiroshima mon amour*, it is because Godard had seen and reviewed Resnais' film before starting his own; it is not because Godard is superior to Resnais. So if you want to become very well known nowadays, don't go in for anything creative, but enter politics instead. The young French cinema is the work of very different personalities, and yet remains to a certain extent a collective work. There are those who go a little further, and those who go a little less far; the difference is quantitative.

What I have just said is wrong, because Godard, typically, brings off the tour de force of being both highly Rossellinian and not Rossellinian at all. That is why one often thinks of Resnais. Godard observes reality in minute detail, but at the same time he attempts to recompose it by means of flagrantly artificial devices. All debutant directors, fearing the unpredictability involved in shooting a film, tend to plan their movies carefully and go in for flashy stylistic devices. In *Charlotte et son Jules*, for example, we discovered a scientific use of décor as sophisticated as that of Lang. This also explains the editing style of *À bout de souffle*, in which very brief shots alternate skilfully with very long-held shots. Because the characters' behaviour results from a series of moral incongruities, the film is a series of jump cuts. The point is, though, that these jump cuts are beautiful and delightful. But in fact the least novel aspect of the film is the systematic and simplistic expression of the subject matter through the *découpage*, editing and choice of camera angles. It is not terribly clever to stick in a low-angle shot every time a character is in a fix. Robert Aldrich, André Berthomieu and René Clément have done it throughout their careers, and it rarely has much effect. There is a similarly facile device when, in the course of a single pan shot, we jump from Seberg and Belmondo on the Champs-Elysées to a brief glimpse of Charles de Gaulle and Dwight Eisenhower driving up the same thoroughfare, then back to Belmondo and Seberg on the same Champs-Elysées, the message being that the only thing that matters is oneself, and not politics, in the field of foreign and social affairs. And the censors, by cutting out the shot of the two presidents, reduced them to the state of mere entities, or ludicrous puppets, the meaning being that the only thing of our times that will survive will be *À bout de souffle*, and certainly not either de Gaulle or Eisenhower, pathetic and necessary figurines like all statesmen. Another device used by Godard comes when, in a very different way from the camerawork in Alfred Hitchcock's *Vertigo* (1957) or Chabrol's *Les Cousins* (1958), the great Raoul Coutard's lens whirls round and round reflecting the central characters' state of mind. That has a very precise meaning. It is a very classical expression of a modern form of behaviour.

But what gives *À bout de souffle* a slight edge over that other formulaic film, *Hiroshima mon amour*, is that with Godard spontaneity is more important than the formula, which complements and summarises it, whereas with Resnais the only spontaneity centres on the direction of the actors. Another facet of Godard's superiority is that he tackles something concrete, whereas recollection, oblivion, memory and time are things which are not concrete, which do not exist, and which, like Christian didacticism or communism, are not serious enough to be treated by such a profound language as that of the cinema. The inability of *Hiroshima mon amour* to evoke such elements in concrete fashion is incidentally quite fascinating: it even aids the expression of something quite different.

Godard may not have felt self-confident enough to express the disorder of our times in a clear fashion and with static shots; and he called technical facility to the rescue. There is no contrast between the camera's viewpoint and what is shown, as there is with Truffaut; but perhaps that is the price to be paid for utter sincerity – though in my opinion *À bout de souffle* would have been just as brilliant a movie if it had not relied on such devices.

The reconciliation of man with his epoch

I think in fact that *Hiroshima mon amour* proved that it was necessary to resort to certain tricks in order to reproduce a vision of our contemporary world, in which a considerable number of artifices condition the way we look at things both physically and morally. Cinema filmed at eye level eventually went out of fashion. And in an area where Resnais half-succeeded, and where his imitators – snobs like Jean-Daniel Pollet (the excellent *La Ligne de mire*, 1959), and impulsive directors like Marcel Hanoun (*Le Huitième jour/The Eighth Day*) or Edouard Molinaro (*Une Fille pour l'été*, 1959) – failed lamentably, Godard has succeeded in getting us to admit that our modern universe, as metallic and terrifying as science fiction, and marvellously represented by Seberg, who is less 'lively' than she is with Preminger and more lunar in the way she breaks down her character, is a wonderful universe full of beauties. Godard is a man who is in tune with his time, as can be seen from the high regard in which he holds certain aspects of truly modern civilisations, such as cars or strip cartoons in the daily newspaper *France-soir*. For the true civilisation of our time is not the reactionary, right-wing civilisation embodied by the weekly *L'Express* or Jean-Paul Sartre's plays, characterised by a rejection of what exists and a morose form of intellectualism, but the revolutionary, left-wing civilisation represented by those celebrated strip cartoons, among other things.

This is why it is wrong to see a link between Godard and Jean-Jacques Rousseau. Whereas Rousseau advocates nature as against artifice, Godard is 100% in favour of modern civilisation, with its big cities and artificiality. Following the American tradition – in the noblest sense – of Walt Whitman, Carl Sandburg, King Vidor and even Howard Hawks, he performs art's highest task, that of reconciling man with his time, with this world of ours which so many of our uptight scribblers see as a world in crisis – and who are often in no position to pass judgment since they know no other – or as a world that crucifies man. They fail to see that man is more capable of revealing himself in a world that seems to harass him. In Godard's view, the 20th century is not a gigantic slap in the face for our Maker; one just needs to know how to see and admire. The power and beauty of his *mise-en-scène*, which is incapable of imposing any image other than that of serenity and optimism, reveals to us all the profound charm of our apparently terrifying world, through the poetics of the jump cut and perdition.

*   *   *

À bout de souffle
RAYMOND BORDE (1962)*

Clumsy, halting and as badly put together as a page written by a six-year-old, *À bout de souffle* has had such an impact on the French cinema-going public that I feel bound to say a few words about this curious product. I realise that the critics almost unanimously, at least to start with, swallowed the colossal piece of advertising bluff that accompanied its release; and I realise that *Le Monde*, no less, not a newspaper given to going over the top, devoted half a page to the launch of the film – which is saying a lot. However, the conditioning of audiences cannot in itself explain the craze for the movie, which has in many cases been of a passionate nature.

À bout de souffle is an affectionate portrait of a small-time conman. It is a 1960 version of *Le Roi des resquilleurs* (*The King of the Gate-Crashers*). Belmondo plays a young hood who practises, with great skill, what is known in Italy as *l'arte di arran-*

---

* *Cahiers du cinéma*, No. 138, December 1962, pp. 41–59

Jean-Paul Belmondo in *À bout de souffle* (1960).

giarsi (the art of pulling a fast one). Taking his cue from Milton [a French music-hall artist of the twenties and thirties], who sang a song called 'J'ai ma combine' ('I've got my little ploys'), Belmondo has his own little trick for telephoning without paying, taking a taxi without paying and making love without paying. From time to time he nicks a car. His little scams say everything there is to be said about him. His life is entirely focused on wangling. He cannot keep up a conversation for more than two minutes. He has become totally alienated by his constant stream of petty lies.

He has been described – laughably – as an anarchist. He has a series of gags up his sleeve that guarantee him a reputation for being someone who couldn't care less about anything: he goes around lifting women's skirts in the street, refusing to give someone a light and telling off a taxi-driver. But it does not go further than that. He even insists that he likes the police – the very police who go after him – and he thinks society works pretty well: everything is in order and everyone is in their place. He strongly reminds one of a paratrooper on leave, with his exaggeratedly tough-guy attitude, his thick-skinned stupidity and his vague anxiety about being let loose among civilians. He feels lonely like a paratrooper who has been cut off from his unit, and who, behind his rascally mask, strongly believes in the values of law and order.

He is someone who is of no interest to me. And yet he appeals to the public, mainly because the gullible see him as a hero who lives up to their pathetic dreams; those who are regularly conned recognise him as someone they will never be, a conman, and I can just imagine shopkeepers feeling a tingle of jealousy at the nonchalant way he nicks cars. But there is another reason: Belmondo exhibits a certain spinelessness that is very much of our time. Behind his scheming, laid-back and provocative ways, he is an anxious, hounded and conformist individual. When he imitates Humphrey Bogart, he deludes himself and others into thinking he is a free man. When he has a serious problem on his hands, he puts on a show of not caring. A smart guy in a fix, he magically denies his status as a smart guy. For most French people, he is not a stranger, but one of them. For several years now, they too have evaded their responsibilities and hidden their heads in the sand, and any twinges of conscience they may have felt end up being brushed aside by cynical flippancy, a guffaw, listlessness or a falling into line. Belmondo plays the role of a respectful cheat, and in that sense he serves as an alibi for them.

A word about Jean Seberg. According to ancient law, you cannot both give and withhold. Here, Godard both gives and withholds. He proceeds in gingerly fashion. He shows us a woman who is not a woman, but a tomboy with close-cropped hair. Belmondo romps with an anti-woman – and this takes much of the punch out of the daring portrayal of sex the film claims to offer. Here again, Godard has cheated.

He has also cheated by slapping together bits of film shot at random. He must have said to himself that there were bound to be a few naïve people who would hail the birth of a new style. He calculated correctly. With the advent of the Nouvelle Vague, contempt for the public has become the attitude that pays off the most. That is why the camera wobbles so much. I can accept that the cinema is a spontaneous art, or rather that it deludes people into thinking it is. But when taken to such lengths it is sheer amateurism. […]

* * *

'Le Quai des brumes 1960: *À bout de souffle* by Jean-Luc Godard'

GEORGES SADOUL (1960)*

À *bout de souffle* has revealed to us an indisputable and very great talent, Jean-Luc Godard, who is still in his twenties. He is a '*bête de cinéma*': he has got film-making in his blood.

Godard, who was born of Swiss parents in Paris on 3 December 1930, was a journalist and film critic on *Arts* and *Cahiers du cinéma* before embarking on a career in the cinema. He began by making four short films: *Opération béton* (*Operation Concrete*, 1954), *Tous les garcons s'appellent Patrick* (*All the Boys Are Called Patrick*, 1957), *Une histoire d'eau* (*A Story of Water*, 1958) and *Charlotte et son Jules* (*Charlotte and Her Boyfriend*, 1958).[1] I have seen only the second of these films, which is engagingly casual, but has a vapid and even vulgar storyline. There is nothing in it that suggests the subsequent success of *À bout de souffle*, to which the following words might apply: 'Apart from one or two technical rules, nothing of what the earlier school had so gradually elaborated remained in place. It marked the collapse of the old principles.'

Victorin Jasset wrote those words in 1911 with reference to *L'Assassinat du Duc de Guise* and the 'new wave' triggered by so-called 'art films'.

From a technical viewpoint, no director under the age of thirty has recently dismantled the old Meccano-set of film-making with such consummate skill. Godard has consigned all the existing grammatical and syntactical rules of the cinema to the dust-heap.

The camera, carried by Raoul Coutard on his shoulder and constantly wobbling as he walks and breathes, is never motionless. Its perpetuum mobile in the street scenes is in keeping with the constant bustle and traffic of Paris. His lens suddenly leaves the two central characters on the pavement of the Champs-Élysées and pans to show Generals Dwight Eisenhower and Charles de Gaulle driving up the same avenue.[2] As the camera noses its way round a hotel room, it lets one of the characters move out of frame (except for a cheek and an ear). It is a neat way of getting out of filming a long piece of dialogue through the device of cross-cutting, that old convention which the very rigorous Robert Bresson always uses legitimately.

---

* *Les Lettres françaises,* No. 818, 31 March 1960.

Jean-Paul Belmondo in *À bout de souffle* (1960).

A qualified film editor could not watch *À bout de souffle* without wincing: half the shots do not follow on from the ones that precede them. No matter: these are not spelling mistakes, but stylistic turns of phrase, something similar to the use of spoken language in literature.

The same tone can also be found in the dialogue and dramatic construction. Tension is reinforced by the fact that traditional devices to create suspense are dispensed with. We fear all the more for the crook on the run because he does not seem to care that the police are after him. The dialogue uses everyday expressions and avoids self-conscious apophthegms. This marks an (apparently) complete break away from the scintillating dialogue of 1930s films, where characters come back at each other like Davis Cup tennis players. In *À bout de souffle*, the characters flit from one topic to another in their conversation and listen to themselves talking rather than answering.

François Truffaut and Claude Chabrol acted as a guarantors for Godard – Truffaut as a scriptwriter and Chabrol as an 'artistic and technical adviser' – in a purely friendly capacity designed to reassure the film's financial backers. As far as sheer competence is concerned, Godard could teach Truffaut and Chabrol a thing or two: their first films were clumsy efforts compared with *À bout de souffle*. Having said that, I prefer the sincerity of *Le Beau Serge* (*Bitter Reunion*) or *Les Quatre cents coups* (*The 400 Blows*) to Godard's stunningly successful film, whose central characters do not appeal to me any more than their adventures.

Its plot could be summarised as follows: a sympathetic murderer is hounded by the police, wanders aimlessly around the big city and encounters the love of his life. He is willing to make a bid for happiness 'somewhere else ', when he meets his death. Message: 'You can't escape your fate.'

You will have recognised the theme, which has regularly featured in American, French, Italian and British films over the past twenty years. *À bout de souffle* is yet another reworking of our good old *Le Quai des brumes* (*Port of Shadows*), as Godard has been the first to admit.

In this connection, may I quote what I wrote as a young film critic on 26 May 1938, after the première of Marcel Carné's movie:

> The characters in *Le Quai des brumes* are delinquents from a good back-ground, second-rate intellectuals, crooks, fences, prostitutes or aspiring prostitutes. The film describes not a society, but the dregs of a society (...). The villains are the most successful characters, those that the director and scriptwriter apparently most cared about.
>
> Such a degree of 'realism' inevitably brings other shortcomings in its train. In the absence of any true humanity, the makers of the film are content to trot out silly sentimental remarks about little old ladies who have lost their little doggies in rainy streets and pathetic platitudes about death and what 'is hidden behind things'. And it is a pity.
>
> It is a pity, too, that the fog in the port gives off a stench of death and fatality in all its forms from which man cannot escape, whether it be murder or suicide. The authors seem to think that fatality is man's only reason to live. One hopes that in the near future Carné will embark on the road towards genuine realism. His youthful talent will surely go very far once he uses it to depict characters other than a floozy and a down-and-out.

Two years later, the ideologues of the Vichy regime proclaimed: 'It was the fault of Jean-Paul Sartre and *Le Quai des brumes* that we lost the war.' I would have looked pretty silly if some Pétainist journalist had used my indictment to counter Carné when he retorted (with considerable courage) that the filmmaker's noblest mission was to act as a barometer set to measure the *Zeitgeist*.

According to an ancient Greek proverb, 'the flight of the owl heralds dusk'. Minerva's instinct does not solely predict victories. Jean Renoir's *Le Crime de Monsieur Lange* (*The Crime of Monsier Lange*) and Jean Grémillon's *Le Ciel est à vous* foreshadowed the Popular Front and the Liberation, and yet they were no less realistic than *Le Quai des brumes* and *La Règle du jeu* (*The Rules of the Game*), which portended the fateful horrors of the terrible years with their depiction of 'the dregs of a society' (people from the underworld or high society). In the review I wrote in May 1938, a few superficial observations combined with a metaphysical view of optimism led me to draw conclusions that were as categorical as they were absurd. In 1960, I should perhaps be wary of making equally peremptory and cursory remarks about the New Wave.

In his 1960 version of *Le Quai des brumes*, Godard reacted not against Carné and Jacques Prévert's creations, but against the stereotypes that certain profiteers subsequently derived from them. His writing method involved not careful preparation, but free improvisation based on a three-page synopsis written by Truffaut. According to an interview Godard gave to Georges Bratschi (*La Tribune de Genève*, 3 February 1960): 'When he felt inspired, he dashed off his dialogue while visualising each shot. He occasionally gave the actors lines he had thought up during shooting. These were of course very simple 'real-life' remarks that bore no relation to the carefully crafted witticisms of a scriptwriter like [Michel] Audiard.' Audiard was a favourite target of Godard and his friends, because he wrote dialogue in the style of 1938-vintage Henri Jeanson (or Prévert). Godard the critic may have shot down such scriptwriters in flames, but surely Godard the director rifled their pockets?

His zealous police inspector is reminiscent of the Inspector Slimane that Jeanson thought up for *Pépé le Moko*. Belmondo, as he stands in front of a poster proclaiming 'Live dangerously right to the end', is a carbon copy of the jobless Gabin that Charles Spaak and Julien Duvivier, in *La Belle équipe* (*They Were Five*), place in front of a poster bearing the words 'Go in for winter sports and stoke up your health'. When the couple in *À bout de souffle* slip under the sheets to make love, the radio starts blaring 'And now for our programme 'Music While You Work', the sort of joke you might find in the *Almanac Vermot*, and one already used in countless really bad French films. The 'audacity' of the young man's remark to his girl, 'Do you mind if I pee in your basin?', shocked some people. What I chiefly hold against this hygienic detail is the fact that over the past fifteen years it has constantly popped up in various (audacious) novels and even in stories published by the weekly *Le Canard Enchaîné*. If, as it would seem, *À bout de souffle*'s considerable success can be put down to its free improvisation, any old hack director will ape its sloppiness in future. The same goes for the style of its photography and editing. Such anti-clichés are in danger of becoming the clichés of tomorrow – not that that would detract in any way from the merits of their inventor.

Could it be that Godard, starting with a hackneyed situation, has succeeded (as Carné did with apparently traditional 'underworld characters') in expressing certain concerns or feelings? I simply ask that question. It is up to young people to answer it. Those present at the previews of *À bout de souffle* were divided, some of them praising it to the skies, others loathing it. We shall learn later on whether a film like that was really able to transcend a trivial story about a petty crook and mirror the anxieties of some members of the younger generation.

In any case, I do not like its two central characters. Unlike Prévert, who used to contrast goodies with baddies, Godard intended to show that there is good and bad in all of us. To demonstrate his theory, he made a very judicious choice of his two main actors. Belmondo, who is excellent, plays the same sort of role he performed in Chabrol's *À double tour* (*Web of Passion*), even using the name of the character he played in that film, Laszlo Kovacs, as an alias. And it was certainly quite an achievement to transform Jean Seberg, a cold fish in *Bonjour tristesse*, into a brightly coloured, scintillating and lissom trout wriggling in a stream. However attractive she may be, her character turns out at the end of the movie to be a perfect 'bitch'.

Some people were prepared to find excuses for her behaviour. But Godard discouraged them by declaring at a *ciné-club* projection that the young woman had 'emancipated' herself by turning informer. As for his central character, he was quite right to say 'I like cops', because it is traditional to criticise them, as does the whole of the national press. Someone sitting next to Godard added that he hated the conformism of Luis Buñuel, who attacks policemen and priests. Here again, one view is as valid as the other. That form of anti-conformism is worse than the worst conformism.

Godard may have been likening himself to his central character when he told *La Tribune de Genève* that he had stolen ciné-cameras from the Zürich television channel, broken into a safe, worked as a navvy, sold some works by Renoir (Pierre-Auguste) that he had nicked from his banker grandfather and walked off with *Cahiers du cinéma*'s petty cash. After that, according to various rumours, he was arrested (as a deserter) and locked up in a Geneva prison. The insolent way the central character of *À bout de souffle* resorts to paradoxes, his love of mystification and his swingeing black humour are not, however, enough to endear him to me. It would be unfair to see this first film as no more than an illustration of the notion that 'one view is as valid as the other', or a mere revamping of old merchandise in new packaging. Its plot is one that has often been used in the past. But whether or not one likes the characters in *À bout de souffle*, they are not conventional, and they possess a very rare gift: life. Godard has gone into print in these pages as saying: 'I've made the anarchist film I dreamed of.' All very well, but we may fairly conclude that his rebellion is far from being left-wing.

If we are to believe Luc Moullet, the two central characters 'endanger their own lives, as if it were some kind of game. The confusion of extremes, which is admirably reflected in the dying central character's comical grimaces, is here targeted at its equivalent on a moral plane.'

Godard did not think up some latter-day Lafcadio – as though reworking André Gide's *Les Caves du Vatican* (*The Vatican Swindle*) – for the purposes of his (anti-)moral message. His central character is not guided by the wager of the 'gratuitous act', or by the 'philosophical' motivations which, in *Rope*, lie behind the murder, for kicks, of a person chosen at random. The murderer in *À bout de souffle* is not driven to kill out of a desire to become a superman, but out of fear and an undoubted feeling of despair. He falls in love while denying the existence of love, or else making fun of it. His cynicism masks a great deal of sentimentality and even naivety. I have encountered quite a lot of youngsters like him, who confine themselves to petty thieving, which they regard as a challenge to established laws.

What is even more interesting and fascinating than the characters themselves is their relationship, though this is too obviously systematised at the dénouement of the movie, when they each carry on with their monologue without hearing the other. The best part of the film is its 'second act', which takes place in a hotel room. Many find this scene too long, an opinion I do not share. In the course of this double soliloquy on the incommunicability of two lovers, a genuine drama unfolds, which is more important and more profound than the pretext for a manhunt and a murder.

If this long sequence were cut, what would remain of *À bout de souffle*? A brilliant exercise on a prefabricated theme and a certain way of looking at Paris – though it has to be said that the Champs-Élysées had already been portrayed in a more original manner by Louis Malle and Henri Decae in the finest sequences of *Ascenseur pour l'échafaud* (*Lift to the Scaffold*). Could it be that Godard, a laconic figure behind his tinted glasses, is a prisoner of his own insolence (or shyness)? His ambiguity is not easily penetrated. Is he or is he not sincere? After spending two months pondering this matter – quick thinking is not my strong point – I have not yet managed to solve this dilemma, which could also be expressed in the following terms: have we witnessed the birth of a great new auteur? Or have we been dazzled by the brilliance of yet another excellent talent?

In any case, why should they be mutually exclusive? This new director – like his characters, like anyone – has qualities and faults, in other words contradictions. *À bout de souffle* may annoy, irritate or even shock. And yet it is in some respects touching. Where will the director go from here? What will the 'political film' he dreams of making be like? Only the future, or more precisely what Godard develops into, can answer that question. As time and events go by, anyone can improve or decline.

Notes

1. The dates of the last three films vary according to the sources consulted
2. In the version of *À bout de souffle* released in France, the censors cut out the part of the shot showing the two presidents

III

THE MISSING PERSPECTIVE: GENDER, POLITICS AND THE NEW WAVE

Introduction

GINETTE VINCENDEAU

The French New Wave was predominantly a white male phenomenon, both in terms of filmmakers and, for a long time, critics and historians writing about it. However, as detailed in the introduction to this volume, since the 1990s, the impact of feminist film theory has led to important challenges to traditional historical accounts and filmic analysis, which in the case of the New Wave privileged authorship (romantic visions of brilliant and embattled male artists) as well as stylistic and formal approaches that put the accent on innovative *mise-en-scène* linked to the use of different kinds of equipment and narrative techniques (shooting on location, rule-breaking editing, etc.). Feminist scholarship by the likes of Sandy Flitterman-Lewis (*To Desire Differently: Feminism and the French Cinema*) and Geneviève Sellier (*Masculine Singular: French New Wave Cinema*) turned the spotlight on the films' gender politics and their construction of femininity.

It seemed, therefore, that a new section putting the accent on gender would be welcome and address the desire among those teaching and studying the French New Wave to introduce more diversity in their approach to the movement, including a wider range of critical material. While the recent feminist scholarship importantly enables such approaches, we wanted to explore the vision of gender politics *at the time*. Going back to the archives of texts written in the 1950s and 1960s, we found that there was a statistically modest yet real and exciting input by women writers that had been obscured by the high-profile male critics anthologized in this volume (Truffaut, Bazin, Sadoul...). We also found that discussions of gender were not completely absent from mainstream film and cultural journals, including *Cahiers du cinéma* and *Esprit*. Concurrently, in view of the growing importance of Agnès Varda in perceptions of the movement, we wanted to revisit the earlier writings on her work. In turn, this encouraged us to look for material on the small number of other women directors of the time, notably Jacqueline Audry and Paule Delsol.

Pierre Kast's 'Il est minuit, Docteur Kinsey…' was published in *Cahiers du cinéma* in December 1953. This early, pre-New Wave article by a future New Wave filmmaker is a rarity for the period in addressing the representation of women from an analytical perspective. A notable exception at the time in *Cahiers du cinéma* (January 1954) is Jacques Doniol-Valcroze's 'Déshabillage d'une petite bourgeoise sentimentale', which we hesitated to include in this selection. However, while Doniol-Valcroze's analysis is interesting in its own right, our opinion was that Kast's article was more incisive.

While Kast's piece is written in a sardonic tone, he raises important issues, pinpointing the generally reactionary and self-serving approach to female characters by male writers and filmmakers. The piece displays an awareness of gender that would later be submerged under the auteurist polemics of *Cahiers du cinéma*. The singularity of the piece is less surprising when taking into consideration Kast's political background: as a former Resistant and communist-sympathizer, he cut an unusual figure among his predominantly right-wing colleagues at *Cahiers du cinéma*. A collection of Kast's writing edited by Noël Burch was published in 2014 by L'Harmattan. In this respect, a reassessment of his New Wave films (in particular *Le Bel âge*, 1960; *La Morte saison des amours*, 1961 and *Vacances portugaises*, 1963) is long overdue.

Ginette Vincendeau

11 The Time Has Come, Doctor Kinsey…[1]

PIERRE KAST (1953)[*]

I am always a bit suspicious when an argument benefits its author. It would be much more satisfying intellectually if the well-intentioned people who find anti-clericalism passé were atheists. Similarly, it would be less irritating if those who declare feminism old-fashioned did not happen to be the authors of saucy novels. […][2]

Of course, women can vote, run a business or write books. Yet, this does not mean that women's problems are over, far from it… The French in Casablanca think nothing of talking about primary schools for 'natives'. Intelligent people, members of the elite, say and believe that women 'also' have the right to be intelligent and to have ideas about other things than cooking, love, doing a wash or redeeming coupons. For goodness sake, this is not 1939.

In real life, in politics, and especially in the private sphere, only a tiny number of men truly recognise these rights – meanwhile, vigorously ignoring what they entail. Equality at work, that's just about OK, but sexual equality, honestly, can you imagine? A jury composed of honourable family men and one woman for good measure, judged Pauline Dubuisson[3] guilty largely because the prosecutor or the judge (or someone of that ilk) revealed that she had had five lovers! A 28-year old woman! Which one among those dinosaurs or their ancient relatives had only had five mistresses? Women's magazines and romance novels would not be so massively successful without the persistence in our society of the myth of masculine pre-eminence. Women are made by men and for men – who, as doctor Kinsey explains so well, can do without them very well.

---

[*] *Cahiers du cinéma*, 30 December 1953, pp. 50–3. (Translated from the French by Ginette Vincendeau)

Pierre Kast.

Men 98% – Women 0.001% – Don't know 1.999%

Fortunately, they say, writers are not like that. […] Many women, it is true, write what they want and in the style of their choice about their own problems. Leaving aside its compilation aspect, *The Second Sex* by Simone de Beauvoir is a landmark in female lucidity. Since then, it has been practically impossible for young male writers to refuse, without, or more often with, bad grace, the principle of equality with 'Women'. Naturally, we are not talking about girls here. Like André Malraux's character Ferral,[4] when these men meet a virgin they try to imagine her face during orgasm.

The Maurras-inspired Hussards,[5] in their serious articles, show that they realise things have changed. Dozens of press clippings prove that writers like Roger Nimier, Jacques Laurent and others are perfectly *au fait* in this respect. But they have to make a living, and, as we know, one doesn't make a living from writing articles. These young men therefore write books. I have no idea whether they will invoke some kind of double-dealing as an excuse, but it must be said that the idea of 'Woman' we find in their works, from *Le Hussard bleu* to the *Caroline* series is nothing but that familiar, pre-war figure, woman-as-object.

The issue is very different in the cinema. Films are almost entirely made by men. Women in films are thus exactly women as seen by men. Scripts by Thea von Harbou, Claire Booth and Anita Loos signal no turning point in the representation of women on screen. A lot of women write 'men's books' and adopt a male perspective. There are very few women directors. They make men's films. We know the kind of amused indulgence and smugness men display towards female homosexuality. Without judging the quality of *Mädchen in Uniform* or *Olivia*,[6] neither film is going to destroy this complacency.

Anyone talking about women and cinema without specifying first who the women in question are, and that these women are seen and *shown* by men, is guilty of a first-class fraud. Maybe this is self-evident. But I cannot believe that to be a film director you need a vocation, or that it is a question of nerves or physiology. The truth is that the cinema is the preserve of men because the key issue is the representation of female characters. In short, their mystification.

The Imaginary Harem

'Big Louise', star attraction of the brothels in Lunéville[7] dressed up, by popular demand, as a peasant from the Balkans or a Roman slave. In this way, the French army learnt about geography and history. The relationship between spectators and characters on screen does not have that classic simplicity. However simple-minded and gullible, the Lorraine soldiers could still recognise Louise under the various disguises. Faced with so many choices and an extraordinary diversity of faces, accoutrements and accessories, cinema spectators are made to feel like kings. This is because women in films are not just made by men, they are above all made for men.

This does not mean that I am impervious to the 'spell-binding magic' of the cinema, nor that, out of Cartesian prejudice, I forsake the attraction of images.

I am also perfectly able to understand that the cinematic representation of women offers something unique, unparalleled by anything else in the world. I can analyse movement. I can understand, and experience, the shock of a face, of a figure, of a detail. I know very well the value of people and can distinguish it from its travesties. Louise Brooks, Cyd Charisse, Katharine Hepburn (in *Little Women* and *African Queen*), Pier Angeli, even Rita Hayworth: I can see what is unforgettable about them and when I read here and there the words 'divine' or 'magic', I don't smirk; I know what they are talking about. However, I lack lyricism.

When working on his 'Imaginary Museum', Malraux is free to establish links between morality and aesthetics. But film spectators have to endure passively the imaginary harem. For reasons that are both clear and obscure, admissible and repressed, they may believe that they are making choices, and yet the characters that these actresses embody in fiction films are indistinguishable from fantasy creatures devised by delirious fanatics. It is also the case that the gay men who are passionate fans of Garbo unconsciously use their love for the star to justify the basically infantile and ridiculous characters she embodies – and the same can be said of other actresses.

I do not deny that *amour fou* or some magic communication may occur between spectators and the moving shadows on screen; but I think that without analysing in detail the basis of these communications, we conceal the most astonishingly self-serving device used by contemporary males, that is, a poisonous picture of women's condition that is spread over hundreds of kilometres of film stock.

Days of Sodom

Having assembled the objects of his lust, the Marquis de Sade's Duc de Blangis told them: 'Feeble, enfettered creatures destined solely for our pleasures, I trust you have not deluded yourselves into supposing that the equally absolute and ridiculous ascendancy given you in the outside world would be accorded you in this place [...] Ceaselessly bear in mind that we will make use of you all'.[8] Needless to say, all these objects were women. Film spectators with a modicum of insight into what they are presented with would not need to change a word to this tirade.

Think, first of all, of the cohort of sweet, pale and charming creatures who are chained, beaten, kidnapped and destined to satisfy, within the limits of morality codes, the most covertly aggressive instincts. There are several versions of the damsel-in-shackles: the most touching is Lilian Gish. Sometimes they undergo surprising transformations; Jane Wyman, comprehensively tortured in *Johnny Belinda*, later put on lurid tights in Technicolor films. But why should we be surprised?

The character of the gold-digger or man-eater is the requisite counterpart of the homely ingénue and her delicious home baking. Femmes fatales, vamps, heart-breakers, freely deliver equally exciting suffering. Besides, they are themselves often punished, so everyone is happy.

Should we conclude that only sadists and masochists will be satisfied? In what category should we put the legions of busy and diligent housewives who are serially betrayed in hundreds of vaudeville farces? The carefully balanced, combined pleasures of activity and passivity lead from brutal beatings to pure victimhood. The traditional range of theatrical roles – ingénues, maids, etc. – cannot be imported into the cinema.

The visual glutton is the only truly satisfied spectator. Eroticism on screen is voyeuristic. I am not thinking only of music-hall peep shows or Pietro Aretino's[9] etchings. You only need to experience once a close-up of a pair of eyes or of a mouth to understand the secret of how the mechanism works. There is practically no film without an enthralling moment for the visual glutton. This is why he keeps going to the cinema.

Love that kills

One of the things that drives burlesque cinema is the mocking of this gallery of portraits. The platinum blondes in the Marx Brothers films, Martha Raye in *Monsieur Verdoux*,[10] were born of a tiny slippage: their traits are not exaggerated, they look like the heroines of countless famous films; it's the context that has changed.

Is it really impossible to find a film heroine who is not an object? One who acts and thinks? Of course, there is Marie Curie, or Joan of Arc, at a pinch. They are real persons, subjects – however, like the heroines of Soviet films, who are also real persons and subjects, love is forbidden to them. If they are granted the right to think they are denied the right to fuck; they can never have both at the same time. And even the right to think is granted them parsimoniously: it is strange that a country like the USA, where a large number of women are integrated into the social and economic fabric of the country up to high-ranking posts, can only show women at work for comic effects. As for the right to sexual freedom, those who have been granted it are cruelly punished: they are unhappy, punished, or they die of it. Hepburn's Rose in *The African Queen* (1951) appears to be the only one who can enjoy the man she wants without horrible consequences. But to succeed you can see that John Huston had to use comedy as a cover.

'Love' is the word that recurs most frequently in film titles. Here is a great topic for research for an expert statistician. But the love in question is the love of men, for which women are the indispensable, yet despised, instrument. As in life, films exclude or suppress women who dare assert their desire. By 'sensuality' what is meant is a man enjoying a woman or bestowing pleasure on to her – never a woman enjoying her own pleasure.

The most violent manifestations of cinema's erotic power are the films of Erich von Stroheim and Luis Buñuel. But valuable, perceptive and coherent as they are, they are still displays of masculine eroticism. It would be ridiculous to associate von Stroheim and Buñuel with the stupefying eroticism of ordinary films, although I am not denying their liberating value. Valmont and Dolmancé are men. We are still waiting for a Merteuil or a Juliette.[11]

Notes

All notes by editor Ginette Vincendeau – except Note 10, by author Pierre Kast.

1. Kast's original title, 'Il est minuit, Doctor Kinsey...' is a pun on the title of Gilbert Cesbron's 1952 play *Il est minuit, docteur Schweitzer*, about a well-known Alsatian doctor who worked in colonial Africa, and Alfred Kinsey, author of the 'Kinsey reports' about human sexual behaviour (published in 1948 and 1953). Cesbron's title signals that a crucial moment has come for the hero; Kast thereby suggests that the time for a change has come, here in the representation of women.

2. Please note that this text has been edited. Kast's original included a number of digressions into literary, artistic and political considerations that by today's standards are quite obscure and, moreover, did not directly relate to the main topic of the article.

3. Pauline Dubuisson was condemned to forced labour for life for shooting her lover to death, though as Kast says, judgment of her character weighed heavily in the jury's decision, which was judged excessively harsh at the time. She was released for good conduct in 1960 and later pardoned. Dubuisson is one of the models for the character played by Brigitte Bardot in Henri-Georges Clouzot's *La Vérité* in 1960.]

4. *La Condition humaine/Man's Fate*, first published in 1933.

5. The Hussards refers to a right-wing literary movement of the 1950s, inspired in part by the Monarchist author Charles Maurras (1868–1952).

6. *Machen in Uniform* (Leontine Sagan, 1931); *Olivia* (Jacqueline Audry, 1951).

7. A formerly important garrison town in Lorraine, eastern France; it is not clear to what period Katz is referring, possibly the 1870 war.

8. Marquis de Sade, *The 120 Days of Sodom*, First Start Publishing, 2012.

9. Italian artist, 1492–1556.

10. *Monsieur Verdoux*, Charles Chaplin, 1947.

11. Valmont is the exploitative male hero of Pierre Choderlos de Laclos's novel *Les Liaisons dangereuses* (*Dangerous Liaisons*, 1782); Dolmancé is a male libertine character in de Sade's *La Philosophie dans le boudoir* (*Philosophy in the Bedroom*, 1795); the Marquise de Merteuil is a manipulative, sexually experienced woman in *Les Liaisons dangereuses*; Juliette is the debauched heroine of de Sade's 1797 eponymous novel.

'Identikit of the New Wave heroine', by the feminist sociologist Evelyne Sullerot, was first published in *France Observateur* on 27 April 1961. It arose from a much wider sociological survey of filmic representations by a team including Edgar Morin alongside Sullerot. It is a key document for a gendered approach to the New Wave, that has been commented on by later feminist scholarship, but has not been anthologised, even in French, probably because it was published in a weekly cultural magazine that is difficult to get hold of. Sullerot offers a trenchant analysis of the representation of women in New Wave cinema up to 1961, pointing to the contrast between their noticeable presence in the films and surface modernity, with the more traditional aspects of their representations. Sullerot unfortunately did not pursue work on film. However, she became one of the leading feminist sociologists in France, writing numerous works on the media (in particular those targeting women) and women's condition, notably issues of birth control.

Ginette Vincendeau

12 Identikit of the 'New Wave' Heroine

EVELYNE[1] SULLEROT (1961)*

The Centre d'Études des Communications de Masse at the École des Hautes Études,[2] on the initiative of Mr Edgar Morin, has launched a survey of film contents, which will enable the analysis of all French films produced within one year. This study is centred on the 'heroes' of individual films: each protagonist is assessed by three analysts using a meticulous questionnaire; they then produce an index card for each of them. An identical study will then take place further afield, with the help of the same questionnaire, in a dozen countries in Europe, Asia and America. The French team, who devised the original questionnaire, have used it to carry out a comparative study of the heroes of New Wave films with those of other productions. The results of this study have already been detailed in a report at the Sorbonne, and will be published by the Centre d'Études des Communications de Masse at a later date. Mrs Sullerot, who worked on the project with Mr Brémond and Miss Berton, examines below the New Wave heroine, as she appears in the study.

* * *

Why 'the New Wave woman'? Undoubtedly because, during the comparative study of the 55 main protagonists from films that clearly belong to the New Wave, and 55 from French films from the same period (1958–1959) that are not labelled New Wave, I was surprised to note that the New Wave group contained a significant number of female protagonists. Considering that the studies conducted up to now on film protagonists revealed male characters winning by a crushing majority, this phenomenon seemed even more novel.[3] How could spectators not find such a result strange? For years, have they not been either bludgeoned, or jaded, by

---

* *France Observateur* [*L'Observateur littéraire*], 27 April 1961, pp.17–18. (Translated from the French by Jennifer Wallace)

Jeanne Moreau in *Ascenseur pour l'échafaud* (1958).

the never-ending, excessive promotion of (female) eroticism on screen? What a line-up of women, of stars! (And we readily think of the word 'star' as feminine).

Who are these heroines?

Bearing in mind, however, that cinema is, in a certain way, a reflection of society, then we must recognise that the society in which we live, here in France, is very clearly 'masculine'. It was therefore all the more interesting to see that the New Wave's little glimmer stands out in this respect, giving us 24 heroines in 18 films.

Through analysing New Wave films and their contents, we wanted to know whether the movement was as 'revolutionary' as it claimed to be, and not just in a technical sense. Did it, or did it not, feminise the population on screen? And why? Who were these heroines, seen in increasing numbers, and what novelty were they bringing to French cinema?

The first observation was disappointing: amongst my 24 heroines, only 14 were the main protagonists of the film, whereas, amongst the male heroes, 22 occupied that prime position. The same old two-thirds proportion strikes again. And we undoubtedly owe the existence of these female 'other-halves' to the New Wave's unique predilection for films containing sexual themes.

Nevertheless, these 24 women were not mere surface illusions. They were sometimes so important that they determined the whole orientation of the film – as in *Les Amants* (*The Lovers*, 1958) or *Hiroshima mon amour* (*Hiroshima, My Love*, 1959), two films where the script, incidentally, was written by a woman…[4] Others were the subject of an entomological study of a certain category of young women: *Les Bonnes femmes* (*Good Time Girls*, 1960).[5] Many others were important players, capturing our attention just as much as the hero of the couple, as in *Ascenseur pour l'échafaud* (*Lift to the Scaffold*, 1958), *Les Liaisons dangereuses* (*Dangerous Liaisons*, 1959), *À bout de souffle* (*Breathless*, 1960), *Une fille pour l'été* (*A Mistress for the Summer*, 1960), *L'Eau à la bouche* (*A Game for Six Lovers*, 1960), and *Les Jeux de l'amour* (*The Love Game* 1960).[6]

Who were these 24 women and what did they have in common? My 24 perforated index cards were ready to tell me. Were they indistinguishable from one another? Or very differentiated? In fact, when the spotlight was aimed on these 24 files, brimming with all kinds of data, it exposed similarities so striking that we can, justifiably, talk of stereotypes. But at other times the light refracted in all directions

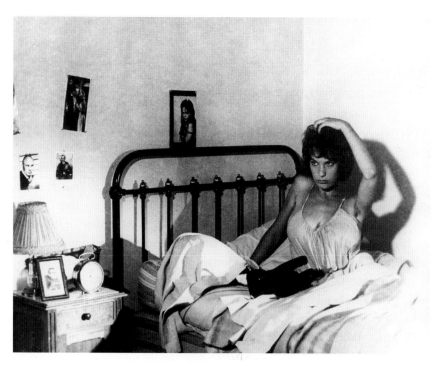

Bernadette Lafont in *L'Eau à la bouche* (1959).

and split into many distinct cases. The range of examples thus obtained was sometimes interesting for their exaggerated and heavily stereotypical aspects, sometimes for their stubborn minority elements, and sometimes because the examples could be divided into sub groups that were noticeably differentiated and contradictory.

If it is not particularly remarkable to observe that our New Wave heroines, 99% of the time, are attractive and nice to look at, it is more interesting, however, to find that these women are overwhelmingly 'lovers'. In all other cinematic production, including mainstream French production, we normally find roles, be they large or small, for action heroines, little girls or elderly mothers. Here, all the female roles are lover roles. And they are nearly always played with the same tragic overtones (only two are comic, in *L'Eau à la bouche,* and *Le Bel âge,* 1960)[7]. But when we say 'lover' and 'tragic', that doesn't mean that our New Wave heroines experience great romantic passion – far from it: only one-third of them are offered a 'great love', and the remaining two-thirds are scattered amongst short-lived affairs, serious (or not) flirtations, lukewarm romances, and loveless sexual relationships (7 out of 22).

During their brief filmic lives (as New Wave films have, indeed, a tendency to build intrigue over just a few days, or even a few hours), two-thirds of our heroines change their partners at least once, or even a few times. This is something new, and it underscores that the treatment of male and female characters is almost comparable when it comes to sex: a sort of de facto equality in terms of sexual behaviour, which is in itself revolutionary. In mainstream productions this kind of dithering and uncertainty, this opportunity to 'practice', is generally reserved for male heroes.

Furthermore, the depiction of these imperfect attempts, of this search for love, so far from the usual model – that is, woman as the known and fixed entity – doesn't shy away from going into detail. Two-thirds of our heroines have sex *during the film* (and we are shown as much of the act as is allowed), and two-thirds again *specify* that they have had sexual experiences (outside of marriage) before the start of their 'filmic life'. It is imperative that *we know* that they are not virgins, or that they are adulterers. Besides, out of our 24 heroines, there is not one who is still a virgin by the end of the film (whereas the young virgin, the ingénue, is very popular in both non-New Wave French films and foreign productions).

Is it because of her age that the New Wave woman is predisposed toward making the search for love or a sexual partner her 'constant primary value' (22 out of 24)? It is true that we are dealing with young women: there are no little girls, only two women in their forties, and the rest are under thirty. By contrast, mainstream productions generally privilege women between thirty and forty, the typical age of the established 'big star'.

Their 'values'

Yet there is also a worrying void. No religious values: only two are *'practising'*, and three are *'overt non-believers'*. As for the rest, the issue is so non-existent that no indication is given to us whatsoever of their religious backgrounds or beliefs. Political values? Only one film alludes to the theme: the 'Nevers' heroine of *Hiroshima, mon amour,* an atypical example and therefore rich with insight. Ambition? None are interested, except in two cases. Money? No, for these women it's irrelevant.

Nevertheless there exists a small, separate group of heroines, who, whilst looking for love, simultaneously throw themselves into the search for independence, self-esteem and individual pride. To reach this goal, they sometimes go as far as to commit an *acte gratuit*.[8] Is it surprising that these six women see their 'individual' value as being in conflict with their value as a 'lover'?

On the opposite side of these unresolved, painful, psychological conflicts (all resolved *'without emotional happiness'*), we note the total absence of the usual group of women who suffer and *'sacrifice love out of notions of duty'*. And this is glaringly obvious when considering the list of things New Wave women hold in 'contempt': half of them consistently scorn *'lawfulness and conformism'*, and half again express their contempt for virtue and traditional *'moral values'*.

So what then of family values, friendship, compassion? This ocean of human tenderness where, for example, the population of female heroines of romance novels dwell. Our New Wave heroines show little appreciation for them. Parents? For two-thirds of them, in spite of their young age, no indication of their family background. Eight are married: six of them have a lover, five have serious marital problems, and three are divorced or dreaming of divorce. So that's about it for marriage.

Children? Only five of them are shown with a child, and if this child is no longer a baby, there is always some emotional conflict between mother and child. The New Wave mother is truly monstrous: Mme Doinel in *Les Quatre cents coups* (*The 400 Blows*, 1959); Thérèse Marcoux in *À double tour* (*Web of Passion*, 1959); Paule in *Une fille pour l'été*, etc.[9]

There are some vaguely sketched friendships, or amiable relations between brothers and sisters or cousins, but these are pittance when compared to the tragic and sustained condemnation of marriage and motherhood.

'Little women and grand women'

Work? Half of them don't work. Which literally means they do nothing, not even housework. Amongst those who do work, there is a clear division between the 'subordinates' who work to earn a living (*Les Bonnes Femmes*, young Véro in *Ascenseur pour l'Echafaud,* Prudence from *L'Eau à la bouche* etc.), and the oth-

Yori Bertin (left) and Georges Poujouly (right) in *Ascenseur pour l'échafaud* (1958).

ers, who, if they're not some kind of undefined student, generally do 'interesting', glamorous, original jobs: artist, antique dealer, interior decorator… But sadly we don't know anything about how they practice their professions. We don't know why they work, nor whether their job is meaningful to them. We don't know if it creates conflicts, nor if it makes them happy in any way.

So, no information on their careers, and no information regarding money either. Nineteen of our 24 heroines live in great comfort, or don't care in the slightest about their finances.

As for our 'little' women from modest backgrounds, who don't have any money, and who, to earn some, work in unglamorous jobs (shop assistants or waitresses), well goodness me! They have practically no education and their problems are 'little' too. We are entertained over and over with their stupidity and their limited horizons. This disparity in treatment is further heightened because the 'little' women are often put in parallel with the 'grand' women (who are rich, idle, refined). The conclusions drawn from this contrast are simplistic, and of highly dubious social morality: for the 'ladies', great love stories 'with class', but the 'little' women have to make do with common or silly romances. (For example, the parallel couples of *Ascenseur pour l'échafaud*, *L'Eau à la bouche* and *À double tour*).

This famous notion of 'class', which has the power, via aesthetics, to elevate the crimes, infidelities, and scandalous behaviour of some characters, is ruthlessly denied to others. This is a total departure from the (perhaps) populist aesthetic that audiences were used to seeing in the French, pre-war, naturalist school of cinema, and its aftermath. In New Wave films, working-class heroines and everyone underneath are easily ridiculed, and their behaviour is depicted with a dry cruelty.

It is only through cross-referencing and comparing these films that this implicit caricature of 'social problems' is revealed: our New Wave heroine, for her part, doesn't worry herself about such issues. Just as she doesn't worry about money, her job, her family, and even less her morality, faith or politics. And yet these women are depicted as living in a clearly recognisable present day.

The self-searching woman

Madame Nouvelle Vague does have certain taboos. But they are not sexual taboos, they are social taboos.

Love, on the other hand, is her domain, and here, at last, there are no limitations. Her progress in this domain knocks down a series of myths, one after the other like vulgar plaster statues: virginity, female monogamy, everything-is-wonderful motherhood, and marriage-is-the-only-solution.

Thus, we see the disappearance of two complementary figures: the ingénue and the prostitute, old accessories that are now useless. There remains only a woman in search of herself in all forms of love, with a mix of ennui and anguished diligence, almost like a man. She is often just visiting, on vacation, or foreign, which means she doesn't have a family or a past, and she is curious, avid, available, and always on the go as well.[10] When she is a foreigner, she keeps her accent and struggles with her vocabulary. A whole new semantics of love is thus suggested. Facility with the body would appear to compensate for any language barriers. But no, in the end love is frequently discussed, and words are even more laden with meaning, seemingly reinvented when translated from an exotic mentality.

Films emphasize distance, so that communication is even more extraordinary and yet simultaneously simpler. The guttural 'Tu-es-une-belle-femme' (you-are-a-beautiful-woman) spoken by the Japanese man in *Hiroshima mon amour*, and the nasal 'ça a gazé?' (how did it go?) of the American woman in *À bout de souffle*, are brand new, justified by the thousands of kilometres that the woman has travelled to end up in this bed, speaking this dialogue, with this new identity of hers that she's crossed the world to find.

Notes

All notes by editor Ginette Vincendeau, except notes 3 and 10 by author Evelyne Sullerot

1. In the original version of this article, Sullerot's first name was Eve; however, as she is everywhere else credited as Evelyne, we adopted this better-known version.

2. The Study Center for Mass Communications, situated within the Ecole Pratique des Hautes Etudes (its full name), a prestigious graduate school, specialising in social sciences

3. Smythe, in the US, analysed characters who were 'indispensable to the action' of 86 television dramas, discovering that of the 476 people therein, two-thirds were men. A simple example that can be proven with many other references. Furthermore, in the comparative sample of 55 protagonists of non-NW films from 1958–1959, that we selected and analysed as representative of an average French production, this disparity remains: 36 male heroes and 19 heroines.

4. *Les Amants*, directed by Louis Malle, with dialogues by Louise de Vilmorin; *Hiroshima mon amour*, directed by Alain Resnais, with a script by Marguerite Duras.

5. *Les Bonnes femmes*, directed by Claude Chabrol.

6. *Ascenseur pour l'échafaud*, directed by Louis Malle; *Les Liaisons dangereuses*, directed by Roger Vadim; *À bout de souffle*, directed by Jean-Luc Godard; *Une fille pour l'été*, directed by Edouard Molinaro; *L'Eau à la bouche*, directed by Jacques Doniol-Valcroze, and *Les Jeux de l'amour*, directed by Philippe de Broca.

7. Le Bel âge, directed by Pierre Kast.

8. Term used by the writer André Gide to designate utterly unmotivated behaviour that defies routine, custom, and normal explanations.

9. *Les Quatre cents coups* (1959), directed by François Truffaut; *À double tour* (1959), directed by Claude Chabrol.

10. For example in *À bout de souffle*, *Les Dragueurs* (*Young Have No Morals*, 1959) directed by Jean-Pierre Mocky, *Hiroshima mon amour*, *L'Eau à la bouche*, *Le Bel âge*, *On n'enterre pas le dimanche* (*One Does not Bury Sunday*, 1960) directed by Michel Drach, *À double tour*, *Les Liaisons dangereuses*, *Sait-on jamais* (*No Sun in Venice*, 1957) directed by Roger Vadim.

Marie-Claire Ropars-Wuilleumier (sometimes called just 'Ropars') is famous as an eminent theoretician of film and literature. It is generally less well-known that for ten years, from 1958 to 1968, she was the film critic for the centre-left intellectual and literary journal *Esprit*. As a result, her work on the New Wave has not had the exposure it deserves.

Her article 'A cinematic language', published in *Esprit* in June 1960 is a remarkable exploration of what she sees as a revolutionary new film language emerging in New Wave films, concentrating on the work of Alain Resnais, Agnès Varda and Jean Rouch, the so-called 'Left-bank New Wave' and touching also on Robert Bresson and Jacques Tati. She discusses the changed relationship between speech, writing and film language, and defines New Wave modernity in the way it 'shows thought in action rather than events in motion', while offering a sophisticated analysis of the preeminent role of time and space in the films under consideration. In this respect, this piece is an important theoretical contribution to the thinking on the New Wave as part of post-war modernist cinema, and it anticipates the concerns of the philosopher Gilles Deleuze in his book *The Time Image* (1985).

Ginette Vincendeau

13 A Cinematographic Language

MARIE-CLAIRE ROPARS-WUILLEUMIER
(1960)*

A chance encounter, love at first sight, the radical impossibility to live together or apart, is that the story of *Les Amants* or *Hiroshima mon amour*?[1] Alain Resnais's basic theme does not appear more revolutionary than that of Louis Malle, and a technical analysis of the films would not help any further in solving this question. Resnais and Malle sufficiently master their craft for their films to be seen as more than a demonstration of virtuosity or the affirmation of formal principles. The era of style manifestos has been and gone, and the same goes for controversies over editing, decoupage and depth of field; modes of expression have become standardised, a certain type of '*écriture*'[2] today seems to have become the norm in the cinema. And yet, it would be hard to find two types of filmmaking more different from each other than those of Resnais and Malle; the difference however is not to do with a school, a wave or principles, but with language. From *écriture* to language, we move from a technique to an aesthetic, from an instrument to significance. And insofar as cinematic language in Resnais, Jean Rouch or Agnès Varda challenges classic narrative frameworks, it entails a new vision of people in the world. It is on this level that a certain mental kinship between such different filmmakers may be found.

Through their clear-sighted and cruel gaze at friendship, love or childhood, Claude Chabrol, Malle or François Truffaut may well try to achieve a filmic humanism, but this novelty belongs to morality rather than aesthetics. This is because their conception is rooted in the logical unfolding of a clearly situated action, and their characters, while they appear contemporary, are still controlled by the laws of classic psychology: archaeologist or society woman, dandy, graduate student or abandoned child, they have a well-defined personality, however com-

---

* *Esprit*, Nouvelle Série, No. 285 [6], June 1960, pp. 960–67. (Translated from the French by Ginette Vincendeau)

plex it may be, they belong to a social milieu, and they live through precise and dramatic events, within a specific time and space.

On the other hand, the language of Resnais, Varda or Rouch, like that of Jacques Tati or Robert Bresson before them, exists on a different level from drama, it goes beyond action or events. We do not see the protagonists of *Hiroshima mon amour* meet, separate or accomplish anything; Resnais himself says that at the editing stage he systematically removed anything connected to the plot and kept only details. This is why, to interpret the film in terms of the literal unfolding of the narrative can only lead to misinterpretation: the love story in *Hiroshima* is of no interest. Similarly, the couple in *La Pointe Courte*[3] are not having a relationship, they are merely performing dialogue through a landscape: 'I don't like telling a story,' writes Varda, 'but rather what happens in between the important moments in a story: what Antonioni does in filming weak time. I would like to explore the moments nobody expects anything from but which end up being more touching than others.' Weak time, *temps morts*, what matters is the 'in between', the moments that stretch through time and remain unfinished, like the interminable separation in *Hiroshima mon amour*, 16 hours of time to kill, during which the man and the woman wander through the city – a waiting room, a café, the banks of the river –, separate and find each other again, without rhyme or reason. A few sequences in *Les Quatre cents coups* or *La Tête contre les murs*[4] give an idea of this kind of time stretching, this inconclusiveness: witness the long flight of the child in the former or of the young man in the latter, which lead nowhere. But what constitutes just a moment in Georges Franju or Truffaut's films becomes the core of Resnais and Varda's universe – it is in fact symptomatic that we can talk of a 'universe' after just one feature film. There is no Chabrol or Malle universe, they just tell stories. Neither *La Pointe Courte* nor *Hiroshima mon amour* tells a story; they simply show two characters permeated by time and space, overwhelmed by the world which, in a classical drama, would function merely as a framework but which here, invades the characters and shatters them.

'If you were to break people open, you would also find landscapes' (Agnès Varda). Inside the husband in *La Pointe Courte*, there is first of all a fishing village; inside the Japanese man in *Hiroshima mon amour* there is Hiroshima, inside the French woman the city of Nevers. Characters are no longer situated in a social milieu but in a landscape – such as the fish and dead cats, the burning sun, that echo the collapse of the couple, the two lovers looking for each other through Hiroshima destroyed and Hiroshima rebuilt. The landscape becomes a visual counterpoint, or even an obsession: the Japanese man keeps saying, 'You saw nothing in Hiroshima', but he has never seen Nevers. Nevers, Hiroshima, two sides of history, one derisory and the other massive, their reflections contrasting

Eiji Okada (left) and Emmanuelle Riva in *Hiroshima mon amour* (1959).

each other. In the end, what matters in *Hiroshima mon amour* is neither love nor Hiroshima, but the connection between the two, the fact that the city 'is made for love', a love that stretches along interminable walks, just as in *La Pointe Courte* the couple walk slowly through the village in search of themselves, or that in *Moi un noir*,[5] Robinson finds himself in his own dreams through the streets of Abidjan.

The landscape is no longer the frame for the action but the site where characters both find and lose themselves; for this foregrounding of space is accompanied by a temporal deepening: time is at the core of Resnais, Varda and Tati's films – not the relentless time that rushes past but on the contrary immobile time (that of M. Hulot[6]) or the time that has already passed (*Hiroshima*). Only landscape can materialise the temporal dimension of 'memory still present in action': the images of Nevers that erupt suddenly in the middle of Hiroshima are the spatial sign of memory, just like the village of *La Pointe Courte* signifies childhood. The present disappears under the invasion of the past, and in the world of *Hiroshima* or *La Pointe Courte*, like that of Robinson or Hulot, it is impossible to live in the present. 'Why deny the evident necessity of memory?'. The woman in *Hiroshima* destroys her love in the present with the memory of her love in the past, at the same time as she betrays that youthful affair with a German soldier by bringing it up in, and associating it with, Hiroshima.

Silvia Monfort (left) and Philippe Noiret (right) in *La Pointe Courte* (1954).

As she narrates her Nevers story, she evokes her past experience in the present tense, and speaking of the German soldier she addresses her Japanese lover: 'I am beginning to remember you less well'. In Hiroshima, as in love, it is impossible to forget, and memories invade even the future: 'when I have forgotten you, says the Japanese man, I will remember you like the forgetting of love itself'. The past vanishes, the present is hollowed out, the future does not exist.

Through this extraordinary confusion of moments, places and characters, time dissolves completely in space, while space becomes both the visual sign of the past and the place where the present elongates and melts away. For the couple of *La Pointe Courte*, the present is devoured by the past, in the same way as Hulot has no memory: time is dissolved at the point it meets the real world, it has become just space, streets, roads, a village, a beach where everything seems to spread out and stand still in long, silent, static shots.

The confused time frames and hybrid spaces of these films gradually construct a haunting universe in which the key issue is not to confront characters with a drama but, in Varda's words, 'to unravel the connections between a man and the world'. The *Hiroshima mon amour* couple, like the one in *La Pointe Courte*, is anonymous, classless, borderless sometimes, situated in a landscape rather than a milieu; they are free and their own masters, and yet unable to live freely (Who are we? Where do we come from? Where are we going?). Resnais, Varda and Rouch's characters define themselves as 'anti-heroes'. They are not people coming to terms with their destiny, but are rootless and foreign to the world; and the visual presence of this world, the constant weight of time and space, underlines how estranged they are from it. The question in *Hiroshima mon amour* is not love but the possibility to exist, the possibility to live in the moment, to escape the endless destruction of the present by memory, and of memory by the present. A profound connection between Hiroshima and love then exists: there is of course no comparison between the German or Japanese love affairs and the death of Hiroshima, yet in both cases memory is destructive and necessary at the same time. The city, like the woman, has disintegrated – and here maybe lies the meaning of the opening shots of the film, the burnt flesh and the smooth flesh, the passage 'from skin as source of extreme pain to skin as source of extreme pleasure'.

The uprooting of Robinson, *Moi un noir*'s Nigerian in Treichville (Abidjan), the disintegration of the couple in *La Pointe Courte*, the collapse of the woman in *Hiroshima mon amour* (where the man is merely a spectator), the theme is always the same: people in search of themselves who lose themselves in the process; they evaporate in time and merge with the landscape, until the present time is just a smooth and empty space. This is the external space of Michelangelo Antonioni[7] and Tati, where the physical presence of the characters and of the world corresponds to a spiritual void. This space by contrast becomes internal in Resnais and Bresson's films, through speech.

For Bresson and Resnais, indeed, speech enables the search for the self. Bresson may use the cinema as a form of *écriture* (writing), while Resnais tries to suggest the equivalent of *lecture* (reading) on screen, the difference between the two is only a question of point of view. The former insists on the creative process, the latter on the role of the spectator, but their field of exploration remains the same. Across immobile faces and through speech they both try to evoke a sense of inner duration that is close to meditation, very distinct from dramatic time. But here end the similarities between Bresson and Resnais, since they concern process rather than meaning. The inner quest of Bresson's hero in *Un condamné à mort s'est échappé/A Man Escaped*[8] ends with the certainty of liberation, of a victory over destiny. For the couple of *Hiroshima* however there is no fate other than to exist; their encounter's only outcome is the uncertainty of their final hours together, when time stretches without coming to an end. If Bresson's film has the classical beauty of a Racine tragedy, it is because for him speech, like the image, remains subjected to an inner meaning, it is primarily the sign of a spiritual presence. For Resnais, on the contrary, speech oddly plays the same role as silence in Tati's films:

in their different ways, both try to suggest a worldly abstraction, characters merging with the surface of the world where they live. Silence destroys Hulot's universe, speech destroys that of *Hiroshima*. Existential problems are echoed by difficulties in expressing oneself and there remains two options: silence or incantation[9]. Tati's characters lose themselves in silence, those of Resnais – like the Knight in *The Seventh Seal*[10] (though Ingmar Bergman's quest remains dramatic) – struggle with speech, which constitutes both their downfall and their last chance to find themselves. Speech for Bresson and Resnais is never simply the functional expression of a situation; but in Bresson it embodies an inner truth, whereas for Resnais it acts like incantation to describe a condition.

Incantation is the only term that can exonerate Resnais from the 'crime' of literature. Going beyond the obsession with the 'theatrical', he uses speech in an audacious way, but the dialogue of *Hiroshima* (unlike that of *Les Amants*) remains authentic insofar as, while it does not always fit the images, its lyrical tone echoes the musical structure of the film. As the author of the dialogue Marguerite Duras[11] put it, 'The text is the verbal equivalent of the images, like an exaltation of the images to come'. The point is correspondence and harmony, not expression or translation: images, like speech or rather voices, are variations on the same theme, and one cannot exist without the other. From this musical perspective, speech runs along scales, like singing, and goes from simple modulation to the most exalted lyricism ('I am going to stay in Hiroshima', 'I think I love you', 'impossible to leave you'); only through these different tonalities can the shifting complexity of the character's quest be suggested. Just like Mother Courage sings the song of Capitulation[12], the woman in *Hiroshima* 'sings' the song of contradiction, the central theme of the film: 'I meet you, I remember you. You are killing me, you are doing me good'. The incantatory effect produced by endless repetitions alone can translate the obsession with time: 'Like you, I know forgetting. Like you I have a memory. Like you I have forgotten. Like you I fought against the horror of not understanding any more the reason for remembering'. It is not pure coincidence if the language of Marguerite Duras resembles the spontaneous poetry of Robinson's commentary as he watches the film of his life go by, spoken and intoned, monotonously and repetitively, about his past, his hopes and his disappointments: 'I did everything men are supposed to do, but it doesn't matter, I am still the same... I am brave – I am a man — I have nothing, I am poor. I am poor but still I am brave. All this is nothing, Petit Jules, let's go home. Everything depends on God. Everything is God'. Robinson, too, 'sings' his song of contradiction.

Why these similarities? Because the lyrical language and recitative tone indicate that the characters achieve self-discovery; in turn, they find, destroy and liberate themselves through the incantation of words. This verbal counterpoint enables

Robinson in *Moi un noir*, the woman in *Hiroshima mon amour* and the couple in *La Pointe Courte* to detach themselves from their lives and contemplate themselves with lucidity, the only achievement and the only salvation in a world in which characters are 'mired' and run the risk of vanishing in the flow of images. In Resnais' words, these are 'characters who adopt a tone of lyrical recitation, plan their gestures but try to preserve the truth in their hearts, and who can appear, depending on the text and the moment, authentic or mythical'. Keeping ambiguity at the heart of truth is the only way to make it meaningful. However, the only possibility of reaching this lucidity is to keep a distance, because, if words express the truth, only formal narration can enable characters to access it. This is why the films of Resnais and Rouch, as well as those of Bresson, work on two levels. To the eye of the camera, acting as an impersonal witness, is added the narration of characters who relive their past; the ambiguity resides in the contamination between the two. The passage from drama to narration produces not just a new film language, but also a new meaning, that of a universe in which characters cannot exist, but like Robinson, can only replay their life and watch themselves live it.

To show thought in motion rather than events in action, to look for the spatial and temporal depths of a world in which people feel the very basis of their lives being questioned, to express through a verbal flow the ambiguity of duration, is this not in the end the challenge to representation already attempted by novelists such as William Faulkner, Virginia Woolf and Marcel Proust? Oddly, it seems that a whole sector of contemporary cinema is taking up the baton from the novel, while, by contrast, the novel[13] is trying to borrow techniques from film. Why this exchange? The answer is that the novelist's ideal is to reach absolute objectivity, to remove, from the space between the work and reality, the distorting mirror of the writer's conscience or style – isn't all writing subjective? About Alain Robbe-Grillet, Roland Barthes wrote that the novel 'teaches us to look at the world no longer with the eyes of a confessor, a physician, or of God – all significant hypostases of the classical novelist – but with the eyes of a man walking in his city with no other horizon than the spectacle before him, no other power than that of his own eyes.'[14] The gaze of a man walking through a city, the painstaking analysis of every detail of concrete reality, the refusal of style which now retreats into geometric precision, nothing apparently distinguishes the novelist from a camera. This systematic withdrawal of the novelist's intervention is the last stage in his or her self-renunciation in the face of reality. For the cinema, however, objective reality is an obstacle, and if film borrows language from the novel, it is in order to explore the inner duration that seemed blocked by the concreteness of the image. So that in the eyes of the novelist the purest truth can only be found, if at all, in photography, whereas for the filmmaker truth becomes more profound if the image appears, primarily, as a subjective vision. What the former wants to reject the latter tries to conquer. But the withdrawal of the novelist, and thus of a subjective conscience, cannot be absolute: the gaze, in *La Jalousie*,[15] is not that of a camera but of a jealous individual – indeed this is the beauty of the novel. This is why the cinema, by taking on board the ambiguity of language together with the accuracy of images seems closer to the truth, and it is no coincidence that writers such as Jean Cayrol and Marguerite Duras seek new forms of expression in the cinema; this may enable them to combine the concrete presence of the world and the vision of uprooted individuals confronted with this world, and whose only salvation is lucidity.

Whatever judgment we may pass on these contradictory endeavours, they suggest similar anxieties. If the novel and the cinema have recourse, as a last resort, to techniques that are not natural to them, it is because they are forced to do so through feelings of uneasiness: both engage with a world in which human beings feel both estranged and compromised. Absence in the novel and speech in the cinema tragically bear witness to this contradiction.

Notes

All notes by editor Ginette Vincendeau

1. *Les Amants/The Lovers* (Louis Malle, 1958); *Hiroshima mon amour* (Alain Resnais, 1959).
2. The French word *écriture*, which means literally writing, has been kept here to indicate Ropars-Wuilleumier's use of the term, closer to 'style', which amalgamates the literary and the filmic.
3. *La Pointe Courte* (Agnès Varda, 1954).
4. *Les Quatre cents coups/The 400 Blows* (François Truffaut, 1959); *La Tête contre les murs/The Keepers* (Georges Franju, 1959).
5. *Moi, un noir/I, a Negro* (Jean Rouch, 1957).
6. Ropars-Wuilleumier refers to the character Monsieur Hulot, played by Jacques Tati in *Les Vacances de Monsieur Hulot/Mr Hulot's Holiday* (1953) and *Mon oncle* (1958), both also directed by Tati.
7. Ropars-Wuilleumier does not specify wich films by Antonioni, but writing in 1960 it is likely she is referring to *Il grido* (1957) and *L'Avventura* (1960) which was shown at the Cannes festival in May, a month before the publication of this piece.
8. In *Un condamné à mort s'est échappé/A Man Escaped* (Robert Bresson, 1956), the hero is a member of the Resistance who escapes from a Nazi jail during the German occupation of France.
9. 'Chant' in French means 'singing', but as the point is developed, it is clear that the author is referring to the incantatory nature of the verbal delivery by the actors, who do not sing. Thus the word 'incantation' is more appropriate.

10. *Det sjunde inseglet/The Seventh Seal* (Ingmar Bergman, 1957).

11. The novelist Marguerite Duras wrote the script and dialogues of *Hiroshima mon amour*.

12. The heroine of Bertold Brecht's play of Mother Courage and her Children/*Mutter Courage und ihre Kinder* (1939).

13. Although there is no mention of the *Nouveau roman* (New Novel) in the article, Ropars-Wuilleumier is clearly referring to this movement in French literature of the 1950s and 1960s – confirmed by the reference to Alain Robbe-Grillet further down, one of the leading figures in the *nouveau roman*.

14. In Roland Barthes, *Critical Essays* (Evanston: Northwestern University Press, 1972), translated from the French by Richard Howard, p. 24.

15. *La Jalousie*, a novel by Alain Robbe-Griller (1957).

The importance of Michèle Firk cannot be underestimated and yet she is relatively unknown outside France. Firk was one of the few regular female critics writing in major film journals at the time (*Positif* in particular), as well as an intensely political figure, involved in anti-colonial struggles. The short pieces here are a sample of the many she wrote. The first is an early analysis of three 'tragic' female characters published in 1957: Livia in Luchino Visconti's *Senso* (1954); Maria in Joseph Mankiewicz's *The Barefoot Contessa* (1954); Lola in Max Ophüls' *Lola Montès* (1955), which she compares in terms of the cinema's penchant for the victimisation of beautiful women. The second piece, published in 1958, is a review of Chris Marker's film *Lettre de Sibérie* (a 'Left-Bank' New Wave filmmaker not yet represented in this book). The third is a poignant letter she wrote to her fellow film critics at *Positif* in 1967, before joining the Revolutionary Armed Forces (FAR) in Guatemala, fully aware that it would mean risking her life. In the letter, she denounces the 'armchair revolutionaries' in Europe. In Guatemala, she took part in the kidnapping of the American ambassador and soon afterwards, just as she was about to be arrested by the Guatemalan police, she shot herself to avoid falling into their hands.

Ginette Vincendeau

14 Three Pieces by Michèle Firk

MICHÈLE FIRK (1957, 1958, 1967)

Three Tragic Heroines: Livia, Maria, Lola*

Women often make for the greatest tragic characters, because they are more demanding than men in their quest for the absolute, thus finding happiness creates problems for them that are rarely resolved.

Following in the footsteps of theatre, then the novel, it seems that it is now cinema's turn to offer women the ideal way to express their suffering. As proof, I only need to point to three of the most recent cinematic masterpieces: in *Senso* (1954) by Luchino Visconti (Italian), *The Barefoot Contessa* (1954) by Joseph Mankiewicz (American) and *Lola Montès* (1955) by Max Ophüls (French), the display of suffering is virtually the main goal.

Livia, Maria, Lola: three beautiful, desirable, intelligent, and sensitive women, who seem destined to be happy – the kind of women we envy. However, their lives will only be a series of disappointments, which will eventually end in a final, irreparable, definitive failure. For all three, even though they live in different eras, different social milieus, and in different contexts, the cause of this failure is always the same: the impossibility of acting upon their closely-held values in a corrupt society, the impossibility of meeting a man who knows to look beyond their appearance and thus love them selflessly. In a nutshell, the world's inability to face up to women it doesn't understand.

Livia, the Countess Serpieri (in *Senso*), is very different from the other two, and closer to a Stendhal heroine. She is a young woman from the 19th Century Italian nobility, married, in all likelihood, without ever having been asked her opinion, to a man who is old enough to be her father. She has therefore never had the opportunity to question her situation and she lives in a semi-lethargic state, meaning she doesn't suffer. She is, in Willy Acher's words,[1] an 'un-awakened' woman, with only a superficial life, satisfying her implicit yearning for idealism through her equally superficial patriotism. It is only once she becomes conscious of herself that she starts to suffer, and earns the epithet of tragic heroine. And, as her newfound

---

* *Bulletin du CCU*, 14 March 1957. (Translated from the French by Jennifer Wallace)

Alida Valli (left) and Farley Granger in *Senso* (1954).

consciousness is all the more powerful for coming late, Livia throws herself into making up for lost time, and gives herself body and soul to the man who awakened her. But she does this so wholeheartedly, so frenziedly, that she will not be allowed a second chance. Which is why, when she realises that she has been humiliated, has betrayed her friends and suffered for something that was not worth it and didn't even exist, all she can do is destroy her lover (by denouncing him as a deserter) and destroy herself in the process. She goes mad with grief.

Peter Ustinov (left) and Martine Carol (middle) in *Lola Montès* (1955).

However, Visconti's Marxist approach which connects the Countess Serpieri's dreadful unravelling to the finals days of a decadent, doomed aristocracy, means that his film is not as desperate as those by Ophüls and Mankiewicz.

Lola (Montès) could have become a sort of Countess Serpieri if she hadn't resisted marrying the old man that her mother chose for her. But, she is a strong-willed, middle-aged woman who wants to be happy. As she is too pure to make any concessions, she rebels and declares war on society by embarking on a 'scandal-ous' life. Yet, if her husband had been worthy of it, her first love could have been her only love. Lola is all of a piece: she gives herself completely without a second thought, but she is also capable of picking herself up and starting again when she thinks she's been wrong, or someone has wronged her. She is always honest and always frank (for example, her reaction when she learns that the conductor she loves is married). But she cannot play this dangerous game with impunity. Each experience leaves Lola more and more weary. The constant wear and tear leaves her depleted, because of how fully she gives herself. Then, when she finally thinks she has found security and happiness in a bourgeois relationship with the old and

Ava Gardner (left) and Humphrey Bogart (right) in The Barefoot Contessa (1954).

whimsical king of Bavaria, society and fate – out of jealousy – take their vengeance and destroy them. Lola, the tragic heroine, was not made to be happy. At the end of her tether, exhausted, she cannot start again ('something is broken within me', she says). She has become a kind of puppet, incapable of reacting, and she can only, in a pathetic echo of herself, re-enact old gestures in a hellish circus, itself a pathetic echo of her past… The ringmaster is perhaps the only person who understands what she truly represents; he loves her and destroys her at the same time.

Lola is ruined for not wanting to cheat. Lola is chastised for wanting to be free.

Maria Vargas, the 'barefoot Contessa', remains more mysterious, because everything we learn about her comes from testimonies and memories of unknown origin (*Senso* was written in the objective-subjective tone of Stendhal or Flaubert, whereas *Lola Montès* is entirely in the first person, as Lola mentally relives moments from her past).

A sort of modern Lamiel[2], Maria gives her body to a lot of men, but she says it's 'a sickness': a physical need that doesn't affect her fundamental purity. Besides, she only gives herself to simple and hearty men (gypsies and servants…) and she refuses, horrified, the advances of men who are rich and corrupt…those who pay, those who want to buy her. Like Lola, she wants to be free, and she only superficially gives her body to others. Maria waits and vehemently protects her heart and her rich interiority. Only two men are worthy of her, but, in a cruel twist of fate, she only feels friendship for the first man, and the second, whom she loves completely, is unable to satisfy her physically. She suffers more than Lola or Livia, because she will never know the relief of giving herself entirely, even just briefly, to one man. The denouement for her is the most brutal: torn between the desires of the flesh and the heart, Maria dies for having tried to bring the two together with a ruse, the first in her life.

Tragic heroines are rare and precious: the ability to suffer is a gift, and only the few who possess this gift can bestow dignity upon mankind.

* * *

Lettre de Sibérie (**Letter from Siberia, Chris Marker, 1958**)[*]

When we watch a documentary, we are subjected to either folky '*cinémas-copades*'[3] with costumes and accessories generously distributed by Fox studios (amongst others), or serious, irreproachable studies, with statistical references provided by scholarly institutes. And so, viewers have come to the conclusion that a geo-cinematographic documentary is either imbecilic or boring, and that we are obliged to swallow it passively between newsreels, ice-cream, and hair gel adverts, before we are eventually allowed some Sofia [sic] Loren or Fernandel.

Yet, for a few years now, this well-established notion has been increasingly in need of revision. As a matter of fact, a number of young directors are no longer making documentaries as if it was a chore – they are making them with love. Furthermore, they are imprinting their unique style onto them, which makes the genre almost as unlimited in scope as the thriller.[4] It is impossible to confuse the works of Jacques Dupont with those of Jean Rouch, or Bernard Taisant with François Reichenbach, just as, for example, we never confuse Bresson with Hitchcock.

Down with objectivity! It claims to be scientific, but it fails to conceal behind its hypocritical and impersonal tone, the dull impotence and dishonesty of certain directors.

These young documentarists are not objective: they speak in the first person. Reichenbach gave us his 'impressions' from America[5], and Chris Marker, after

---

[*] *Cinéma 58*, No. 32, December 1958, pp. 111–13. (Translated from the French by Jennifer Wallace)

having spent a *Dimanche à Pekin* (*Sunday in Peking*, 1956), sends us a long *Lettre de Sibérie* (*Letter from Siberia*, 1958). 'I am writing to you from a far-off country...', 'I am writing to you from the end of the world...' Only the phrasing is borrowed from Michaux[6] but the 'I' who is talking is Chris Marker, and, if any film deserves the label of an 'auteur film', it's this one. The rare pleasure we feel when we read Madame de Sévigné's letters[7] is very difficult to translate onto the screen. But my goodness! Perhaps Marker has succeeded in making the first epistolary film. And the miracle is even more impressive considering it's a full-length film: if we magnanimously ignore Disney and the Italians, *Le Monde du silence* (*The Silent World*, 1956)[8] is still, to this day, the only successful feature-length documentary.

And Marker, for an hour and a half, leads us through a tumbling torrent of observations, of impressions that rush past or suddenly warrant a pause, of non-sequiturs that follow his ever-fluctuating train of thought, with forward and backward leaps through time and space. Thank god, there is no structure in the traditional Cartesian sense, the kind that's demanded in essays for French class and philosophy dissertations. Marker displays all the lack of discipline and extreme brilliance of the gifted schoolboy who makes his teacher fearful of losing his scholarly authority and of a bad influence on the dunces. The teacher isn't wrong, because not everybody is gifted enough to handle fireworks (Hulot[9] taught us that). And anyone who tries to follow in Marker's footsteps and produce an animation film about 'the mammoth... the mammoth...' or to the glory of the reindeer; or pause to follow the sexual antics of a short-haired bear; or suddenly, good-naturedly mock Bernard Buffet[10]; or invent dreamlike newsreels; or observe the strange ballet of monstrous cranes: these people seriously risk making fools of themselves. Chris Marker seems to be constantly improvising and spontaneously composing his letter – with his pen (sorry, his camera), but this insouciance hides much real art.

We are told that this film is the first shot by a foreigner on Siberian soil. There is always something awkward about people writing about or filming 'what-goes-on-behind-the-iron-curtain.' It's hard to tell the difference between *En liberté sur les routes d'URSS* (1957)[11] and an ode to Stakhanovism. By contrast, in a section of *Lettre de Sibérie* dedicated to the little town of Yakutsk, we see the same shots in sequence, repeated three times: the only things that change are the commentary and the light. Through the persuasive voice of the narrator, we find the same image of a banal bus, either miserable, luxurious, or uninteresting. It all depends on whether we look at it with soviet-phobic eyes, soviet-loving eyes, or 'objective' eyes. But we also understand that the real truth lies in a fourth way, which consists of looking at people as they are, not as abstract things that are conduits for conventional ideas...or politics.

The tone is of a very personal sense of humour, a little in the style of Queneau[12]. Ironic but not scathing. Besides, this irony must hide a certain tenderness, since it provokes a desire to run to Siberia as soon as we exit the cinema…The ironic tone is also prepared to turn on itself: 'Our irony is perhaps more naïve than their enthusiasm', the voice-over states at one point, in response to the pride that the villagers feel for their modern installations. Irony is only a tone after all – something akin to a discreet stylistic clause – as sentimentality is more fatal than ridicule in our world, and especially because this is in Chris Marker's nature.

I am a bit worried that the sparkling commentary showcased by the beautiful voice of Georges Rouquier, which always narrates a little ahead the images, goes beyond them and grants them a more profound significance, might also be going over the heads of some spectators who are used to falling asleep in their seats.

And as this 'letter' is full of surprises, Chris Marker and Sacha Vierny shot remarkable Eastmancolor images (keeping in mind that they recorded in 16mm that was blown up afterwards), interrupted from time to time by sequences in black and white (for example, the mammoths), or even in inverted black and white taken from coloured negatives (the imaginary newsreel). This enables them to obtain unusual, yet essential effects which help make this film what I have wanted to call it since the beginning: a cinematographic poem. Some grumpy critic might note that, with the exception of the popular Russian songs, the music (by Pierre Barbaud) is inferior to everything else and seems to come straight out of a John Ford film, but this is beside the point.

If you want to know the figures for the population of Siberia, the results of the recent Five-Year Plans, and the average salary of a gold miner: don't read this 'letter'. If you're looking for information on the hellish world of the Bolshevik, the sad life of the kolkhozes, or the misfortunes of Boris Pasternak: don't even glance at it. But if you like birch forests, little beavers, wide-open, frozen horizons, and the memory of Michel Strogoff[13] in Irkutsk; and if, with understanding and camaraderie, you want to bond with people who roll their r's, have slanting eyes, and wide smiles that centuries have imbued with wisdom, and whose modern lifestyles contradict their beliefs and legends: then read and reread this *Lettre de Sibérie.*

* * *

Dear Comrades (A letter to fellow critics at *Positif*)*

I am leaving you this letter because, in case I forgot, the 'Debray Affair'[14] is here to teach us to what extent we must remain vigilant when we choose to give ourselves over entirely, until the bitter end, to the anti-imperialist fight. When the facts are as plain as day, the bourgeoisie strives to distort their meaning so as to limit their impact. They bring the ideas into their own territory so as to better denounce them – as far away as possible from politics.

The Extreme Right have branded Régis [Debray] a traitor to his class and to his country. The *grande bourgeoisie*, more cunningly and hypocritically, are content with reducing him to the figure of a young male dreamer: generous, Quixotic,

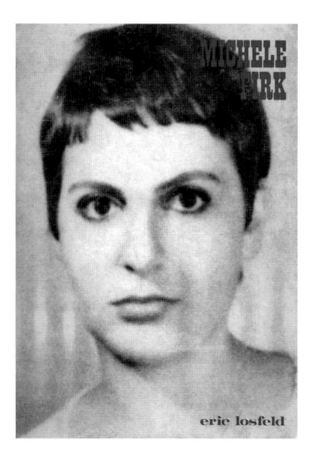

Michèle Firk.

eric losfeld

---

* *Positif*, 17 May 1967, reprinted in *Michèle Firk, écrits réunis par ses camarades*, Eric Losfeld, 1969. (Translated from the French by Jennifer Wallace)

Christ-like – a bit mad perhaps – but essentially redeemable tomorrow, even if they have to keep a close eye on him. Nothing of the sort is in store for me, as I represent everything that terrifies them: shifting terrain, insecurity, instability, 'a-sociability'. This will make it even easier to condemn me on account of my suspicious appetite for 'adventures' and the 'Third World', to make everyone forget that this is, above all, a political fight. Nothing is more important than the fight against the imperialist enemy, because we are surrounded by it, it threatens us, and we cannot choose not to take sides. It is not shameful to make the revolutionary fight the axis of your existence, around which everything else fades in importance, quite the opposite. What is shameful, is to talk about Vietnam with your toes in the sand, without changing anything in your life. To talk about guerrillas in Latin America like the latest Johnny Hallyday concert tour. What is shameful, is to be 'objectively informed', which really means keeping your distance and never taking part. We are citizens of the world and the world is vast: whether it is here or there, it doesn't matter, there is no geographical fatalism. My means are limited and paltry. However, I have put them all into this combat, and I will fight to the death for my convictions in the name of 'Che', Fidel, and the Vietnamese people, which nobody has the right to take away from me. In the fight against American imperialism, all the battle fields are glorious. Even though glory is what we seek the least.

Dear comrades, do not let them turn me into something other than what I am, and what I wish to be: a revolutionary fighter.

As 'Che' says: 'until the everlasting victory, always!'

Notes

All notes by editor Ginette Vincendeau – except Note 4, by author Michèle Firk.

1. Willy Acher, 'Pour saluer Visconti', *Cahiers du cinéma*, no. 57, March 1956, p. 4.
2. Lamiel is the heroine of Stendhal's last, unfinished, novel, published in 1889.
3. Firk is making a pun on 'cinemascope' and 'escapade', referring to the lavishly shot touristic documentaries on distant lands that were shown before main features in cinemas in the 1950s.
4. I'm limiting myself strictly to current French documentaries and putting to one side the question of the drama-documentary.
5. By 1958, François Reichenbach had made 16 documentary shorts, including several on various aspects of the USA.
6. The quotes are from a poem written by Henri Michaux in 1938, entitled *Je vous écris d'un pays lointain* (*I Am Writing To You From A Far Off Country*).
7. The Marquise de Sévigné (1626–1696), one of the most famous French writers of the 17th century, is known for her witty and affectionate letters to her daughter.
8. *Le Monde du silence* is a documentary about exploring the depths of the ocean, directed by Louis Malle and Jacques Cousteau.
9. Monsieur Hulot is the maverick and accident-prone hero of Jacques Tati's films such as *Les Vacances de Monsieur Hulot* (*Mr Hulot's Holidays*), 1953, and *Playtime*, 1967.
10. Bernard Buffet was a fashionable painter at the time.
11. *En liberté sur les routes d'URSS* (['Freedom on USSR roads']1957) was directed by Dominique Lapierre and Jean-Pierre Pedrazzini.
12. Raymond Queneau (1903–1976), a former Surrealist, poet and novelist, known for his wit and play with language. His biggest success was his novel *Zazie dans le métro*, published after Firk's review was written.
13. *Michel Strogoff* is the fictional hero of an adventure novel written by Jules Verne, published in 1876, and set in Siberia.
14. Régis Debray (born 1940) is a French philosopher and intellectual. In the late 1960s he was committed to anti-Americanism and close to Fidel Castro and Che Guevara. A month before Firk's letter, in April 1967, he accompanied Guevara on his last trip to Bolivia and was imprisoned for aiding insurrection, and allegedly tortured by the CIA. He was released in 1970.

Marie-Claire Ropars-Wuilleumier's excellent review of one of the canonical films of the New Wave, François Truffaut's *Les Quatre cents coups*, was published in *Esprit* in July-August 1959. It is a welcome addition to the literature on this film. Among other things Ropars-Wuilleumier astutely articulates the film's quasi-documentary style with the attempt to create the subjectivity of the 13-year old hero. As she points out, 'the camera is ceaselessly complicit with Antoine; just as the adult world is viewed from the outside, Antoine and René are evoked from the inside', noting that the film oscillates 'between two styles – quick shots that copy reality, and tracking shots that sympathise with it.' (in her 'Cinematographic language' piece also in this section, Ropars-Wuilleumier discusses the ending of the film in terms of its deployment of time and space).

Ginette Vincendeau

15 *Les Quatre cents coups* [1]

MARIE-CLAIRE ROPARS-WUILLEUMIER (1959)*

*L*es Quatre cents coups (*The 400 Blows*) tells the story of an unloved child who runs wild in the streets and is sent to a detention centre by his parents: this could be a melodrama à la Delannoy or a film about childhood delinquency in the style of Cayatte.[2] *Les Quatre cents coups* is something quite different: Truffaut says it is a chronicle of the thirteenth year. A chronicle, in other words, is an objective depiction of a series of events that leaves the reader or spectator free to reconstruct the universe and draw conclusions. The word seems apt: Truffaut never moralises nor does he pass explicit judgement. The spinelessness of the parents and their petty fights, and Antoine's incarceration at the detention centre, where we see him locked in a kind of cage and questioned, tested, recorded, judged, classified: this steady destruction of a human being is treated with the objective, rapid style of photographic snapshots. The camera is only there to record. And it is, to say the least, ironic that the film won the prize for *mise-en-scène* (Best Director) at Cannes, as many sequences underline a deliberate refusal of *mise-en-scène*. The static shots with grey, sombre lighting, attest to a documentary style over aesthetics. But the deployment of photographic impressionism here may be a sophisticated creative choice. Little by little, the refusal to evoke sensitivity or pity, and the building of a linear, cold account of a world that isn't awful – just ugly and mediocre – creates an inhumane atmosphere. Antoine is not a 'child martyr', he is just a boy whose mother says to him every night 'Antoine, empty the bins', and on a day when she's feeling tender, 'don't forget to empty the bins, my dear'. A child that isn't physically abused, but is rejected nonetheless. Parents, policemen, judges and carers are not depicted as torturers, but as robots given over to indifference. And the callousness that is attributed to the adult world arises from being observed from the outside: the few scenes featuring only adults are those where Antoine's

---

* *Esprit*, No. 275, July–August 1959. (Translated from the French by Jennifer Wallace)

Jean-Pierre Léaud in *Les Quatre cents coups* (1959).

father and the police officer, or his mother and the judge, discuss various methods of imprisonment.

Perhaps the key to this apparent objectivity is to be found in the interrogation scene, subjected upon Antoine by the psychologist, where he coldly and lucidly judges his parents and shows how well he understands them. If the camera, as it depicts the world of adults, is nothing more than a filmic lens, then this lens belongs to Antoine, a silent, stone-faced witness to his parent's arguments. But this objectivity is just a ruse. This view of the adult world, as realistic as it is, is analogous with Antoine's vision. In *Les Quatre cents coups* the camera is ceaselessly complicit with Antoine; just as the adult world is viewed from the outside, Antoine and René are evoked from the inside. This is unlike the marked distancing of the camera as seen in *Jeux interdits* (*Forbidden Games*), where the efforts of Clément[3] to recreate a child's universe ultimately destroy its authenticity. However, certain conversations between the two friends do not totally avoid the trap: Moussy[4], in his attempt to write dialogue that contains both the seriousness and pretentiousness of adolescence, sometimes puts the viewer in the position of the adult. But this ambiguity does not extend to the on-screen images; the language of the camera is that of adolescence itself, and the viewer is swept along immediately. On the surface, *Les Quatre cents coups* looks like the chronicle of a loveless world that treats children like strangers; but in the end it is also the story of a child who is a stranger in the world of men, who looks onto this world, but lives in another.

This alternate world is that of the thirteenth year, and it is not inhabited solely by Antoine and René. They are shown amongst their classmates of the same age: ink-stained dunces and snitching teacher's pets. And even if they have parents – not everybody can be an orphan as Poil de Carotte[5] would have said – school is still the centre of their universe. The chronicle of adolescence builds across incidental sequences which are scattered throughout the first part of the film, where nothing is just functional, and everything suggests the freedom of living: vertigo from a fairground rotor, chasing after a dog at night, stealing a typewriter or a bottle of milk, delirious, wild-eyed faces watching a puppet show or a film. A world where imagination is the only law, friendship is the only form of love, and the only rules are the rules of the game. A world where stealing is fun, and the death of someone is a made-up excuse or just a story. A world of unconscious freedom and mad dashes through the streets, and where the two friends are filmed in long tracking shots, as opposed to the still images of the adult world.

This struggle between two styles – quick shots that copy reality, and tracking shots that sympathise with it – incarnates Antoine's adventures: from his unconscious freedom to his conscious liberation, after his cruel imprisonment. His long journey inside the police car is shot as a panorama of Parisian streets at night. It is his last goodbye to freedom, and the only moment where he appears on the verge of tears. Afterwards, he enters the world of static images: fingerprints, a headshot against a white wall where he resembles a pinned insect – just as he was pinned by the fairground rotor – an interrogation, becoming an object in front of the camera, as he is now for the psychologist, or maybe for himself. It is only after he runs away, in a protracted race towards the sea, that he finds his freedom once more. But here Truffaut's film changes direction: if it refrained from drama by remaining true to its chronicle style, this is the moment it moves beyond that. Antoine's escape is swift and unnoticed, he finds a fortuitous moment to slip away that's not particularly spectacular. He is not pursued. He runs through the detention centre, then through fields and woods, and finally towards the sea. Running has changed in rhythm and meaning for Antoine: it is no longer a mad dash propelled by an irresistible force as when he ran through the streets of Paris. It is all-out and measured at the same time, intentional and perhaps desperate, unending and yet sustained, surprising, timeless, absolute. Is this freedom's last gasp before it dies? *Les Quatre cents coups* is not the kind of drama with a resolution, it is a snapshot of someone's existence. But a snapshot that risks being definitive. When Antoine arrives at the sea, he steps back and turns to the camera, and his face is replaced by a photo that freezes him before our eyes. The chronicle transforms into a tragedy. The word *fin* is etched onto his frozen face, taking on an ambiguous meaning. His freedom led him to the sea, but what lies beyond it? Even if he is not recaptured, this shot suggests that he has been compromised by the adult world, and there is something inexorable about this conclusion.

Only this last image allows for tragic hindsight. Throughout the film, the spectator, just like the camera, is made to be Antoine's accomplice. They both adopt his point of view on the world, and are denied pity and tenderness just as he is. But this shot, in separating Antoine from the spectator, makes one realise that a child can be suffocated by indifference from others, and that this suffocation possesses a tragic significance. Even if Truffaut's style is influenced by Vigo and Franju,[6] his originality lies with how he plays with appearances and points of view to create truthful emotion through the matter-of-factness of his testimonial. Ultimately, *Les Quatre cents coups* is a tragedy of the thirteenth year, because the tone of its chronicle evokes what it is like to be thirteen. Furthermore, if it looks so natural, it is because Truffaut often let his lead actor, Jean-Pierre Léaud, improvise based on his own experiences. For example, Antoine's answers to the psychologist's questions might have been scripted, but Léaud's smart and aloof tone, and his half-embarrassed, half-ingratiating smile, are real. The result of the collaboration between an adolescent on the cusp of adulthood and an adult who remembers his adolescence, *Les Quatre cents coups* is perhaps, fundamentally, an exorcism.

Notes

All notes by editor Ginette Vincendeau.

1. The film is spelt *Les 400 coups* in the original French text, a common erroneous spelling; the correct one has been restored here.

2. Ropars-Wuilleumier is alluding to Jean Delannoy's *Chiens perdus sans collier* (*The Little Rebels*, 1955), a mainstream melodrama about delinquent children. André Cayatte's *Avant le deluge* (*Before the Deluge*, 1954) also dealt with delinquent youth, in the didactic style Cayatte was known for.

3. René Clément's 1952 drama *Jeux interdits* (*Forbidden Games*) set during the German occupation, portrays two young children whose misdemeanours are contrasted with the cowardice and mendacity of the parents' generation.

4. Marcel Moussy, the adapter and dialogue-writer for the film.

5. Poil de Carotte is the young hero of Jules Renard's 1894 eponymous novel about a maltreated child, the victim of his mother's hatred and father's indifference; the novel was adapted to film several times.

6. Jean Vigo and Georges Franju both directed films about unhappy youth; respectively *Zéro de conduite*, 1933, and *La Tête contre les murs* (*The Keepers*), 1959.

Françoise Audé was one of a small band of female film critics working at *Positif* from the 1970s onwards, until her accidental death in 2005. Her book *Ciné-modèles cinéma d'elles,* published in 1981, was the first French-language examination of films about and by women from a feminist perspective. Although *The French New Wave, Critical Landmarks* is devoted to writing that was contemporary with the New Wave, we decided to include this piece because, although published in 1981, Audé in it discusses *Hiroshima mon amour,* one of the great New Wave classics, from her perspective as a woman spectator of 1959. As she puts it at the beginning of the article, 'I am only trying to explain, as close to my subjective point of view as possible, and as a spectator at the time, the shock of *Hiroshima mon amour* for me.'

Audé's text is not only personal but deeply political. In particular, she reads the film as a metaphor for France's unacknowledged guilt for its 'dirty war' in Algeria.

Ginette Vincendeau

16 The Heart and the Mind: *Hiroshima mon amour* [1]

FRANÇOISE AUDÉ (1959–81)*

Alain Resnais' *Hiroshima mon amour* (1959) is based on a script by Marguerite Duras. The film, which premiered 'out of competition' at Cannes in May 1959 (where it won the Fipresci prize and the Film Writers Award), was released in Parisian cinemas on June 10th. Initially, the producers (Dauman, Halfon, Lipschitz and Fouet)[2] wanted a documentary about the atomic bomb, but Chris Marker, with whom Resnais had begun to plan the project, found the idea to be impossible. Marguerite Duras and Alain Resnais agreed upon the notion that 'the main aim of the film was to have done with the description of horror by horror' (M. Duras).[3]

Consequently, *Hiroshima mon amour* was a passionate love story. My comments below are not meant as a retelling or an analysis of the film, which has already been done with great thoroughness and skill.[4] It is not necessary to go over the details as was the case for *Et Dieu… créa la femme* (*And God Created Woman*).[5] I am only trying to explain, as close to my subjective point of view as possible, and as a spectator at the time, the shock of *Hiroshima mon amour* for me.

'Elsewhere'

I remember what overwhelmed me, in 1959, in the provincial town of Dijon, where I first saw the film. Firstly, it was the situation: the miracle of this real, intense love between a woman and a man, who are utterly different from one another, in an absolute 'elsewhere'. That is, an elsewhere where everything is so alien, to the point that it would be absurd to use any notion of exoticism to understand it. An elsewhere related to melodrama, meaning it is cerebral rather than geographical, where the two lovers have 'broken ties' with their connections, their pasts, and

* Françoise Audé, *Ciné-modèles cinéma d'elles*, Lausanne: L'Âge d'homme, 1981, pp. 35–9. (Translated from the French by Jennifer Wallace)

they are new and pure for each other, because the magical place of their meeting has made it possible ...

It was also the limited duration, the tragic brevity of their union, a unique parenthesis within two lives – a parenthesis that is both closed in on itself, and open to changing times: the time before, the present time, and after.

I wasn't affected by the film because I felt a literal identification with the woman (played by Emmanuelle Riva), but because of a broader identification/projection with her starting hypothesis. The novelistic element, which is the least commented upon aspect of the film, is what swept me away/moved me. And I think this reaction is specific to women.

We know now – since *Le Camion* (*The Lorry*, 1977) – that Marguerite Duras lends her voice to her characters. *Hiroshima mon amour* was an Alain Resnais film, but within it we hear her words. At the time, I don't know if I was able to formulate my gratitude to Resnais for the service he was rendering her in bringing her the images and the language of cinema. I knew of *Nuit et brouillard* (*Night and Fog*, 1956), where, in much the same way, he gave Jean Cayrol's text its true significance, its profound resonance, and its intensity. It seemed natural to me that he had succeeded again in organically synthesising the writer's ideas and lyricism. Today, knowing that each separately constructed their work, we can better appreciate the

Emmanuelle Riva (left) and Eiji Okada in *Hiroshima mon amour* (1959).

director's role – a show of such skilfulness that the film has not aged a day – and the specific contribution of the screenwriter.

The clarity of the couple's love affair was specifically feminine to me. They each shared fundamental things about themselves. They knew one another. She knew he was married and happy, and she saw his house and where he lived. He knew the same things about her. This kind of love was so adult. This kind of love was responding to – and still responds to – a rigorous call for the truth. I marvelled at the fact that right from their first exchange there was a political undertone. He knows that she is shooting a pacifist film, and he 'doesn't scoff at films about peace.'

Even though they only had a short time together, this reciprocal knowledge is what made it possible for something so intimate to bloom between them: something that resembled each individual's true self. We learn her truth, the French woman from Nevers, but we know less about him. We assume he carries with him the immense tragedy of his city, that he has suffered unlimited tragedies. Tragedies that words cannot describe. He was therefore at once devastating, non-human, and yet so weighed down with humanity, that you could tell him everything, because he had been through it all.

From this a priori situation, which made their communication extraordinary, 'Elle' (She[6]), the woman, succeeded in confronting the challenge that he gave her. She answered, in her own way, in her own poor, paltry, questionable way, his 'you saw nothing in Hiroshima.' Of course she saw nothing, but at least she found a way to imagine it, not by Seeing, but by Feeling Hiroshima.

Resnais took exception to the fact that her individual tragedy (her love affair with a German soldier and the humiliation of her head shaving in 1944) could be compared with the collective destruction of Hiroshima. He was right, the two are not comparable. The film doesn't posit their relationship in terms of comparison, but, instead, of communication. It is this specific and improbable area that he shared with Marguerite Duras (and we know how critical the elimination of geographical and temporal distances is to her own work). By focusing on the character of a woman, an individual whose education and social function mean that she is normally destined to be left out of history, Resnais and Duras established a connection between genocide and the doomed sexual affair of a female collaborator.[7] Between her, on her own, and the others, who were all obliterated.

And yet, the possibility that an event of such all-encompassing horror could have a personal echo, and that this echo was found within a person who is rarely, or never, 'authorised' to be its receptacle, connected to contemporary issues.

Addressing the Present Day

While evoking the immediate post-war years and the bomb, the main themes of *Hiroshima mon amour,* however, spoke to my generation: that of the colonial wars, and, in particular, Algeria. Shot in 1958, the film was directly addressing French citizens who were collectively responsible for the dirty war that nobody dared name. In rereading articles from 1959, I am struck by the film's dual resonance. The disparity surprises me – between the reactions of those for whom this film reflected their guilty conscience about the Liberation of France and the atomic bomb – and mine. To me, the film reflected my guilty conscience regarding Algeria.

Hiroshima mon amour engages with the intellectual climate of a young audience for whom history was not rooted in what-happened-after-the-war, but the years 1956, 57, 58, 59: the time of a never-ending conflict that was rotting French politics to the core.

After having been pelted with tomatoes when visiting Algiers, Guy Mollet,[8] who was elected to make peace, turned instead to war and torture. On the 13th May, 1958, the Fourth Republic collapsed. On the surface, the film is not connected to these events. However, in terms of its subjectivity – its essence – it evokes them.

For those who claimed to oppose the war that France unleashed upon the Algerians, the film dealt with a central issue that they understood well. They were against 'pacification', torture, and genocide: a stance that clashed with the wilful ignorance of France as a whole. They spoke of things that broke the country's silence on the matter, despite witness accounts and information published by the Editions de Minuit, Maspéro, and the left-wing press. Yet, even when faced with these facts there was a moratorium, a refusal to know and to imagine what was happening. How, in these conditions, could horror be brought to the surface? How was it possible to provoke a simple reaction that would finally be a sign of recognition for the dirty role the French army played in Algeria?

Hiroshima mon amour did not respond in any specific way to these questions. But the film does show one particular situation – that is not necessarily exceptional – of the moment when the floodgates opened, and the dam broke. The woman, who, in the past, was responsible for an irrational, yet unacceptable affair with a German soldier; this woman, who was on the wrong side of history, just as France was in 1959 vis-à-vis its colonial disputes; this woman still managed to reach an understanding, and to react to the tragedy of Hiroshima's victims. Psychology – or possibly guilt – were irrelevant. Only her full, quasi-absolute, commitment to life, mattered.

It was significant and far-reaching to claim, 'You saw nothing in Hiroshima' at the very moment when it was unbearable that nobody saw anything in Algeria. As the French woman from Nevers managed to eliminate the distance from her past

– the fourteen years from the day of the bomb to the day of her delirium in the rebuilt city – the time would have to come when the population of France would stop feeling so far from Algeria. *Hiroshima mon amour* pulled off the unthinkable: Nevers and Hiroshima co-existed in suffering. The time would have to come when the French would understand that Algeria wasn't French but *within* France. Tortured and humiliated, Algeria was the country's own pain and profound suffering.

Rapture and Politics

In 1959–60, *Hiroshima mon amour* was an adult film for an adult audience. Its heroine, plucked straight from the intellectual world of Existentialism, turned her emotional turmoil into a real-world presence. She was made of flesh, emotions, and subjectivity. And this baggage did not impede her path to liberation.

She was pulled out of her delirium by one of those rare slaps in cinema that is not just tritely misogynist. A slap that doesn't end a dialogue, or stop a conflict, but is instead an opening: the start of a cathartic and revealing story.

'Lui' (Him), the Japanese man, slaps her at the moment she loses herself, at the moment she identifies with the corpse of her previous lover. She is dispossessed of herself. He doesn't remain a spectator. He is not passive/unconcerned. The 'rapture' which he opposes is more than an escape or a betrayal of the real. It is, quite simply, death. The brutal gesture doesn't serve to punish her. It is so she can find herself again, reintegrate into the world. She comes back into herself. She is a person in whom everything is at stake: the body, the heart, and the mind. Someone who is situated amongst others and in the present. She is a political being.

She is one of the most beautiful protagonists in French cinema, a woman. A woman who comes out of herself, freed from her ego, her Nevers and her silence. She speaks, and she is whole once more. Today, when, the search for identity is a major preoccupation for women, this fleeting visitor to Hiroshima is a sister. She seems to me closer, and more immediately connected to the present, than most of the depictions of women that claim to take into account the 'newly born women'[9] of the 1970s.

* * *

From 1944 to 1959, from Nevers to Hiroshima, from Resnais to Duras: something strong and irrepressible circulates. And now Duras and so many others – some are female directors, some are male directors – so many others are starting to speak a different language. A continuity emerges between 1959 and the present day.

Everything stems from those pivotal years that ended the post-war era. New women asserted their independence, their freedom, and their principles. And cinema captured their reflection. Did it, as much as we had hoped, disseminate their image? Alas, no. The New Wave, heir to these initial shockwaves, did not advance things further in its own films. It was the beginning of fifteen sad years.

Notes

Notes 1 and 6 are by the author Françoise Audé; other notes by editor Ginette Vincendeau.

1. The heart and the mind: *Hearts and Minds* (1974) is the title of a beautiful film by Peter Davis that is apt for a study on *Hiroshima mon amour*. The American film analyses the Vietnam War – the role of American mothers and Mother America – with an emotional approach that takes us back to Alain Resnais' film.

2. Anatole Dauman and Samy Halfon are credited as producers of the film; Lipschitz and Fouet could not be traced.

3. Marguerite Duras, *Hiroshima, Mon Amour and Une Aussi Longue Absence* (trans. Richard Seaver and Barbara Wright), London: Calder and Boyars, 1966, p. 10.

4. In her original piece, Audé mentions a special issue of *L'Avant-Scène du cinéma* (Nos. 61–2), July–September 1966. Since then, numerous articles and books on the film, on Alain Resnais and Marguerite Duras have been published, among which: Jean-Louis Leutrat, *Hiroshima mon amour, Alain Resnais: étude critique*, Paris: Nathan, 1994. For Duras's text, see note 3 above.

5. A reference to the author's analysis of this film (directed by Roger Vadim) in the volume from which this chapter is extracted.

6. The two main characters are not given a name and are referred to as 'Elle' (she) and 'Lui' (him).

7. In the original French, Audé makes an untranslatable pun playing on the idea of 'death' in genocide and sexual ecstasy, which can be referred to as 'petite mort' (little death).

8. Socialist Prime Minister.

9. Audé is referring to *La jeune née* (*The Newly Born Woman*), a landmark feminist text of 1975, by Hélène Cixous and Catherine Clément.

'Birth of a cinema' by Marie-Claire Ropars-Wuilleumier, published in *Esprit* in July-August 1967 is a remarkably prescient article for two reasons. First, and unusually for the time, the author turns to a film by the Francophone African filmmaker, Ousmane Sembène, *La noire de…/Black Girl* (1966) and analyses it as part of the larger movement, the rise of African cinema. She is particularly interested in the construction of the heroine's subjectivity and her alienation in terms of language. Although the article, inevitably, bears the mark of the author's Eurocentric perspective, it should be remembered that this was one of the first sustained analyses of the film, written long before post-colonial studies. Secondly, Ropars-Wuilleumier, while being attentive to *La noire de…* as an African film, situates it also within the larger New Wave context, notably through a comparison with Jean Rouch's *Moi, un noir* (1958).

Ginette Vincendeau

17 Birth of a Cinema (Ousmane Sembène's *Black Girl*)

MARIE-CLAIRE ROPARS-WUILLEUMIER (1967)*

L
a Noire de… (*Black Girl*),[1] the first full-length feature film from an African director, follows in the footsteps of a series of short and medium-length films, mostly from Senegal and the Republic of Niger, which have been paving the way for the birth of a Francophone Black African cinema for a dozen years. Only by referencing this context, the subject of a recent retrospective organised by the Cinémathèque Française, can we understand the

Ousmane Sembène.

* *Esprit*, Nouvelle série, No. 362 (7/8), July–August 1967, pp. 135–140.
(Translated from the French by Jennifer Wallace)

true impact of Ousmane Sembène's film. It is relevant not only from a purely sociological standpoint, but also because the expressive features of the film are illuminated and authenticated when understood alongside the African sources that saturate it.

The schematic nature of the plot, as well as the absence of any psychological nuance or even personal point of view, might at first disappoint a European spectator. The film's subject touches on a current problem: it is about a young African maid, exiled in France, isolated within a French family of *coopérants*[2] who exploit her, who then commits suicide out of despair. The classical narrative structure, however, with a steady continuity of sequences illustrating the logical unfolding of the plot, and the neutral stance of the shots, where the camera records images without trying to inflect them through its own gaze; all these intrinsically visual elements turn the work into a drama made all the more traditional by a long interior monologue, artificial in tone, and often lyrical in nature, which is meant to express the tragic feelings of the young woman, while only music intervenes, from time to time, as a direct African voice.

Any disappointment could be a measure of certain illusions. Over the last ten years, the development of a free, direct, cinema of reportage and *vérité*, with a liberated camera, with editing unburdened by the need to dramatize, with an attentive and mobile gaze, and unscripted, spontaneous speech: all of this has enabled the discovery of different – formerly hidden and forgotten – worlds. Through this new cinematic language, Lozère farmers, the mentally ill and ancient societies have acquired, little by little, the right to be visible and the power of speech. And the ethnographic film, such as was practised by Jean Rouch, was expected to be taken into African hands, enabling African filmmakers to express a subjectivity that European documentarists could only ever approach with the risk of falsifying it. It is a tell-tale sign that *Moi, un noir (I, a Negro)*[3] which appeared, to the eyes of French critics, as the first example of the collaboration between filmed men and men who film, was harshly criticised by Africans who saw it as a misrepresentation, all the more dangerous for its appearance of authenticity.

Because there is no more persistent cinematographic illusion – illusion being at the heart of the visual nature of cinema – than to confuse looking *at* men with how *these* men look. Jean Rouch himself, after several attempts at *cinéma vérité*, went back to a more objective technique, as he recognised the limits of his own creation. A truly honest ethnographic film, because it will always remain outside of what it is showing, must signal its exterior perspective. This is a gesture of respect for the barrier that could only be crossed by someone who would be simultaneously on both sides, who would participate in both languages, and understand both visions – for example an African director. But if burgeoning African cinema hasn't yet responded to this expectation, it is undoubtedly because it has not yet been able to access the right means of expression, but also because perhaps this expectation is the last vestige of a conception alien to Africa, still trying to enforce its rule by enforcing such criteria as the only way to express reality.

Documentary style, however, is not absent from African cinema – quite the opposite – and even if it is out of technical or financial necessity, the core of African production is in the form of news and reporting. The pilgrimage of the Mourides in Senegal (Blaise Senghor: *Grand Magal de Touba* [*The Great Pilgrimage to Touba*, 1962]); African wrestling (Paulin Vieyra: *Lamb*, 1963); the reconstruction of a large hut in Cameroon (J.P. N'Gassa: *La Grande case Bamiléké*, 1965): such topics transmit an immediate reality, often picturesque, and certainly authentically African. Even more ambitious films, where fictional storylines are attempted, remain connected to current problems of Black Africa. Whether it's the attempts of a young fisherman to modernise his boat (P. Vieyra: *Môl*, 1966); the hardships of a former sergeant in the French army, who returns to his bush village to civilise it, and is persecuted by spirits (Momar Thiam: *Sarzan*, 1963); or the folly of a young man who brings back Cowboy costumes and guns from America to arm a gang, to then re-enact, in real life, a murderous western (Mustapha Alassane: *Le Retour d'un aventurier* [*The Return of an Adventurer*, 1966]): it is always the conflict between the old and the new; the ongoing shock of two civilisations that finds itself depicted on screen, frequently to the detriment of a vigorously condemned white myth. But what the majority of the fictional storylines have in common, just like news reports, is that the visual reality is presented primarily as the backdrop to, or at the most an illustration of, an already established schema channelled through verbal commentary or speeches, and they alone position, explain, and inform the film. Instead of investigative works, in which cinema would use the visual powers at its disposal to capture, show and listen to life, this style is far more literary. The reigning power of speech manifests itself through the voices of the characters playing their roles, and the voice of a reporter or storyteller, who may not directly express his or her own feelings, but who explains what is in front of them, judges and filters what he or she sees, and only sporadically and superficially actually shows things.

However, it would be wrong to view this as only another sign of the alienation of a society whose own culture, stifled for so long, cannot access newer means of expression. Quite the opposite, these films draw upon their own African traditions. To prove it you only have to read the folk tales and short stories which are at the heart of African literary expression, and which films like *Sarzan* or *La Noire de...* draw from. The structure of an African folk tale adheres to a pure dramatic style, where the unfolding of events and discourses is largely symbolic, accompanied by a narrator who, depending on the scenario, adopts a humorous or lyrical tone. The narrator, visible or not, is the director of actions and words – a concept that has left its mark in the style of news commentaries; while the style of the folk tales informs theatre and poetry more often than the novel. Thus, we find a declamatory tone in a drama like *Sarzan*, giving it weight, and at times, a tragic grandeur. Alternatively, the charm of *Le Retour d'un aventurier*, influenced by the Western, whilst simultaneously condemning it, lies with the fact that only the structure of the folk tale is used, without the intrusive presence of a narrator. In this way, poetic and mythical touches in the folk tale are revealed, whilst also, as is the case here, the myth is destroyed.

In *La Noire de…* the recourse to this expressive tradition illuminates the dramatisation of the story, the lack of psychological nuance or a personal gaze, and the inflation of an interior voice; analysis gives way to the expression of a grievance, often ending in a lament. It is not an individual's time nor their perspective which gives the story its rhythm, but, as in the whole African literary tradition, a collective spirit which needs to be expressed. And through the manifestation of this spirit, and by the film's very nature, *La Noire de…* takes on a previously unknown dimension compared to other African films.

Through commentary or performance, most of these films reveal, despite an abundance of words, silence from Africa. Evidently, if a director is speaking via the film, then it is an African who, in refusing to speak about himself, is reflecting on the ancient ways of a civilisation and the current problems of its evolution. But neither the civilisation nor its evolution directly express themselves, as they are hidden off-screen. This is because the drama lies solely in the *mise-en-scène*, which refuses any kind of subjective expression that only an individual vision could communicate. Civilisation and its evolution are also denied expression, since only the narrator or a few characters may talk, and everyone else stays silent. Evidently, in many cases this is for technical reasons. Most films are post-synchronised, therefore it is easier and less expensive to post-synchronise just a few voices. But, isn't this post-synchronisation also linked to a language problem that prohibits a direct understanding of most characters? If bush villages are sometimes shown, or if expressive faces sometimes emerge in front of the camera, they remain, however, elusive – as the few films with recorded sound testify, about half of them, 'in dialect'. The dispersion of dialects contributes to the isolation of a large sector of the population, a population that filmmakers can only put in front of the camera as décor or background noise, or who can only be featured through theoretical ideas or having actors play their roles. Because the only viewers currently imaginable are French viewers, or at least French speakers, to whom you have to speak French. And if the spoken unification of Africa is achieved through the development of this language, it will always remain, for many, a foreign language.

Mbissine Thérèse Diop in *La Noire de ...* (1966).

Thus is revealed, through most of these films, the central problem of Black Africa: communication. But where most films show this unease with a discrepancy, imposed rather than voluntary, between the silence of men and the presence of speech, Ousmane Sembène takes control of expressing this discrepancy through both the structure and the subject of *La Noire de...,* as it is the story of impossible communication as well as alienation. He does this first of all through a visual symbol, presented in the opening image, which structures the dramatic construction of the story. The young woman offers an African mask to her employers when they hire her, and she takes it back from them before she commits suicide. It is an African mask, but also the mask of a spirit or a ghost, so a white-coloured mask. At the end of the film the young woman's little brother grabs the mask from the employer when he returns her belongings to her mother, and he holds the mask over his face as he follows the employer, in a long sequence, across the Medina of Dakar. A musical theme syncopates the rhythm with increasing force as the slow pursuit ends with the final shot: the child takes off the white mask, showing his black face. Added to this visual and arresting symbol of complex alienation and potential liberation, there is a more subtle but profound symbol, authenticated by the very subject of the film. Because she does not speak French, and because she does not know how to write, the heroine of *La Noire de...* finds herself in France in a situation of exile, deprived of communication, dispossessed of her own language, and on the receiving end of malicious remarks or indifferent comments from her employers. The young woman silently testifies to her imprisonment by language – as absolute as the prison of the walls of the apartment – by not speaking for the entire film: she offers only her impassive face. And if her interior monologue reveals her thoughts and identity, in an increasingly lyrical fashion, it is through an artificial white voice[4], and therefore it is a white woman who speaks for her: the credits state 'with the voices of'. This contrast was deliberately crafted by Ousmane Sembène, as, on the contrary, in his remarkable short *Borom Sarret*, he is one of the rare examples of an African filmmaker who has recreated, in approximate French, the language of a Dakari artisan. The interior monologue in *Borom Sarret* provides us, alongside a rigorous criticism of the social situation, with one of the most charming voices in Africa. In *La Noire de...*, however, the interior monologue's lack of realism is signalled by its tone and its lyrical richness, yet its insertion into the story, and onto the subject, makes it even more tragic, and her silence even more desperate. The literary tone, which betrays itself from the moment it is used, becomes all the more necessary given that Ousmane Sembène, when writing, avoids it.

A black face and a white voice, a white African mask on a black boy: the film traces a series of sensitive counterpoints, many more of which could be detailed. They work together to suggest, with contrapuntal language, the impossibility of a unified tongue and manner of expression. Thus, the banal images are contrasted with the lyricism of the monologue, which is itself inconsistent with some awkwardness in style; and just as, in two flashbacks, the anonymous Antibes apartment where the young woman is trapped transforms into Dakar, the two musical themes heard on the soundtrack are of exile and nostalgia.

By drawing, like most African directors, on historical structures of African expression, Ousmane Sembène succeeds in introducing, at every moment, discrepancies of expression, mirroring a continent that, through masks and languages, is looking for its true face while looking for its own language. If African cinema has yet to engage with realism, then this lack is found in the history of all cinemas, where the transmission of reality is always the goal, and a major step in their evolution. But Ousmane Sembène has taken this current weakness, painful in nature, and given it its most symbolic manifestation.

Notes

All notes by editor Ginette Vincendeau.

1. Released in 1966 in Senegal and April 1967 in France.
2. White professional workers sent overseas in the immediate post-colonial period.
3. Jean Rouch, 1957.
4. Although Ropars-Wuilleumier's point about Diouana being 'imprisoned' by language is correct, and the voice-over is in French, which Diouana does not speak, the voice dubbing Diouana's thoughts is that of the black Haïtian actress Toto Bissainthe.

The second part of this new section on gender, politics and the New Wave is a case study devoted to women directors. Inevitably it is dominated by Agnès Varda, whose presence in New Wave scholarship has continued to grow since the 1990s. Varda's eminence is totally justified and she is undoubtedly the only filmmaker who was fully part of the New Wave movement, but she is sometimes wrongly presented as the only woman filmmaker in early post-war France. There were quite a few others, such as Nicole Védrès and Yannick Bellon, who worked in documentary before the New Wave, and of course many more would emerge from the late 1960s onwards. Here however we wanted to pay tribute to Jacqueline Audry, the only woman filmmaker working in the mainstream film industry in France from the late 1940s to the 1960s. Audry made typical 'Tradition of Quality' films, that is, costume films adapted from literature, including *Olivia* (1951) a story of lesbian desire in a boarding school (mentioned by Pierre Kast in this volume), although her most successful films were adaptations from Colette: *Gigi* (1949), *Minne, l'ingénue libertine* (1950) and *Mitsou* (1956). Audry made one New Wave film, *Les Petits matins* (1962), a light-hearted feminist road movie. The film however was not a success and it does not appear to have given rise to any sustained writing at the time. It has taken until 2015 for Audry to be the subject of a monograph, by Brigitte Rollet. It is from Rollet's book that we extract the text that follows, the transcript of a radio talk given in 1955 in which Audry reflects on being a woman director.

Ginette Vincendeau

18 CASE STUDY

WOMEN DIRECTORS (JACQUELINE AUDRY, AGNÈS VARDA, PAULE DELSOL)

I am a woman director [1]
JACQUELINE AUDRY (1955)*

I am a woman director, which is why I think that *mise-en-scène* as an art is feminine and masculine in equal measures. I am therefore going to try and demonstrate that the place of a woman can be besides my camera. For this, all I need to do is think about the qualities required to become a perfect director and thereby prove that nothing prevents a woman – because she is a woman – from directing films. Apart from the basic qualities inherent in each sex, one must find in the filmmaker a happy balance between so-called masculine and so-called feminine qualities; I say 'so-called' because I have reservations. Clearly there are masculine and feminine characteristics. Yet, when you look closely, you discover that, either some of these traits are shared by both sexes, or that the feminine is defined simply as the absence of any marked characteristic; which means that there is not much left for women and that, as a result, any noticeable trait in a woman is considered a masculine quality.

To start with, I will list the fundamental, essential and vital qualities for both male and female directors. You must, first of all, and above all, love the cinema, have a calling for it; you must put at its disposal your intelligence, artistic flair, the visual skills that make you want to express yourself in images rather than in any other way, a sense of observation, an enduring interest in studying the behaviour of human beings, and, when the right moment comes, the ability to remember and apply these observations. You need sensuality, a passion for forms, nuances,

---

* Radio transcripts from Brigitte Rollet, *Jacqueline Audry, La femme à la camera* (Rennes: Presses Universitaires de Rennes, 2015). (Translated from the French by Ginette Vincendeau)

Edwige Feuillère (left) and Marie-Claire Olivia (right) in *Olivia* (1950).

reflections, materials, the substance of things. You also need a lot of intuition: the director needs to be a clairvoyant, bent over a crystal ball; officiating with the help of a screenwriter,[2] he or she must predict the future of the project they have chosen on behalf of a more or less blind film industry. The director must be able to have a split personality, imagine how the film will be made and how it will be received while keeping enough spontaneity to react like the first spectator at an imaginary screening. I probably forget some of these fundamental qualities, but you will agree with me that the ones I have mentioned can be found equally in men and women. We now get to the delicate point. Film directors need so-called masculine qualities and, believe-me, in this profession, they must not be watered down: creative spirit, daring, courage, strength, brutality even, the authority of a ship commander and nerves of steel. This is already quite a lot but there remains for me to mention some other, so-called feminine qualities, not the least important ones.

Imagination, sensitivity, tenderness, delicacy, patience, tenacity, seduction, allied to the ability to spin fairy-tales. And above all, you need what is wrongly (in order to make it the preserve of women) called passivity. This passivity in fact is nothing of the sort. It is the opposite of activity, but only insofar as the force of attraction relates to the force of propulsion, like the positive to the negative in electricity. It means in fact receptivity, open-mindedness, the gift for letting oneself be permeated by things and people, in order to imitate and express them better as a result. This is where my demonstration begins. If a human being, whoever they are, cannot muster in themselves so many possibilities…[3]

[…]

To sum up, just like the man who has all the musical instruments on his back is a one-man-band (*homme-orchestre*), the director, following his or her innate aspirations will select topics that are violent or tender, cruel or sentimental, profound or light-hearted. But within the chosen subject, the man will inevitably need to deal with scenes that are full of gentleness and love, and the woman will have to face violence and horror. As film directors, we are a one-man or one-woman band.

Agnès Varda's first feature film, *La Pointe Courte*, is rightly hailed as an exceptional achievement in its own right and is increasingly celebrated as the starting point of the French New Wave. At the time of shooting it, the young Varda was a novice in film, having studied art and trained as a photographer but with no experience of film technique or film history. She made the film on a small budget and crew on the margins of the industry. *La Pointe Courte*, shot on location in the eponymous Mediterranean village which Varda knew as a child, combines documentary views of the fishing village and of its inhabitants with the intense conversations of a middle-class, intellectual couple (these conversations are discussed by Marie-Claire Ropars-Wuilleumier in 'A Cinematographic Language' in this volume).

Here are gathered three reviews of the film written when it was first shown in 1955–1956. Annette Raynaud's review is notable for being written by a woman at *Cahiers du cinéma*, a rarity at the time (and since), and also as a very complimentary review with identifies several aspects of the film's originality. André Bazin's review was written for the daily *Le Parisien libéré*, one of the popular newspapers in which the prestigious critic and editor of *Cahiers du cinéma* also wrote. Bazin gives the film high praise, calling it 'miraculous' and pointing to its specificity as a woman's film. Martine Monod's short review, published in the communist cultural journal *Les Lettres françaises* is critical of some aspects of the film, but recognises its originality and the quality of its documentary images. Remarkably the writer also identifies the talent of the filmmaker at this very early stage, hailing 'the birth of a cineaste'. Although Varda's film was ignored for a while, both on account of its botched release and of sexism in the film world, these early pieces show that her talent was nevertheless recognised.

Ginette Vincendeau

Agnès Varda: *La Pointe Courte* (1954)

To Give Them to the Other *
ANNETTE RAYNAUD

La Pointe Courte resembles several other recent films conceived as studies of human nature. As seen in *Les Vacances de Monsieur Hulot* (*Monsieur Hulot's Holiday*)[4], and primarily *Voyage en Italie* (*Journey to Italy*)[5], there is a new style of cinema involving a densely woven documentation of the real. But although these two films are natural extensions of Neo-Realism, *La Pointe Courte,* even more stylised in form, doesn't easily fit into the current cinematic landscape.

Dreams, like any uncertain endeavour that disappears into the ether, never make it into history. Agnès Varda's film seems to emerge from a dream-like, backward-age where many women's creative lives have been wasted. It comes from out of the blue, a hodgepodge of photography, modern philosophy, the works of Faulkner, and poetry; one only needs to read *Le Cimetière marin* (*The Graveyard by the Sea*)[6] and watch the film to feel how the use of light and the unfolding of images evoke a poetic charge originating from the same soil: *La Pointe Courte* was shot close to Sète. Combine an artist's touch and a taste for observation, and everything and nothing come together to give this film meaning.

Within this strange mix of styles, the broad strokes of the plot are the same as *Voyage en Italie*. A man and a woman, married for several years, quarrel and then miraculously reunite during a holiday, able to experience anxiety and joy once they have navigated the existential heaviness that surrounds them, as if their holiday location functioned as an oracle.

The couple are a pair of (talkative) intellectuals, and the themes of village life that intersect with their marital crisis are as meaningful as the protagonists of the story. So much so that the film seems to establish a system of equivalences whereby the actions of the couple, with their hesitant, spontaneous mysticism, are of no more importance than the daily happenings and movements of the village. This creates a basic filmic material, amorphous in itself, but which the formal rigour of the *découpage* and framing inevitably 'poetise'. Thankfully, it is through this technique that from the dark, existential substance of the film, a shape emerges, and it allows us to penetrate deeply into the images. Images like that of a boat, difficult to separate from its poetic symbolism as both a cradle and a grave, take on an alluring vibrancy.

---

* *Cahiers du Cinéma*, No. 53, December 1955. (Translated from the French by Jennifer Wallace)

Silvia Monfort (foreground) and Philippe Noiret in *La Pointe Courte* (1954).

Instead of falling back into obscurity, shots are imbued with acute meaning. If the art of *mise-en-scène* is to link symbolic images to one another, then rarely has this been executed with so much love. At times 'the divergences and the convergences [...] that determine signs'[7] are pushed towards the limits of the two-dimensional frame in almost abstract patterns; at times, they expand in depth.

A passionate geometry prevails in sequences where pain is the dominant emotion. Characters are reduced to silhouettes, they are traversed by brief convulsions, or the couple is flattened into a monstrous composite face. Objects become cleverly-crafted traps, horizontally and vertically dominating the shots. When the atmosphere lightens, on the other hand, the structures on screen become ethereal. The film offers us images of animals moving around, happy crowds, the rolling tide; but under the widening rings in the water, there is something unsettling about the depth beneath. Tension is built through the assembling of unusual symbols on brightly lit stretches against a dark background, suggesting something underneath the surface.

The melodic line from symbol to symbol also functions as counterpoint. When they are happy, the couple resemble stone effigies, as if in their joy, they had accepted 'the ultimate possibility' that death offers the living.

Thus, the deliberate formalism of the images remains excessive; but these flat perspectives are used so relentlessly that the auteur seems to convey the message of an existential unveiling rather than a study of human nature. The passing of time in the film echoes that of reality; it flows eternal, slow and monochromatic. Space is also recognisably human, it tends to constitute a world, not just a backdrop. It is intentional that the man in the couple is viewed as part of the landscapes of *La Pointe Courte,* his birthplace, and a picture of unchanging truth. He is the land-scape. He reignites the early passion of their love by offering this part of himself to his wife; as those who want to be loved must 'be those whose function is to make trees and water exist, to make cities and fields and other men exist, in order to give them later to the Other who arranges them into a world.'[8]

It is essential to praise the female character, conceived by a female auteur, as an authentic creation. She is a female subject, capable of realising her full poten-tial without ceding her ground to the man in terms of the power and privilege of thought. She is a straightforward, open individual, even capable of evolving; in a derisory way perhaps, but what real evolution is not derisory? In the long run, since to insist on dreamy idealism leads to nothingness, it is courageous folly to break the spell to 'try to live'[9] by simply embracing hope.

It took great courage on the part of Agnès Varda to depict an intellectual woman on screen; what she gains in pathos with her moving portrayal of a woman trying to keep the love within her alive, she also risks losing in provoking the irritation of many viewers. Hopefully the graceful Silvia Montfort will dispel their misgivings. I've barely said anything about the documentary shooting of the village. However, this part of the film, the most understated, is the best.

*　*　*

La Pointe Courte, A Free and Pure Film[*]
ANDRÉ BAZIN

La Pointe Courte is a miraculous film. For its existence and style. For its existence, because you probably have to go back as far as *Le Sang d'un poète* (*The Blood of a Poet,* 1930)[10] to find a film so free from all commercial constraints in its concep-tion. And even Jean Cocteau essentially benefitted from a sumptuous patronage. Those days are sadly behind us. A talking picture costs too much, even for a bil-lionaire's fantasy. Yet, Agnès Varda is a very young woman, whose great talent we already know as photographer for the TNP[11], and who simply felt the need to make this film. Instead of looking for a producer as per the usual process, she

---

[*] *Le Parisien libéré,* 7 January 1956. (Translated from the French by Jennifer Wallace)

Agnès Varda (kneeling behind the camera) shooting *La Pointe Courte* (1954).

justifiably thought that the energy needed to unearth this rare treasure would be better spent on taking care of it herself, with her own means. She convinced a few friends to work with her in a cooperative, and that's how, with just a little money, but with a lot of courage, imagination and talent, *La Pointe Courte* saw the light of day. This first miracle led to the second. By this I mean a total stylistic freedom, rarely found in cinema, which gives us the feeling that we are in the presence of a creation that obeys only the will of its creator, without any outside interference. A creation as free in its inspiration as the book Agnès Varda could have written on the same subject.

If *La Pointe Courte* is an 'avant-garde' film, it is not, however, in the traditional sense of the word, which is still more or less confused with the aftermath of Surrealism, or at least the destruction of plot and storytelling. The story that Agnès Varda tells is the simplest story in the world, and it's a love story. A man and a woman are on the verge of separating after four years together. The man spends his holiday in the village where he was born, a fishing village, near Sète, named

La Pointe Courte. The woman comes to join him before their potential definitive separation. They walk together, dreaming of their past, confronting their emotions, in an uncertain pursuit of themselves and their truth. However, alongside them, mysteriously both in harmony with their story and indifferent to it, village life unfolds. Shellfish fishermen in muddy ponds fight with civil servants from the hygiene department. A child dies, a couple marries, there is jousting on the Sète canals for the holidays. The couple weave their destiny into this human tapestry. At the end of this dreamlike journey, they find themselves once again reunited.

Naturally, we can't help but think of *Voyage en Italie* (*Journey to Italy*) by Rossellini (which, by the way, for chronological reasons,[12] could not have influenced Varda), because there is a comparable counterpoint between the protagonists' emotions and the geographical and human environment. This comparison honours both films. However, Agnès Varda's film is very different in tone and technique. Firstly, it is a woman's film, and by that I mean in the same way that there are women's novels, which however is quite unique in cinema. Next, the auteur has adopted a bias in terms of the image. In this respect, Agnès Varda may not have shed her talent as a photographer quite enough. But there is, however, admirable dialogue. The protagonists only speak of needless yet essential things, like words that elude us in our dreams.

Alongside *La Pointe Courte*, the Studio Parnasse presents the always admirable *A Propos de Nice* by Jean Vigo.

*   *   *

Birth of a Cineaste [*]
MARTINE MONOD

Today Agnès Varda, long-time photographer for the TNP (Théâtre National Populaire), unveils her talents as a director. A rather singular director at that, as she does away with a producer, managing the whole enterprise with the help of her network of technicians and actors.[13] Quite the charming and sympathetic initiative.

The plot of *La Pointe Courte* is perfectly simple. A man and a woman, who have been married for some years, believe that their relationship is over. Not because they hate one another, but because their marriage has lost its sense of passion, discovery and wonder. He goes on holiday to 'La Pointe Courte', the traditional

---

[*] *Les Lettres françaises*, 12 January 1956. (Translated from the French by Jennifer Wallace)

fishing neighbourhood in Sète where he spent his childhood. She, before making a final decision as to whether to end the relationship, joins him. Together they observe the locals. They see the landscape in which they work and play, all the while confronting their own problems too. By the end of the film they decide to stay together. The honeymoon period may be over, but their relationship is not, and they are ready to move forward, hand in hand. The wisdom of middle age supersedes the ardour of youth.

I like the story. In fact, I like nearly everything about the film, I only wish I could say I like all of it!

Agnès Varda has a lot of talent, intelligence, sensitivity, and a deep connection to her work. I feel like nothing she creates could ever be meaningless. And once she has gotten rid of certain aesthetic touches that weaken rather than enrich her work, we are in for some truly great films. Everything about local life in *La Pointe Courte* is excellent – above all at the end of the film, with scenes of the jousting competition in Sète's harbour, a local dance, and boats sailing into the night along the canal. But the way in which she deals with the plot of the protagonists exposes two shortcomings.

Firstly, the couple's storyline is so disconnected from that of La Pointe Courte, that it's almost as if we are watching two separate films that don't ever overlap. Secondly, the highbrow, verbose way in which they talk strips the emotion from what is otherwise a realistic and deeply-felt drama. The dialogue is full of impressive figures of speech, but they are just that – figures of speech. Even interesting moments of grand, dramatic intensity fall flat. Are the actors at fault? Certainly, some blame lies with Phillippe Noiret, who is excessively pompous in style, but not the enthralling Sylvia Monfort (who should be seen more often on screen). I think it's rather a problem of direction, moreover the very concept of the film.

However, even with my reservations, I think one should go and see *La Pointe Courte*. Its authenticity largely overrides its artifice, and there are more things in it to like than dislike. One day, I'm sure we will see a wonderful film from Agnès Varda.

To our delight, the film is screened alongside *À propos de Nice* by Jean Vigo and an irresistibly funny short from Buster Keaton.

By the time she made *Cléo de 5 à 7* in 1961 (the film came out in 1962), Agnès Varda had made several documentaries, including the celebrated *L'Opéra Mouffe* in 1958. She had also been integrated into the 'Left-bank' New Wave group, and in *Cléo de 5 à 7*, she pays tribute to the friendly relations in the New Wave as a whole, in the short mock silent film seen by the heroine. Among her friends were Alain Resnais, who had edited *La Pointe Courte*, and Chris Marker, and Jacques Demy was her partner in life – they married in 1962. Although Varda's marginalisation from New Wave scholarship (until reclaimed by feminist scholars) tends to suggest that she was ignored at the time, the reviews of *Cléo de 5 à 7* tell a different story. If the film's score at the box-office was modest, it was a critical success, signalled by its nomination for the Palme d'Or at the Cannes film festival of 1962 (although it did not win it). The two reviews of the film selected here are by high-profile film writers and both recognise and celebrate the film's stylistic originality, affecting story and social relevance.

In 'The Tell-Tale Heart of Agnès Varda' published in *Les Lettres françaises*, Georges Sadoul, one of the important historians of French cinema, briefly recaps Varda's career and deplores the fact that her first feature *La Pointe Courte* had not been fully appreciated, including by himself. He then proceeds to a perceptive analysis of *Cléo de 5 à 7*, especially in relation to the way its story is embedded in current events, notably the Algerian war (contrary to most New Wave films which ignored it). One of the most famous quotes about the film, 'Ninety minutes in the life of a *Parisienne* can contain the anxieties and preoccupations of a nation – France' comes from this article. The second review, '*Cléo de 5 à 7* is a masterpiece' was written by novelist and star film critic Jean-Louis Bory, and published in *Arts*, then an important cultural publication. Bory is particularly attentive to textual details and style, and he writes about the modernity of the film and its complex representation of time and duration. At the same time, remarkably, while not writing explicitly from a feminist perspective, Bory identifies the major themes that future feminist critics will focus on, in particular the crucial turning point when the heroine appropriates the gaze: the moment she tears her wig off and starts looking around her, as opposed to being looked at, that is where she goes from objectification to subjectivity.

Ginette Vincendeau

Agnès Varda: *Cléo de 5 à 7* (1962)

The Tell-Tale Heart[14] of Agnès Varda – *Cléo de 5 à 7* *
GEORGES SADOUL

Only a few films, perhaps *Peter Ibbetson*[15], have so profoundly moved me as *Cléo de 5 à 7* (*Cléo from 5 to 7*). Cléo from 5 to 7: the film's subject is contained entirely in the title. A woman's life between five and seven in the afternoon (or more precisely until 18h30). The duration of the film corresponds to her schedule. From time to time subtitles remind us that it is 17h45 or 18h22.

What happens during the 90 minutes that we share with Cléo (Corinne Marchand)? She is, like the actress, a young singer. She is at the beginning of quite a promising career. She was worried about her health. The doctor ordered a biopsy. She will know, at around six in the evening, if she has cancer or not…

The idea of sickness, of death possibly just around the corner, haunts her. She comes home to her studio on the rue Huyghens, next to the Rotonde café, in Montparnasse. She rehearses a few verses with her pianist (Michel Legrand) and her songwriter[16]. She spends ten minutes with her lover (José Luis de Vilallonga), still a seductive man, who showers her with luxurious gifts and attention. And then, unable to handle any more stress, she goes to find a friend (Dorothée Blanck), who is a model in a sculptor's studio. The two women go to the cinema rue Delambre, opposite the Dôme café, where they watch an old silent film (meant to go before the main feature), recreated by Agnès Varda with Anna Karina, Jean-Luc Godard, Eddie Constantine, Sami Frey, Yves Robert, Jean-Claude Brialy, Danièle Delorme, etc.) Cléo swiftly leaves the cinema and her friend.

Her anguish leads her to the Parc Montsouris. Here, on this beautiful day, the first day of summer, she meets a young man (Antoine Bourseiller). They engage in conversation. They like each other. He is a soldier. He has to leave that very night for Marseille, then onto Algeria. He still has a little bit of time left. He accompanies her to the Salpêtrière Hospital, where she will learn the results of the biopsy. They wait, on this June afternoon, in the large hospital garden, as empty as a graveyard. She stops a busy doctor in his tracks. He talks about radiotherapy treatment. He employs the kind of language that masks the truth behind incomprehensible scientific words, so that the truth is left vague. He flees. Cléo

---

* *Les Lettres françaises* No. 922, 12 April 1962; reprinted in Georges Sadoul, *Ecrits 1, Chroniques du cinéma français 1939–1967* (Paris: Union Générale d'Editions, 1979, pp. 266–72) (Translated from the French by Jennifer Wallace)

Corinne Marchand (centre) and Antoine Bourseiller (right) in *Cléo de 5 à 7* (1962).

knows she has cancer, is doomed, and now she has to leave this soldier, who is leaving too, perhaps to his death...

Agnès Varda, who proves she is one of our best auteurs with this film, is a unique woman. She was born on the 30th May, 1928, in Brussels, but her parents were Greek, from Crete I believe[17]. She has the same look and profile as *La Parisienne,* the figure named by the workers who discovered her, in 1880, in King Minos' palace[18] . She is often dressed like the Jack of Diamonds.

That doesn't mean to say that she always wears the same skirt (or the same trousers). The card character, an emblem chosen by the Russian Avant-Garde painters in 1910, dresses in very different costumes depending on the game and the country. And sometimes Varda adopts other costumes too. I saw her arriving one winter's day, dressed like an Eskimo, with her baby on her back. She had just crossed the Bois de Vincennes in the snow to see her friends, the Bazins[19].

I was with André Bazin when I met Agnès Varda for the first time. One afternoon, on rue Troyon, near Place de l'Étoile in Paris. She had just presented her first film to the critics, a full-length feature: *La Pointe Courte*. She had filmed it in Sète.[20] It was both a documentary about a poor neighbourhood and a drama about incommunicability (the word had yet to be invented). A couple talk a lot, for a long time, in a very literary style. At first we didn't understand this contradiction between reality and an excessively flowery style (intended by the auteur). Agnès Varda had hoped that her *Pointe Courte* would be presented in one of the cinemas taking part in the *cinéma d'essai* initiative, linked to the French Association for Cinema Critics. She had to make do, three years later, with a mediocre venue.[21]

The film was edited by Alain Resnais. We were wrong to not have understood in 1956 that *La Pointe Courte* was the beginning of an era: that of the New Wave, more so than *Et Dieu…créa la femme* (*And God Created Woman*, 1956) by Roger Vadim or *les Mauvaises Rencontres* (*Bad Liaisons*, 1955) by Alexandre Astruc. Shot on a very small budget, totally independently, with no stars (but with the excellent Silvia Montfort, then not well-known), *La Pointe Courte* prefigured, in both its production method and style, developments in French cinema around 1960.

The cinemas that missed their chance to screen this film to the public at the time (partly my fault), should show it today. If there is one film that influenced *Hiroshima mon amour*[22], both in its conception and style, this is it. Its only fault was to come too soon.

Undoubtedly, *La Pointe Courte* would have been better understood in 1960 than in 1956 by the public, and by critics – prisoners of their judgemental ways – always late to identify a movement, no matter what it is.

This singular woman, a stage photographer for the TNP (Théâtre National Populaire), was not discouraged by her first failure, even though there was no chance of funding another feature-length film, not even with money from friends.

She agreed to make documentaries commissioned by the tourist board: *Ô saisons, ô châteaux* (1958), about the Loire Valley and *Du côté de la côte* (1958), about the Côte d'Azur, that she wanted to call *La Cocotte d'Azur*.[23] An honourable success in Tours,[24] but no prize at Cannes.

And yet, with her sharp wit, the director had managed to transcend the commission, with its drastic list of specifications imposed by the institutional sponsors, and she showed the unexpected side of these touristy postcards, whilst expressing her own convictions and feelings. *L'Opéra Mouffe*, (1958), dedicated to the rue Mouffetard in Paris and to her pregnancy, did not have any more luck and only reached a tiny audience. What a shame for the public. And for the critics.

The New Wave, that she, more than anyone else, contributed to shaping, finally ended up supporting her. Last year she found a producer and a modest, but sufficient budget, to make *Cléo de 5 à 7*, for which she wrote the script and dialogue.

It didn't win the Delluc, nor the Vigo prize, in spite of some sincere advocates, but there were always a few votes missing to secure a majority. What a shame, not for the film, but for those jury members who were concerned about the prestige of their award. They will regret it in the future for *Cléo* as they regret it now for

Lola (1961). It's no secret that the director, Jacques Demy, is now Agnès Varda's husband. In the future, their two films will be rightly celebrated. We are the ones who didn't get it right.

Certain clever folk, who are in the know about this marriage, will think that Lola is the older sister of Cléo. I don't think so. A person's private life has nothing to do with this kind of thing. Those who are determined to prove that Elsa Triolet is influenced by Aragon's *La Semaine sainte* in her novel *Les Manigances*[25] (or vice versa), are wasting their time. They are both wonderful books, but without literary parentage. It's the same for *Lola* and *Cléo,* and I find Cléo closer to Clarisse from *Les Manigances* (without any possible influence).

Cléo unfolds in an hour and a half and Varda would have liked to shoot it in exactly 90 minutes, with a *caméra-stylo*[26] ten times more sophisticated than the primitive mechanics still employed by Leacock and Jean Rouch.[27]

Cléo's reality is, first and foremost, fundamentally our reality: the year 1961, with its never-ending not-so-phony war.[28] It matters that the film, like Dreyer's *Jeanne d'Arc* (1928), was 'shot in the right order', both chronologically and geographically (of course this isn't the only method of making a film). I was part of a group of a hundred or so writers who, on the initiative of *Izvestia*[29] (inspired by an idea by Gorky[30]), contributed to a collective work: the *25th September 1960,* recording how the day was lived in 100 countries around the world. During a week devoted to Hungarian cinema, we saw an excellent documentary (done a disservice with a bombastic commentary) called *Histoire d'une seconde* ('History of a Second'), that showed in slow motion zoo animals frightened by a bomb exploding …

Everything is in everything. A drop of dew can reflect the entire universe, as Eisenstein and Dovjenko[31] liked to say. Ninety minutes in the life of a *Parisienne* can contain the anxieties and preoccupations of a nation – France – even if her universe, for the superficial viewer, is just a small world of florists and dressmakers, songwriters and sugar daddies.

Is this film, which I found overwhelming, without its faults? Fortunately, nothing is faultless. Nothing is more boring than perfection. Heartbeats are irregular compared to the ticking of a clock. What is important in a film (or a novel, or a painting), is that we hear within it the beating of a 'tell-tale heart'.

In the rhythm of the passing minutes, I heard the incessant beating of Agnès Varda's heart, like 'the variations of a violin and a metronome'. Time passes, relentlessly, until the meeting of two victims of two cancers, one of which (that we dared not, and could not, name) is called The Algerian War.

'Cain, what have you done to your brother'? History, or else critics, sooner or later end up addressing this question to writers, to artistic schools, or to a whole era. 'We were, in our own way, in chains,'[32] the New Wave could respond, which rose to prominence whilst massacres were being carried out. 'Don't judge us too severely for remaining in the world of sports cars and white telephones'. Of course, but witnesses must run the risk of having their throats cut. Or at least being censored.

'Don't be too hard on us. During those dreadful times, our best films remain chronicles of their time. Sometimes they are even ahead.'

'Was Godard's *Le Petit Soldat* (1960) – the intimate journal of an OAS[33] killer *avant la lettre* – not extremely topical, and ahead of its time, three years before the true revelation of those three sinister initials? Or *Moranbong* by Bonnardot[34], a great story of love and understanding. Or *Tu ne tueras point* (*Thou Shalt Not Kill,* 1960) by Claude Autant-Lara, which asks the question, can we accept becoming torturers.'

There were a few things I didn't like the first time I saw *Cléo de 5 à 7*. The Montparnasse studio, extremely stylish, truly ravishing, but a little too many flowers and feathers. The attraction (in the music-hall sense) of snippets from a few songs. And I wanted to feel more affection for the soldier played by Antoine Bourseiller, who is a little uneasy in front of the camera.

I may no longer think that when I watch it for the second time. But more importantly, *since watching the film, I still have an open wound in my heart.* No-one has ever shown so well our tragic times[35], with death and torture present on every street corner, in the most banal spectacles. And this anxiety is in no way metaphysical, it's physical.

Am I brave enough to watch *Cléo de 5 à 7* again? This film has touched me too profoundly. And I am not one to suffer. But if you want to know what a real film is, a film that's modern and profoundly of our time, if you want to watch the lives of protagonists that you recognise, and if you also want to have a good time – because the tragic narrative is also very funny – then run, don't hesitate to run and see *Cléo de 5 à 7*, one of the films that by itself will make the season of 1961-1962 a wonderful season.

*   *   *

Cléo de 5 à 7 (Cléo from 5 to 7) is a Masterpiece [*]
JEAN-LOUIS BORY

Agnès Varda's film is the polar opposite of *L'Année dernière à Marienbad (Last Year at Marienbad,* 1959). With the latter, Alain Resnais produced a masterpiece of affected beauty and extreme artificiality; with the former, Agnès Varda gives us a masterpiece of technical freedom and versatility. The most mundane, the

---

[*] *Arts*, 17 April 1962. (Translated from the French by Jennifer Wallace)

most lively, everyday language replaces the haughty poetry of Alain Robbe-Grillet. *Marienbad* and *Cléo* are as different as oil and vinegar. I very much enjoy creating connections between cinema and literature: therefore, without hesitation, I declare that *Cléo de 5 à 7* is to the cinema what *Mrs Dalloway* or *To the Lighthouse* are to the literary canon. Agnès Varda is the Virginia Woolf of modern cinema.

They share the same audacity from the start: Varda, like Woolf, establishes an extremely rigorous chronological framework. As the title indicates, we spend two hours in the company of Cléo – to be perfectly precise: from five o'clock to six thirty. Literally, the ninety minutes that the screening lasts. Varda achieves what classical theoreticians dream of: she matches as precisely as possible the amount of time spent by the spectator in their seat to the time on screen as experienced by the characters. The time of representation is the same as the time represented. Provided the spectator sat down when the first image of *Cléo* appears, as we hear the last stroke of five o'clock, at the end of the film, the spectator's watch and the hospital clock we see on screen would show the same time: six thirty.

First repercussion: no ellipses. Even during the taxi and bus sequences we stay with Cléo throughout, experiencing the real time of her journey. This doesn't mean that the aim of the film is merely to show the passing of time, that would quickly become tedious. Instead, within this objective time, because of how the flow of movement is represented – quickly or slowly – Varda suggests subjective time. One sequence, that is identical in length to another (on screen, subtitles constantly remind us what time it is, matching our time), can feel shorter. Another stretches forth, provoking our impatience, and running the risk of provoking our boredom, just as the real time lived by Cléo provokes her impatience or her boredom (for example the last moments in the taxi back to her house). The first dazzling success of Agnès Varda is that she has, without cheating, represented duration, recreated the passing of time.

To this 'timetable' Varda adds a looming sense of tragedy with the theme of Death. The film opens on a tarot reading framed in an overhead shot: we only see the cards, with their strange, disconcerting illustrations, and the two hands that shuffle and turn them – one young, one old. We only hear two voices – one young, one old. The prophecy is catastrophic: the young client is in danger, and we quickly learn through fragments of her private life that she fears she has cancer, and that she will receive the results of a medical test at seven o'clock. The consultation with the fortune teller triggers her fear. From five to seven, the two hours that separate the tarot cards from the test, the fortune teller from the doctor, occultism from science, Cléo will struggle with this fear. Varda shows us Cléo's internal battle between the superstitious omens by which a music-hall singer of modest origins allows herself to be easily dominated (a broken mirror, unlucky phrases that suggest cancer or the hospital, a sad ballad that mirrors her reality too closely), and the impulse to live that lies within a young and beautiful person like Cléo, in a teeming, vibrant city like Paris, on such a beautiful day, the afternoon of the first day of summer.

Cléo de 5 à 7 is a film about the fear of death. Intermittent bursts of fear break in waves onto carefree shores of gaiety. This obsession with Time, sprung on Cléo by visions of a clock or other related symbols, and nurtured for the spectator through surreptitious subtitles – 17h18, 17h23 – keeps us in a state of anxiety. And it forces Cléo into her haphazard walk across the city to 'kill time', until the potentially fatal results of her medical test.

Under this fearful influence, Cléo undergoes a spiritual transcendence. The passing of time provokes a change in her. Initially, Cléo is a sweet, music-hall doll: capricious, flirty, and completely selfish – for example, she is totally indifferent to the news on the radio during the taxi ride (Algeria, a putsch, various riots, innumerable tragedies). But anxiety forces the young woman out of herself. The change happens the second Cléo rips off her starlet wig and goes out onto the street. She finally sees others, because, perhaps for the first time, she is attentive. She watches them. She hears them. There is incredible diversity before her. 'Today everything amazes me', she says, 'people's faces next to mine'. In its rendering of flickering images; a myriad of reflections; brief oddities in the street; the proliferation of snatches of conversation – everything that the flood of a city crowd sweeps along with it – the art of Agnès Varda seems incomparable. The colourful street opera that Varda previously captured on the rue Mouffetard[36] is seen once again during Cléo's walk. In the midst of this crowd, Cléo abandons her stage name and goes back to being Florence. She has been a kept woman until this moment, will she come to experience real, sincere love? The 'truth' of trees and water (even if they are just in a public park), and the natural openness of a young soldier destined for the war in Algeria (therefore doomed, perhaps, to die) transform Cléo. And if at the end of it all she is no longer afraid, it is not because the doctor promises a cure, but because *another person* exists for her.

Equally admirable is how, without any artificial flash-backs, which would be impossible due to Varda's decision to stick to real time (memories intervene only in brief flashes, quick still images that cut into the rhythm of the editing); without indulgent explanations by third parties; without the intervention of a narrator, we come to know Cléo, her past, her relationships, her vocation, and her hopes. Seeking the warmth of others against the cold that threatens her, she reveals her true self through small acts that may seem insignificant, but constitute the framework of her everyday life. And not just Cléo, but her female companion, her musician friends, her model friend, the cinema projectionist, the official Lover (a

Corinne Marchand (right) in *Cléo de 5 à 7* (1962).

playboy performed with great aplomb by José-Luis de Villalonga) and the con-
script Antoine, remarkably depicted by Antoine Bourseiller: these characters are
alive. And they live because Varda knows how to capture clichés, small gaffes and
the way people speak today; because the cinematography doesn't have the frozen
perfection of a film shot in a studio; and, because finding beauty in the frame is
not synonymous with perfect aestheticism. The game at play between the subjective camera, which shows us what, and how, Cléo sees, and the objective camera,
which shows us Cléo surrounded by others, testifies to Varda's great freedom.

Every detail is remarkable. For those who enjoy in-jokes, look out for the faux
comic silent film sequence: Eddie Constantine, Danielle Delorme, J.-C. Brialy (if
I'm not mistaken) have fun with this pastiche.

The most marvellous thing about the faux film, is that it captures the same light
and outdoor locations as *Cléo*, generating a running impression of unease – of
being out of sorts –which matches Cléo's nervous faux-cheeriness.

I've rarely been this sure of being right: *Cléo de 5 à 7* is a masterpiece.

Agnès Varda's early work, from *La Pointe Courte* to *Cléo de 5 à 7* is synonymous with the New Wave and has found its rightful place in it. However, she also went on to pursue a remarkably long and prolific career until her death in 2019, gathering new audiences and fans on the way, which in part explains her continued visibility and high status. The case of Paule Delsol could not be more different. She made two short films in 1958 and 1961, her first feature *La Dérive* in 1964 and subsequently only one feature (*Ben et Bénédict*, 1977) and a television film in 1985. She later became a novelist. Delsol's main claim to cinematic fame in general and in respect of the New Wave is thus *La Dérive*, an unusual and striking portrait of a sexually free young woman, 'drifting' (the meaning of the title) from man to man in the south of France, shot on location and on a small budget. While the film gave rise to many shocked and disapproving reviews by male critics at the time, the female journalist Michèle Manceaux, in the first article here, offers a sympathetic portrait of Delsol and of her film, based on an interview with her – her interest signalled right from her title, 'Paul Delsol. A woman who understands women' (published in *L'Express* in October 1963). Among other things Manceaux places *La Dérive* within the circumstances of Delsol's life and she discusses the censorship suffered by the film. The second text, by Claude-Marie Trémois, was published in *Télérama* in August 1964. Trémois has had a long and successful career as a film critic and historian (she wrote a book on French cinema in the 1990s). Writing in the early 1960s, she is, like Manceaux, one of the few critics to see the filmic originality as well as sociological interest of this 'portrait of a woman by a woman', as her piece is called. As she astutely says, '*La Dérive* is a rare work in which a woman is depicted truthfully and seen through eyes that are neither contemptuous, nor protective or falsely admiring.' The film unfortunately is still difficult to get hold of and at the time of writing there does not appear to be a version with English sub-titles. One can only hope that, as for Jacqueline Audry and *Les Petits matins*, critical interest in the film and in Delsol may facilitate the availability of *La Dérive* and thus widen our view of the New Wave..

Ginette Vincendeau

Paule Delsol: *La Dérive* (1964)

Paule Delsol: A Woman Who Understands Women[*]
MICHÈLE MANCEAUX

It is wonderful to watch a first film, the first piece of work from an unknown director, and to like it. It's even better to be able to discuss it so that others can discover Paule Delsol for themselves – a young, red-headed, fast-talking woman with a Midi accent.

Paule Delsol lives in Montpellier, where she is raising four children, or four sprogs as she calls them. She is married to a cameraman, which is how everything started.

Everything, meaning *La Dérive*, a sensitive and accurately judged film that succeeds with every shot. *La Dérive* tells a very banal story: a pretty girl from the provinces, specifically Palavas-les-Flots, is bored in her village. The girl is cute, but lazy, with fantasies of a car and the great unknown, and she only has her easy-going, supple body as a means to get them.

A bit foolish, a bit sentimental, but also poetic and rebellious, the heroine, Jackie, hops from bed to bed. Between two disappointing encounters she returns home to her mother. This is not played as sad, or dramatic, just inevitable – she's a listless girl, a dreamer, who goes with the flow.

Paule Delsol understands women. From the opening shots, we feel that she listens to them often, watches them a lot. She wanted to be a psychologist, but in Hanoi where she was raised, it wasn't possible, so she studied Law instead. She never finished because she got married. When she came back to France to work, she became a beautician in Montpellier. This is where she heard a lot of secrets.

'Girls would come in crying, they would wail 'he left me!' I would say 'had you known him long?' They would reply, 'since yesterday', and every time I was flabbergasted. How can someone be simultaneously so naive and so independent? That's where the problem lies.'

'You have to be a little smarter to wield your independence.'

An Inheritance

'The character of Jackie is almost entirely based on a real person. The girl who inspired me was also unable to have children. Maybe it seems arbitrary, doubtless it is, but so what? I didn't want to throw in more complications. The risk of falling pregnant is another story.'

---

[*] *L'Express*, 31 October 1963. (Translated from the French by Jennifer Wallace)

'This girl is truly independent. She's working-class but she has the nonchalance of a girl from a higher social status. By chance, I saw a photo of the actress who plays Jackie in *Le Midi libre*. Her name is Jacqueline Bastide and she wanted to change her name to Linda Vandal. That's my kind of heroine! She wanted to be a Vandal! Now her stage name is Jacqueline Vandal. She compromised with half the name...'

How did you choose the other actors?
'It was a bit haphazard. One for his voice, another because she made a small gesture that I liked, or a smart retort. I used a mix of professionals and amateurs.'

How did you overcome the technical difficulties?
'My cameraman husband helped me. He's fantastic. There is no technical problem he cannot solve.'

Where did you find the money?
'I inherited some money. As I never felt that this money really belonged to me, I wanted to spend it straight away. I checked with the kids, as after all they are the ones who would have benefitted from it. But they wanted me to make a film.'

Do you go to the cinema often?
'No, you could even say I have no cinematic education. Hanoi and Montpellier are not the best places to see films. Apparently, Antonioni and Bergman have great female characters. But, generally, I think women have a false impression of themselves because of how men portray them on screen: they do it badly. They see shrill shrews, fat cows in hair rollers, or seductresses. There's no nuance. You get lifeless, cardboard cut-out portrayals.'

Current Trends

Paule Delsol wrote two books, published by Julliard, in 1958 and 1961. *Adieu et merci* and *Pourquoi j'aime Nine*, which was brought out in paperback in the USA.

'I've stopped writing. Maybe I'll start again when I'm really old. Cinema is so much less abstract, so much more alive.'[37]

To be alive, living: Paule Delsol hums with life. She tells a thousand stories at once.

How will your film be released?
'I don't know. I would like it to be released so I can make another, about students. I only find young people interesting. *La Dérive* was originally going to be released by Gaumont, but then the censorship commission gave it an adult rating. So Gaumont dropped it.'

Jacqueline Vandal (right) and Marc-Hervé Sourine in *La Dérive* (1964).

'They banned it [for under-18s] under the pretext that the heroine was an immoral character. Apparently, it shocked everyone on the commission that she was infertile, even though in the film she explains it's because of a botched operation. It's incredible, someone can plan to murder a man for an entire film and it's not immoral, but a girl who does what she wants with her body, that's shameful.'

Considering your interest in women – they are currently being criticised for acting more like men, do you think that's true?
'Oh! Yes, it's very fashionable to think this. And it's also fashionable for women to complain that there are no (real) men anymore. All of this means nothing to me. Women and men are equal. There is no rivalry. Their differences are what make them equal. We should keep those differences.'

You, for example, were not content with raising four children, you wanted to work as well?
'Oh! I think that by having children we become even more creative, but you know, there will always be those who do everything and others who do nothing.'

Amongst the great dialogue of *La Dérive*, there is a line that touches on this idea in a different way. A boy says to Jackie 'You're the kind of girl to get into trouble', and Jackie replies, 'I'd rather be in trouble than bored.'

*   *   *

A Woman Adrift (*Une Fille à la Dérive*)*
CLAUDE-MARIE TRÉMOIS

The Portrait of a Woman by a Woman

A girl is sitting on a low wall next to a boy who strums a guitar. 'I'm so hungry', says the girl. It's been two years since Jackie left with Pierre. Together they have led a nomadic life. One night here, the next day there. Pierre plays outside cafés. One day they have money, the next they go hungry. But Jackie wholeheartedly enjoys this carefree life. She trails after Pierre. She believes in him. She has faith in his talent. She loves him. This little girl[38], who scandalised her village of Palavas-les-Flots, looks to be outwardly liberated, but she is secretly a faithful woman, utterly devoted to her man. 'We are realistic romantics' says Pierre. She repeats it. And when Pierre, who knows and says he's a street cat, leaves her in a train whilst she's sleeping, she also becomes a street cat, out of loyalty to the man she wants to forget. She starts to drift…

This is how drifting starts in Paule Delsol's debut film, which stars no-one famous.

Paule Delsol, a novelist, shot *Une fille à la dérive* in the Hérault region,[39] where she lives (the title must have been imposed by the distributors. It's a shame. The original title, *La Dérive,* was beautiful). Paule Delsol managed to produce the film herself. She is the complete auteur: both writing and directing.

This film is a portrait, she says, in one of the two intertitles that open the film. It is effectively a portrait without statement or rhetoric, of a woman by a woman. *La Dérive* is one of those rare films where femininity is portrayed truthfully, shown through eyes that are not scornful, nor protective, nor falsely admiring. Paule Delsol didn't see her heroine as an object to be depicted, but as a living being, worthy of respect, whose life we watch.

Jackie is Daring, not Deceptive

Jackie never explains her actions. She wanders here and there, changing lovers on a whim, without ever analysing herself. She lives in the present. Nor has Paule Delsol 'constructed' her film. *La Dérive* is a wandering film, sometimes fast, sometimes

---

* *Télérama*, 30 August 1964. (Translated from the French by Jennifer Wallace)

Jacqueline Vandal (left) and Pierre Barouh in *La Dérive* (1964).

slow, in turn straightforward and meandering. Between each escapade Jackie returns to her mother. She even tries, genuinely, to work. 'But', she says, 'I don't know how to do anything.' And her fear of mediocrity and vulgarity constantly propels her to the next man. She likes money, of course, in the sense that she believes money can save her from mediocrity. But she will always put her feelings before money.

Her mother guilelessly advises her to let herself be bought, to ensure her future. As her daughter has given up the much-vaunted value of respectability, the least she can do is make her indiscretions profitable. But Jackie is simultaneously decent and reckless: to escape boredom and the stifling atmosphere of her family home, Jackie will do anything; but in reality, in all these young men, she is looking for Pierre. If she accepts the protection of an old, rich man, it is only out of despair, after she's twice been abandoned and betrayed. She doesn't have it in her to be deceptive, she is just daring. A naive, young girl whose 'sentimentality leads her to drift', says Paule Delsol. She won't become a harlot, but perhaps, disappointment after disappointment, abandonment after abandonment, she will stoop low, without ever letting it dent her pride. She will always be a street cat who claims to love freedom, but is always ready, for love, to go back to being a submissive woman.

A Fascinating Truth

La Dérive is a clever and tender film, cruel and nostalgic, reflecting the current era. It depicts the conundrum of today's woman. A woman who no longer wants to be an object, but who instinctively reverts to being one for love. Will a man finally see Jackie as something more than a beautiful, wild animal and love her forever? But a woman always needs to ensure the future, as the young painter for whom Jackie abandons everything at the end of the film puts it[40]. A young man, a bohemian – Jackie is drawn instinctively to people like her – struggles to commit to the future. Will Jackie, so generous, so devoted, once again be left to drift?

The auteur never intervenes to moralise Jackie's clumsy quest for love, but the moral of the story is clear. And powerfully so. Jackie is hungry for love, but will never be sated. Her path will never lead to happiness.

Moreover, Paule Delsol's talent lies in suggesting but never explaining. She teaches us to look. With her camera she captures a glance, an expression, a furtive gesture. She catches them as if by chance, without appearing to try. Her film is as fluid as Jackie's roaming soul. The characters exist in a surprisingly vivid world. The authenticity of her work is compelling. All it takes is one clumsy, yet honest word from Jackie, a childish gesture, a flutter of her eyelids, to show us the conflicting feelings that are splitting her in two. And Jacqueline Vandal, new on the scene, is here to stay[41]. She doesn't resemble anyone else. She's carving out her own space.

La Dérive is both a poetic and realist film. Paule Delsol likes even her most pathetic characters, and teaches us to like them too. The tone of the film is discerning, just like the little instinctive animal depicted within it. This is a welcome change from the intellectualism and cult of mediocrity of certain New Wave films. Jackie could be one of their heroines. But the virtue of Paule Delsol is that she likes her protagonist enough to pierce beneath the surface and let us sense her soul.

Notes

All notes, except No. 9, by editor Ginette Vincendeau.

1. Talk given on behalf of the Association of film authors (Association des auteurs de films), Paris Inter radio, 18 December 1955. The talk did not have a title – I extracted it from the first sentence.

2. After the word 'screenwriter', the original transcript indicates, 'laughter in the voice'. This probably refers to the fact that Audry worked with her husband Pierre Laroche, who scripted all her films from her first feature, *Les Malheurs de Sophie* (1946) to his death in 1962.

3. The transcription of this talk is missing its ending. However, on 26 October 1964, Audry gave a similar talk to France Culture radio, reiterating many of the points from the 18 December 1955 talk, as well as emphasizing the importance of collaboration between the director and her collaborators. Below is the conclusion to this second talk, which appears to complete the truncated first text.

4. *Les Vacances de Monsieur Hulot/Monsieur Hulot's Holiday* (Jacques Tati, 1953).

5. *Viaggio in Italia/Journey to Italy* (Roberto Rossellini, 1954).

6. Paul Valéry's 1920 poem, which refers to one of the sea-side cemeteries in Sète.

7. Heidegger, *Approche de Hölderlin*, traduction Henri Corbin, Paris : Gallimard, 1973, p. 59.

8. Jean-Paul Sartre, *Being and Nothingness*, New York: Washington Square Press, 1943, p. 481.

9. *Le Cimetière marin* – Paul Valéry.

10. Directed by Jean Cocteau.

11. Théâtre National Populaire (a prestigious state-subsidised theatre in Paris).

12. *Viaggio in Italia/Journey to Italy*, Roberto Rossellini, 1954. Rossellini's film came out in September 1954, after Varda had shot *La Pointe Courte*.

13. In 1954 Varda created Tamaris films (later renamed Ciné-Tamaris) to produce and distribute *La Pointe Courte*.

14. Sadoul's original title, 'Le cœur révélateur', is an allusion to the French title of Edgar Allan Poe's short story *The Tell-Tale Heart* published in 1843.

15. It was decided to remove Sadoul's development about this film, as not directly relevant to the rest of the article devoted to *Cléo de 5 à 7*. The author said: 'I think this 1935 adaptation by Henry Hathaway (a mediocre director who got lucky) is superior to the George du Maurier novel. It's a passionate love story. A man has loved a woman since childhood. He is separated from her and thrown into an awful prison. Despite shackles, prison bars, space and time, he continues to live close to her, in his thoughts, until he dies.'.

16. Played by the actor and filmmaker Serge Korber.

17. In fact, only Varda's father was of Greek origins; her mother was from France.

18. The figure appears on a fresco, dating from c. 1400 BC; the palace is situated in Knossos, Crete.

19. The film critic André Bazin, his wife and their son.

20. A city on the South-West Mediterranean coast; the film was shot there in 1954.

21. The 'cinéma d'essai' initiative, in which a number of Parisian art cinemas teamed up with the critics' association, led to the Cinéma d'Art et d'Essai movement, founded in 1955. In

fact, contrary to what Sadoul says, the film was shown at some prestigious art cinemas, including the Studio Parnasse and the Cinéma du Panthéon.

22. Directed by Alain Resnais, with a script by Marguerite Duras.

23. A pun on 'Côte d'Azur' and 'Cocotte', in the sense of a 'loose woman'.

24. Referring to the annual short film festival in Tours from 1955 to 1968.

25. Louis Aragon's *La Semaine sainte* was published in 1958, his wife Elsa Triolet's *Les Manigances* in 1962.

26. The *caméra-stylo* is a term borrowed from Alexandre Astruc's article 'The Birth of a New Avant-Garde: *La Caméra-Stylo*' – see section I in this volume.

27. The British-born Richard Leacock and the French Jean Rouch are leading figures in the *cinéma-vérité* movement.

28. Through his reference to the 'funny war' at the beginning of World War II, Sadoul is making a reference to the Algerian war, which ended officially at the Evian agreements on 18 March 1962, shortly before the release of the film in France (11 April 1962).

29. Major Soviet daily broadsheet newspaper; Sadoul here openly acknowledges his Communist credentials.

30. Maxim Gorky (1868-1936) was a major Russian and Soviet writer.

31. Sergei Eisenstein (1898-1948) and Alexandre Dovjenko (1894-1956), two major Soviet filmmakers.

32. Sadoul is alluding to the first sentence of Jean-Jacques Rousseau's 1762 *The Social Contract*, 'Man is born free, and he is everywhere in chains'.

33. OAS stands for 'Organisation de l'Armée Secrète' or Secret Army Organisation, an extreme right-wing French dissident paramilitary organisation, active during the Algerian War.

34. *Moranbong, une aventure coréenne*, directed by Jean-Claude Bonnardot in 1960.

35. In the original article, Sadoul alludes to the title of an 1866 left-wing political song, *Le Temps des cerises*, a wistful evocation of the tragic consequences of social struggle, later associated with the brutal repression of the Paris Commune of 1871 – comparing it implicitly with the repression of Algerian independence fighters.

36. Bory here refers to Varda's documentary *L'Opéra Mouffe/Diary of a Pregnant Woman* (1958), set in the street market of rue Mouffetard in Paris.

37. In fact, Delsol went on to write several books in the 1960s, 1970s and 1980s, including *Horoscopes chinois/Chinese Horoscopes* which was translated into English and reprinted several times.

38. Trémois uses the term 'petite fille', which normally means 'little girl'. Although 'young woman' would be more appropriate, it was decided to keep her phrasing.

39. In South-West France, on the Languedoc side of the Mediterranean coast.

40. The character in the film actually says, 'for women, love means the next day, the future, it's physiological'.

41. Unfortunately, Trémois's prediction did not come true. Vandal's subsequent film career was quite short – she made three films and one television series and stopped in 1968 after *Trois filles vers le soleil/Erotic Urge*, an erotic comedy.

Select Bibliography of Books in French and English

The New Wave

Bazin, André, *Le cinéma français de la libération à la nouvelle vague* (Paris: Cahiers du cinéma, 1983).

Borde, Raymond, Buache, Freddy and Curtelin, Jean, *Nouvelle Vague* (Lyon: Premier Plan, Serdoc, 1962).

Buache, Freddy, *Nouvelle vague* (Paris: Serdoc, 1962).

Cauchetier, Raymond, *Raymond Cauchetier's New Wave* (Woodbridge, Suffolk: ACC Editions, 2015).

Cléder, Jean and Mouellic, Gilles, *Nouvelle vague, nouveaux rivages* (Rennes: Presses Universitaires de Rennes, 2001).

Clouzot, Claire, *Le cinéma français depuis la nouvelle vague* (Paris: Nathan, 1972).

de Baecque, Antoine, *La Nouvelle vague: portrait d'une jeunesse*, 3rd edition (Paris: Flammarion, 2019) [first published 1998].

de Baecque, Antoine & Tesson, Charles (eds), *La Nouvelle Vague* (Paris: Petite bibliothèque des Cahiers du cinéma, 1999).

Douchet, Jean, *Nouvelle Vague* (Paris: Cinémathèque Française/Hazan, 1998). Published in English as *French New Wave* (New York: Distributed Art Publishers, 1999). Translated by Robert Bonnono.

Douin, Jean-Luc (ed.) *La nouvelle vague vingt-cinq ans après* (Paris: Editions du Cerf, 1983).

Durgnat, Raymond, *Nouvelle Vague, the first decade* (London: A Motion Monograph, Motion Publications, 1963).

Frayling, Christopher, Tony Nourmand and Graham Marsh (eds), *French New Wave: A Revolution in Design* (London: Reel Art Press, 2019).

Graham, Peter (ed.), *The New Wave* (London: Secker & Warburg in association with the British Film Institute, 1968).

Greene, Naomi, *The French New Wave – A New Look* (London: Wallflower Press, 2007).

Higgins, Lynn. A., *New Novel, New wave, New Politics* (Lincoln: University of Nebraska Press, 1996).

Kline, T. Jefferson, *Screening the Text: Intertextuality in New Wave French Cinema* (Baltimore: Johns Hopkins University Press, 1992).

Labarthe, André S., *Essai sur le jeune cinéma français* (Paris: Le Terrain Vague, 1960).

McMahon, Orlene Denice, *Listening to the French New Wave, The Film Music and Composers of Postwar French Art Cinema* (Oxford, Bern: Peter Lang, 2014).

Marie, Michel, *La nouvelle vague: Une école artistique* (Paris: Nathan, 1997). Published in English as *The French New Wave: An Artistic School* (Malden: Mass.: Blackwell, 2002). Translated by Richard Neupert.

Mary, Philippe, *La Nouvelle vague et le cinéma d'auteur. Socio-analyse d'une révolution artistique* (Paris: Editions du Seuil, 2006).

Monaco, James, *The New Wave: Truffaut, Godard, Chabrol, Rohmer, Rivette* (New York: Oxford University Press, 1976).

Neupert, Richard, *A History of the French New Wave Cinema* (Madison, Wisconsin: The University of Wisconsin Press, 2002). Second edition, with a new chapter on the Left Bank Group (2007).

Ostrowska, Dorota, *Reading the French New Wave, Critics, Writers and Art Cinema in France* (London: Wallflower Press, 2008).

Rolandeau, Yannick, *Nouvelle vague : Essai critique d'un mythe cinématographique* (Paris: L'Harmattan, 2018).

Schmid, Marion, *Intermedial Dialogues: The French New Wave and the Other Arts* (Edinburgh: Edinburgh University Press, 2019).

Sellier, Geneviève, *La Nouvelle Vague, un cinéma au masculin singulier* (Paris: CNRS Editions, 2006). Published in English as *Masculine Singular: French New Wave Cinema* (Duke University Press, 2008). Translated by Kristin Ross.

Siclier, Jacques, *Nouvelle vague?* (Paris: Editions du Cerf, 1961).

Simsolo, Noël, *Le dictionnaire de la Nouvelle Vague* (Paris : Flammarion: 2013).

Tassone, Aldo, *Que reste-t-il de la nouvelle vague?* (Paris: Stock, 2003).

Individual figures

Alexandre, Wilfrid, *Claude Chabrol, la traversée des apparences: biographie* (Paris: Le Félin, 2003).

Alter, Nora, *Chris Marker* (Urbana and Chicago: University of Illinois Press, 2006).

Anderst, Leah (ed.) *The Films of Éric Rohmer: French New Wave to Old Master* (Basingstoke: Palgrave Macmillan, 2014).

Andrew, Dudley, *André Bazin* (New York: Columbia University Press, 1990).

Andrew, Dudley, and Anne Gillain (eds), *A Companion to François Truffaut* (Malden, MA: Wiley-Blackwell, 2013).

Armas, Miguel & Luc Chessel (eds), *Textes critiques / Jacques Rivette* (Post Editions, 2018).

Armes, Roy, *The Cinema of Alain Resnais* (New York: A.S. Barnes, 1968).

Astruc, Alexandre, *Du stylo à la caméra* (Paris: Archiper, 1992).

Astruc, Alexandre and D'Hugues, Philippe, *Le Montreur d'ombres, mémoires* (Paris: Bartillat, 1996).

Astruc, Alexandre, *Le plaisir en toutes choses : entretiens avec Noël Simsolo* (Paris: Écriture, 2015).

Austin, Guy, *Claude Chabrol* (Manchester: Manchester University Press, 1999).

Ayrolles, François, *Jean-Pierre Léaud* (Châtenay-Malabry: A. Beaulet, 2007).

Bardot, Brigitte, *Initiales BB*. Vol. I (Paris: Bernard Grasset, 1996).

Barnet, Marie-Claire (ed.), *Agnès Varda Unlimited: Image, Music, Media* (Oxford: Legenda, 2017).

Bastide, Bernard, *Bernadette Lafont : une vie de cinéma* (Nîmes: Atelier Baie, 2013).

Bauby, Jean-Dominique, *Raoul Lévy, un aventurier du cinéma* (Paris: Jean-Claude Lattès, 1995).

Bellour, Raymond, *Alexandre Astruc* (Paris: Seghers, 1963).

Bellour, Raymond and Bandy, Mary Lea (eds), *Jean-Luc Godard: Son & Image* (New York: Museum of Modern Art, 1992).

Benayoun, Robert, *Alain Resnais: Arpenteur de l'imaginaire* (Paris: Stock, 1980).

Benezet, Delphine, *The Cinema of Agnès Varda, Resistance and Eclecticism* (New York, Chichester, West Sussex: Wallflower Press, 2014).

Bergala, Alain (ed.), *Jean-Luc Godard par Jean-Luc Godard* (Paris: Editions de l'Etoile/ Cahiers du cinema, 1985).

Bergala, Alain (ed.), *Godard par Godard, les années Cahiers (1950-1959)* (Paris: Flammarion, 2007)

Bergala, Alain, *Godard au travail, les années 60* (Paris: Cahiers du cinéma, 2010)

Berthomé, Jean-Pierre, *Jacques Demy et les racines du rêve* (Nantes: L'Atalante, 2014, 3e édition augmentée).

Blanchet, Christian, *Claude Chabrol* (Paris: Rivages/Cinéma, 1989).

Blanchon, Philippe and Jacques Sicard, *Godard de Manon Lescaut à Manon l'Écho* (Paris: La Nerthe, 2019).

Boiron, Pierre, *Pierre Kast* (Paris: Editions Pierre L'Herminier, 1985).

Bonitzer, Pascal, *Eric Rohmer* (Paris: Cahiers du Cinéma, 1991).

Boulangé, Guillaume, *Jacques Demy – Agnès Varda : Essai de généalogie artistique* (Selena, 2020).

Bounoure, Gaston, *Alain Resnais* (Paris: Seghers, 1974).

Braucourt, Guy, *Claude Chabrol* (Paris: Seghers, 1971).

Braunberger, Pierre, Producteur, *Cinémamémoire* (Paris: Centre National de la Cinématographie/ Centre Georges Pompidoum 1987).

Brink, Joram ten (ed.), *Building Bridges, The Cinema of Jean Rouch* (London: Wallflower, 2007).

Brody, Richard, *Everything is Cinema: The Working Life of Jean-Luc Godard* (London: Faber, 2008).

Brown, Royal S. (ed.), *Focus on Godard* (Englewood Cliffs, N.J.: Prentice-Hall, 1972).

Burch, Noël (ed.), *Pierre Kast : écrits 1945–1983* (Paris: L'Harmattan, 2014).

Cahiers du cinéma, *Le Roman de François Truffaut* (Paris: Cahiers du cinema, 1984).

Cahoreau, Gilles, *François Truffaut, 1932-1984* (Paris: Julliard, 1989).

Cameron, Ian (ed.), *The Films of Jean-Luc Godard* (New York: Praeger, 1970).

Cardullo, Bert (ed.), *Bazin at Work: Major Essays and Reviews from the Forties and Fifties* (New York: Routledge, 1996).

Cardullo, Bert (ed.), *Interviews with Eric Rohmer* (Chaplin Books, 2012).

Cerisuelo, Marc, *Jean-Luc Godard* (Paris: L'Herminier/Editions des Quatre-Vents, 1989).

Cerisuelo, Marc (ed.), 'Jean-Luc Godard, au-delà de l'image', *Etudes Cinématographiques*, No. 194/202 (1993).

Chabrol, Claude, *Et pourtant je tourne, un homme et son métier* (Paris: Robert Laffont, 1976).

Cinémathèque française, *Le monde enchanté de Jacques Demy* (Paris: La Cinémathèque française/Skira Flammarion/Ciné-Tamaris, 2013)

Cléder, Jean, *Duras* (Paris: François Bourin, 2019).

Collet, Jean, *Jean-Luc Godard* (Paris: Seghers, 1963).

Colmant, Marie and Olivier Père, *Jacques Demy* (Paris: La Martinière, 2010).

Conley, Tom and T. Jefferson Kline (eds), *A Companion to Jean-Luc Godard* (Chichester: John Wiley & Sons, 2014).

Conway, Kelley, *Agnès Varda* (Urbana: University of Illinois Press, 2015).

Cooper, Sarah, *Chris Marker* (Manchester: Manchester University Press, 2008).

Costeix, Éric, *Alain Resnais: la mémoire de l'éternité* (Paris: L'Harmattan. 2013).

Costeix, Éric, *Georges Franju : L'image désincarnée* (Paris: L'Harmattan, 2019).

Coutard, Raoul, *L'Impériale de Van Su: Comment je suis entré dans le cinéma en dégustant une soupe chinoise* (Paris: Editions Ramsay, 2007).

Crisp, Colin, *François Truffaut* (New York: Praeger, 1972).

Crisp, Colin, *Eric Rohmer: Realist and Moralist* (Bloomington: Indiana University Press, 1988).

Dauman, Anatole, *Argos Films – Souvenir-Ecran* (Paris: Centre Georges Pompidou, 1989).

de Baecque, Antoine and Toubiana, Serge, *François Truffaut* (Paris: Gallimard, 1996). Published in English as *Truffaut* (New York: Alfred A. Knopf, 1999). Translated by Catherine Temerson.

de Baecque, Antoine and Noël Herpe, *Éric Rohmer: A Biography*, translated by Steven Rendall and Lisa Neal (New York: Columbia UP, 2016).

de Beauregard, Chantal, *Georges de Beauregard* (C. Lacour éditions, 1991).

Delavaud, Gilles, Esquenazi, Jean-Pierre and Grange, Marie-Françoise (eds.), *Godard et le métier d'artiste* (Paris: L'Harmattan, 2001).

Déon, Alice, Clara Robert (eds), *Entretiens avec Jacques Chancel : Jean-Pierre Melville, François Truffaut, Claude Chabrol, Louis Malle, Claude Lelouch* (Paris : Editions de la Table Ronde, 2017).

Dereux, Robin, and Serge Le Péron, *Alain Cavalier: cinéaste et filmeur* (Paris: L'Harmattan, 2014).

DeRoo, Rebecca J., *Agnès Varda Between Film, Photography, and Art* (Oakland: University of California Press, 2017).

Deschamps, Hélène, *Jacques Rivette : théâtre, amour, cinéma* (Paris : L'Harmattan, 2001).

Desjardins, Aline, *Truffaut* (Paris: Ramsay, 1987).

De Vita, Philippe, *Penser vers l'autre: Godard en entretien* (Paris: L'Harmattan, 2017).

Dixon, Wheeler Winston, *The Early Film Criticism of François Truffaut* (Bloomington: Indiana University Press, 1993).

Dixon, Wheeler Winston, *The Films of Jean-Luc Godard* (Albany: State University of New York Press, 1997).

Douin, Jean-Luc, *Jean-Luc Godard* (Paris: Rivages/Cinéma, 1989).

Douin, Jean-Luc (ed.), *François Truffaut: le roman du cinéma* (Paris: Le Monde, 2014).

Dousteyssier-Khoze, Catherine, *Claude Chabrol's Aesthetics of Opacity* (Edinburgh: Edinburgh University Press, 2018).

Dubois, Philippe (ed.), *Théorème 6: recherches sur Chris Marker* (Paris: Presses Sorbonne Nouvelle, 2002).

Duggan, Anne E., *Queer Enchantments Gender, Sexuality, and Class in the Fairy-Tale Cinema of Jacques Demy* (Detroit: Wayne State UP, 2013).

Estève, Michel (ed.), 'Jean-Luc Godard, au-delà du récit', *Études Cinématographiques*, No. 57/61 (1967).

Esquenazi, Jean-Pierre, *Godard et la société française des années 60* (Paris: Armand Colin, 2004).

Estève, Michel, 'Eric Rohmer 1', *Etudes Cinématographiques*, No. 146/148 (1985).

Estève, Michel, 'Eric Rohmer 2', *Etudes Cinématographiques*, No. 149/152 (1986).

Fiant, Antony, Roxane Hamery & Éric Thouvenel (eds), *Agnès Varda: le cinéma et au-delà* (Rennes: Presses Universitaires de Rennes, 2009) [first published 1995].

Fleischer, Alain, *L'Art d'Alain Resnais* (Paris: Centre Georges Pompidou, 1999.

Flitterman-Lewis, Sandy. *To Desire Differently: Feminism and the French Cinema* (Urbana: University of Illinois Press, 1990). [chapters on Agnès Varda]

Frappat, Hélène, *Jacques Rivette, secret compris* (Paris: Cahiers du cinema, 2001).

French, Philip (ed.), *Malle on Malle* (London: Faber and Faber, 1993).

Frey, Hugo, *Louis Malle* (Manchester: Manchester University Press, 2004).

Gauteur, Claude, *François Truffaut : en toutes lettres* (Grandvilliers: La Tour Verte, 2014).

Gauthier, Guy, *Chris Marker: écrivain multimédia, ou voyage à travers les médias* (Paris: L'Harmattan, 2001).

Gillain, Anne, *Le cinéma selon François Truffaut* (Paris: Flammarion, 1988).

Gillain, Anne, *François Truffaut: Le secret perdu* (Paris: Hatier, 1991). Published in English as *François Truffaut: The Lost Secret*, translated by Alistair Fox (Bloomington: Indiana University Press, 2013).

Gillain, Anne, *Tout Truffaut : 23 films pour comprendre l'homme et le cinéaste* (Paris: Armand Colin, 2019). Translated into English as *Totally Truffaut, 23 Films for Understanding the Man and the Filmmaker* (New York: Oxford University Press, 2021).

Gardies, André, *Le cinéma de Robbe-Grillet: Essai sémiocritique* (Paris: Albatross, 1983).

Gouslan, Elizabeth, *Truffaut et les femmes* (Paris : Grasset, 2016).

Gray, Marianne, *La Moreau: A biography of Jeanne Moreau* (Donald I, Fine Books, 1996); published in French as: Marianne Gray, avec la collaboration de Yannick Dehée, *Jeanne Moreau: le tourbillon d'une vie*; traduction Odile Demange (Paris: Nouveau Monde Editions, 2017).

Grosoli, Marco, *Eric Rohmer's Film Theory (1948-1953): From 'École Scherer' to 'Politique Des Auteurs'* (Amsterdam: Amsterdam University Press, 2019).

Gruault, Jean, *Ce que dit l'autre* (Paris: Julliard, 1992).

Guigue, Arnaud, *Truffaut & Godard: la querelle des images* (Paris: CNRS, 2014).

Günther, Renate, *Marguerite Duras* (Manchester: Manchester University Press, 2002).

Handyside, Fiona (ed.) *Éric Rohmer: Interviews* (Jackson: University Press of Mississippi, 2013).

Hill, Lesley, *Duras: Apocalyptic Desires* (London: Routledge, 1993).

Holmes, Diana and Ingram, Robert, *François Truffaut* (Manchester: Manchester University Press, 1998).

Hösle, Vittorio, *Eric Rohmer, Filmmaker and Philosopher* (London: Bloomsbury, 2016).

Ince, Kate, *George Franju* (Manchester: Manchester University Press, 2005).

Ingram, Robert, and Paul Duncan (eds), *François Truffaut: Film Author, 1932– 1984* (Cologne: Taschen, 2013).

Insdorf, Annette, *François Truffaut* (New York: Cambridge University Press, 1994).

Karina, Anna, *Golden City* (Olivier Orban, 1983).

Keeney, Gavin, *Dossier Chris Marker: The Suffering Image* (Newcastle upon Tyne: Cambridge Scholars, 2012).

Kline, T. Jefferson (ed.) *Agnès Varda: Interviews.* (Jackson: University Press of Mississippi, 2014).

Lafont, Bernadette, *La Fiancée du cinéma* (Paris: Olivier Orban, 1978).

Layani, Jacques, *Jacques Demy: un portrait personnel* (Paris: L'Harmattan, 2014).

Lebelley, Frédérique, *Duras ou le poids d'une plume* (Paris: Grasset, 1994).

Le Berre, Carole, *François Truffaut* (Paris: Cahiers du Cinéma, 1993).

Le Berre, Carole, *François Truffaut au travail* (Paris: Cahiers du Cinéma, 2014)

Lefebvre, Martin, *Truffaut et ses doubles* (Paris: J. Vrin, 2013).

Leigh, Jacob. *The Cinema of Éric Rohmer: Irony, Imagination, and the Social World* (New York: Bloomsbury Publishing, 2012).

Le Roy, Eric, *Jean-Pierre Mocky* (Paris: BiFi/ Durante, 2000).

Loshitzky, Yosefa, *The Radical Faces of Godard and Bertolucci* (Detroit: Wayne State University Press, 1995).

Louguet, Patrick (ed.). *Rohmer ou le jeu des variations* (Saint-Denis: Presses Universitaires de Vincennes, 2012).

Lupton, Catherine, *Chris Marker: Memories of the Future* (London: Reaktion, 2005).

MacCabe, Colin (ed.), *Godard: Images, Sounds, Politics* (London: Macmillan, 1980).

MacCabe, Colin, *Jean-Luc Godard: a Portrait of the Artist at 70* (London: Bloomsbury, 2003).

Magny, Joël, *Eric Rohmer* (Paris: Rivages, 1986).

Magny, Joël, *Claude Chabrol* (Paris: Cahiers du Cinéma, 1987).

Martin, Philippe, *Mag Bodard: portrait d'une productrice* (Paris: La Tour Verte, 2014).

Met, Philippe (ed.), *The Cinema of Louis Malle: Transatlantic Auteur* (London: Wallflower, 2018).

Mocky, Jean-Pierre, *La longue marche : entretiens avec Noël Simsolo* (Paris: Neige, 2014).

Monaco, James, *Alain Resnais, The Role of Imagination* (New York: Oxford University Press, 1979).

Morrey, Douglas, *Jean-Luc Godard* (Manchester: Manchester University Press, 2005).

Morrey, Douglas, Christina Stojanova, and Nicole Côté (eds.), *The Legacies of Jean-Luc Godard* (Waterloo: Wilfrid Laurier University Press, 2014).

Narboni, Jean and Milne, Tom (eds), *Godard on Godard: Critical Writings* (New York: Viking, 1972).

Naze, Alain, *Jacques Demy: l'enfance retrouvée* (Paris: L'Harmattan, 2014).

Nicholls, David, *François Truffaut* (London: B.T. Batsford, 1993).

Nogueira, Rui (ed.), *Melville on Melville* (London: Secker and Warburg and BFI, 1971).

Pascal, Michel, *Claude Chabrol* (Paris: La Martinière, 2012).

Perrot, Vincent, *Georges Delerue. De Roubaix à Hollywood* (Paris: Carnot 2004)

Phillips, John, *Alain Robbe-Grillet* (Manchester: Manchester University Press, 2011).

Prédal, René (ed.), 'Le Cinéma selon Godard', *CinémAction* No. 52 (1989).

Proulx, Caroline, and Sylvano Santini (eds), *Le cinéma de Marguerite Duras : l'autre scène du littéraire?* (Bern: Peter Lang, 2015).

Raboudin, Dominique (ed.), *Truffaut par Truffaut* (New York: Harry N. Abrams, 1987). Translated by Robert Erich Wolf.

Robic, Sylvie, and Laurence Schifano (eds) *Rohmer en perspectives* (Paris: Presses universitaires de Paris X, 2014).

Robles, Amanda, *Alain Cavalier: filmeur* (Le Havre: De l'incidence, 2011).

Rohmer, Eric, *Le Goût de la beauté* (Paris: Editions de l'Etoile, 1984 [1979]). Published in English as *The Taste of Beauty* (Cambridge: Cambridge University Press, 1989). Translated by Carol Volk.

Rohmer, Eric and Noël Herpe, *Le Sel du présent, chroniques de cinéma* (Capricci, 2020).

Rohmer, Eric, *Le Celluloïd et le marbre : suivi d'un entretien inédit* (Editions Léo Scheer, 2015).

Rollet, Brigitte, *Jacqueline Audry : la femme à la caméra* (Rennes: Presses universitaires de Rennes, 2015).

Rosenbaum, Jonathan (ed.), *Rivette: Texts and Interviews* (London: British Film Institute, 1977).

Roud, Richard, *Godard* (Bloomington: Indiana University Press, 1970).

Ward, John, *Alain Resnais, or the Theme of Time* (Garden City, N.Y.: Doubleday, 1968).

Roud, Richard, *A Passion for Films: Henri Langlois and the Cinémathèque française* (London: Secker & Warburg, 1983).

Royer, Michelle, *The Cinema of Marguerite Duras: Multisensoriality and Female Subjectivity* (Edinburgh: Edinburgh UP, 2019).

Schilling, Derek, *Eric Rohmer* (Manchester: Manchester University Press, 2007).

Serrut, Louis-Albert, *Jean-Luc Godard, cinéaste acousticien : des emplois et usages de la matière sonore dans ses œuvres cinématographiques* (Paris: L'Harmattan, 2011).

Serrut, Louis-Albert (ed.), *Le Cinéma de Jean-Luc Godard et la philosophie: D'hier à aujourd'hui* (Paris: L'Harmattan, 2019).

Smith, Alison, *Agnès Varda* (Manchester: Manchester University Press, 1998).

Solecki, Sam, *A Truffaut Notebook* (Montreal: McGill-Queen's University Press, 2015).

Stam, Robert, *François Truffaut and Friends. Modernism, Sexuality and Film Adaptation* (New Brunswick, N.J.: Rutgers University Press, 2006).

Sterritt, David, *The films of Jean-Luc Godard: Seeing the Invisible* (Cambridge: Cambridge University Press, 1999).

Sweet, Freddy, *The Film Narratives of Alain Resnais* (Ann Arbor, MI: UMI Research Press, 1981).

Taboulay, Camille, *Le Cinéma enchanté de Jacques Demy* (Paris: Cahiers du cinéma, 1996).

Temple, Michael, Williams, James S., and Witt, Michael (eds), *For Ever Godard* (London: Black Dog Publishing, 2003).

Thomas, François, *Alain Resnais : les coulisses de la création – Entretiens avec ses proches collaborateurs*. Paris : Armand Colin, 2016).

Tourret, Franck, *Alain Resnais : Le Pari de la forme* (Paris : L'Harmattan, 2019).

Truffaut, François, *Les Films de ma vie* (Paris: Flammarion, 1975). Published in English as *The Films in My Life* (New York: Simon & Schuster, 1978); translated by Leonard Mayhew.

Truffaut, François, *Le Plaisir des yeux* (Paris: Cahiers du cinéma, 1987).

Truffaut, François, *Correspondance* (Paris: Hatier-Cinq Continents, 1988).

Truffaut, François and Lillian Ross (eds), *François Truffaut : Textes issus de The New Yorker, 1960–1976* (Paris: Carlotta, 2013).

Truffaut, François, *Chroniques d'Arts-Spectacles 1954–1958* (Paris : Gallimard, 2019).

Vadim, Roger, *Mémoire du diable* (Paris: Stock, 1975). Published in English as *Memoirs of the Devil* (London: Hutchinson, 1976). Translated by Peter Beglan.

Varda, Agnès, *Varda par Agnès* (Paris: Editions Cahiers du Cinéma, 1994).

Varda, Agnès, *Cuba* (Xavier Barral; Bilingual Edition, 2015).

Vetinde, L.J. and A.T. Fofana (eds), *Ousmane Sembene and the Politics of Culture* (Lanham : Lexington Books, 2015).

Vidal, Marion, *Les Contes moraux d'Eric Rohmer* (Paris: L'Herminier, 1977).

Vincendeau, Ginette, *Jean-Pierre Melville, An American in Paris* (London: BFI, 2003).

Waldron, Darren, *Jacques Demy* (Manchester: Manchester University Press, 2014).

Wiles, Mary M., *Jacques Rivette* (Urbana: University of Illinois Press 2012).

Warehime, Marja, *Maurice Pialat* (Manchester: Manchester University Press, 2006).

Williams, James S., *Jean Cocteau* (Manchester: Manchester University Press, 2006).

Wilson, Emma, *Alain Resnais* (Manchester: Manchester University Press, 2006).

Wood, Robin and Walker, Michael, *Claude Chabrol* (New York: Praeger, 1970).

Zarader, Jean-Pierre. *Philippe de Broca: Caméra philosophique* (Paris: Klincksieck, 2019).

Individual films

Amengual, Barthélémy, *Bande à part de Jean-Luc Godard* (Brussels: Yellow Now, Crisnée, 1993).

Andrew, Dudley (ed.), *Breathless* (New Brunswick, N.J.: Rutgers University Press, 1995).

Bailblé, Claude, Marie, Michel and Ropars, Marie-Claire, *Muriel: Histoire d'une recherche* (Paris: Editions Galilée, 1974).

Bastide, Bernard, *"Les Mistons" de François Truffaut* (Nîmes: Atelier Baie 2015)

Bastide, Bernard, *Cléo de 5 à 7* (Paris: Canopé, 2019).

Brunette, Peter (ed.), *Shoot the Piano Player* (New Brunswick, N.J.: Rutgers University Press, 1993).

Carlier, Christophe, *Marguerite Duras, Alain Resnais: Hiroshima mon amour* (Paris: Presses Universitaires de France, 1994).

Cieutat, Michel, *Pierrot le fou de Jean-Luc Godard* (Limonest, Editions L'interdiscipliaire, 1993).

Crittenden, Roger, *La Nuit Américaine* (London: BFI Film Classics, 1998).

Darke, Chris, *Alphaville* (London: I.B. Tauris, 2005).

Ertel, Judith, *Cléo de 5 à 7* (Paris : Atlande, 2020)

Fotiade, Ramona, *À bout de souffle* (London : I. B. Tauris, 2013).

Guillamaud, Patrice, *Les Parapluies de Cherbourg : Jacques Demy* (Liège: Céfal, 2014).

Gillain, Anne, *Les Quatre Cents Coups de François Truffaut* (Paris: Nathan, 1991).

Leutrat, Jean-Louis, *Hiroshima mon amour d'Alain Resnais* (Paris: Nathan, 1994).

Leutrat, Jean-Louis, *L'Année dernière à Marienbad* (London: BFI Film Classics, 2000).

MacCabe, Colin, and Laura Mulvey (eds.), *Godard's* Contempt: *Essays from the London Consortium* (Malden: Wiley-Blackwell, 2012).

MacKillop, Ian, *Free Spirits. Henri Pierre Roché, François Truffaut and the Two English Girls* (London: Bloomsbury, 2000)

Marie, Michel, *Le Mépris* (Paris: Nathan, 1990).

Marie, Michel, *À bout de souffle* (Paris: Nathan, 1999).

Marie, Michel, *Muriel d'Alain Resnais* (Neuilly: Editions Atlande, 2005).

Orpen, Valerie, *Cléo de 5 à 7* (London: I.B. Tauris, 2007).

Ungar, Steven, *Cléo de 5 à 7* (London: Palgrave Macmillan, 2008)

Vaugeois, Gérard (ed.), *À bout de souffle* (Paris: Balland, 1974).

Viment, Pascal, *Le Mépris* (Paris: Hatier, 1991).

Selection of special issues of journals dedicated to the New Wave

Cahiers du cinéma, no. 138 (December 1962).

Cahiers du cinéma, hors série, 'La nouvelle vague en question' (December 1998).

Cinéma 60, 'Aujourd'hui la N.V., no. 42 (January 1960), 43 (February 1960), 44 (March 1960).

CinémAction no. 104, 'Flash-back sur la Nouvelle Vague' (3e trimestre 2002).

Cinema Journal, 49/4, Summer 2010 (In Focus: The French New Wave at Fifty, Pushing the boundaries).

Communications I (1962).

Positif, 'Quoi de neuf?', no. 31 (November 1959).

Positif, 'Feux sur le cinéma français', no. 46 (June 1962).

Premier Plan, 'Marée montante', no. 9 (May 1960).

Premier Plan, 'Cinéma d'aujourd'hui', no. 10 (Juin 1960).

 [N.B. The *Premier Plan* texts are anthologized in the 1962 Premier Plan volume indicated in the first section of this bibliography]

Studies in French Cinema, Volume 17/2 (2017) ('Nouvelle vague, The First Wave').

[see also the bibliography in de Baecque, *La nouvelle vague: Portrait d'une jeunesse*, for a round-up of special issues and dossiers on the various phases of the New Wave].

Other books relevant to, or with sections on the New Wave

Abel, Richard, *French Cinema: the First Wave, 1915-1929* (Princeton; Guilford: Princeton University Press, 1984).

Alexandre, Olivier, *La Sainte famille des Cahiers du cinéma* (Paris : Vrin, 2017).

Andrew, Dudley, with Hervé Joubert-Laurencin (eds), *Opening Bazin: Postwar Film Theory and Its Afterlife* (Oxford: Oxford University Press, 2011)

Armes, Roy, *The Ambiguous Image, Narrative Style in Modern European Cinema* (Bloomington: Indiana University Press, 1976).

Barrot, Olivier, *L'Écran français, 1943-1953: Histoire d'un journal et d'une époque* (Paris: Les Editeurs français réunis, 1979).

Bazin, André, *What is Cinema?*, Essays selected and translated by Hugh Gray, 2 vols. (Berkeley; London: University of California Press, 1971).

Bazin, André, *Écrits complets*, 2 vols, Hervé Joubert-Laurencin (ed.) (Paris: Macula, 2018).

Bazin, André, *Selected Writings 1943–1958*, translated by Timothy Barnard (New Brunswick: Rutgers University Press, 2018).

Bonnell, René, *Le Cinéma exploité* (Paris: Seuil, 1978).

Borde, Raymond, *Les Cinémathèques* (Lausanne: L'Âge d'homme, 1983).

Bordwell, David, Thompson, Kristin and Staiger, Janet, *The classical Hollywood cinema : film style & mode of production to 1960* (New York: Columbia University Press, 1985).

Bordwell, David, 'Godard and Narration', *Narration in the Fiction Film* (Madison: University of Wisconsin Press, 1985), pp. 331-334.

Bourdieu, Pierre, *Les Règles de l'art: génèse et structure du champ littéraire* (Paris: Editions du Seuil, 1992). Published in English as *The Rules of Art: Genesis and Structure of the Literary Field* (Stanford: Stanford University Press, 1995). Translated by Susan Emmanuel.

Brassart, Alain, *Les Jeunes premiers dans le cinéma français des années 60* (Paris: Cerf/ Corlet 2004).

Browne, Nick (ed.), *Cahiers du cinéma 1969-1972, The Politics of Representation* (London: Routledge/BFI, 1989).

Buache, Freddy, *Le Cinéma français des années soixante* (Paris: Cinq continents/ Hatier, 1987).

Buchsbaum, Jonathan, *Exception Taken: How France Has Defied Hollywood's New World Order* (New York: Columbia University Press, 2017).

Burch, Noël, *De la beauté des latrines. Pour réhabiliter le sens au cinema et ailleurs* (Paris: L'Harmattan, 2007).

Caughie, John (ed.), *Theories of Authorship: A Reader* (London; Boston: Routledge & Kegan Paul, in association with the British Film Institute, 1981).

Chabrol, Marguerite, and Pierre-Olivier Toulza (eds), *Lola Montès : lectures croisées* (Paris : L'Harmattan, 2011).

Chion, Michel, *Le Complexe de Cyrano, La langue parlée dans les films français* (Paris : Cahiers du cinéma/Essais, 2008).

Ciment, Michel and Zimmer, Jacques (eds), *La Critique de cinéma en France: Histoire, anthologie, dictionnaire* (Paris: Ramsay, 1997).

Crisp, Colin, 'The classic French cinema and the New Wave', in *The Classic French Cinema, 1930-1960* (Bloomington: Indiana University Press, 1993).

Darke, Chris and Corless, Kieron, Cannes, *Inside the World's Premier Film Festival* (London: Faber and Faber, 2007).

David, Michel, '25 ans de réflexion', in *La Nouvelle vague et après* (Paris: Cinémathèque Française, 1986).

de Baecque, Antoine, *Les Cahiers du cinéma: histoire d'une revue. Vol. I., A l'assaut du cinéma: 1951-1959* (Paris: Cahiers du cinéma, 1991).

de Baecque, Antoine, *Les Cahiers du cinéma: histoire d'une revue. Vol. II., Cinéma, tours detours:1959-1981* (Paris: Cahiers du cinéma, 1991).

de Baecque, Antoine, *La Cinéphilie: Invention d'un regard, histoire d'une culture, 1944-1968* (Paris: Fayard, 2003).

de Baecque, Antoine, *Camera Historica. The Century in Cinema* (Columbia University Press : 2012).

Elsaesser, Thomas, 'Two Decades in Another country: Hollywood and the Cinephiles', in Bigsby, Chris (ed.), *Superculture, American Popular culture and Europe* (London: Paul Elek, 1975).

Esquenazi, Jean-Pierre, '*À bout de souffle* et la société de la Nouvelle Vague', in Jean-Pierre Bertin-Maghit (ed.), *Les Cinémas européens des années cinquante* (Paris: AFRHC, 2000).

Esquenazi, Jean-Pierre (ed.), *Politique des auteurs et théories du cinéma* (Paris: L'Harmattan, 2002).

Frodon, Jean-Michel, *L'Âge moderne du cinéma français, de la Nouvelle Vague à nos jours* (Paris: Flammarion, 1995).ciné

Gimello-Mesplomb, Fréderic, *Objectif49 : Cocteau et la nouvelle avant-garde* (Paris: Séguier Éditions, 2014).

Giroud, Françoise, *La nouvelle vague : Portraits de la jeunesse* (Paris: Gallimard, 1958).

Goubel, François, *Le Cinéma français de 1958 à 1967* (Paris : L'Harmattan, 2019).

Goudet, Stéphane (ed.), *L'Amour du cinéma. 50 ans de la revue Positif* (Paris: Gallimard, 2002).

Hayward, Susan and Vincendeau, Ginette (eds.), *French Film, Texts and Contexts* (London; New York: Routledge, 1990); second, enlarged edition 2000.

Hayward, Susan, *French Costume Drama of the 1950s: Fashioning Politics in Film* (Bristol, UK: Intellect, 2010).

Hedges, Inez, *Breaking the Frame: Film Language and the Experience of Limits* (Bloomington, Indiana: Indiana University Press, 1991)

Herzog, Amy, *Dreams of Difference, Songs of the Same: The Musical Moment in Film* (Minneapolis: University of Minnesota Press, 2010)

Higgins, Lynn A., 'Screen/Memory: Rape and Its Alibis in *Last Year in Marienbad*', in Higgins, Lynn a. and Silver, Brenda R. (eds), *Rape and Representation* (New York: Columbia University Press, 1991).

Hillier, Jim (ed.), *Cahiers du Cinéma: The 1950s* (Cambridge, Mass.: Harvard University Press, 1985).

Hillier, Jim (ed.), *Cahiers du Cinéma: The 1960s* (Cambridge, Mass.: Harvard University Press, 1992).

Hubert-Lacombe, Patricia, *Le Cinéma français dans la guerre froide, 1946-1956* (Paris: L'Harmattan, 1996).

Jeancolas, Jean-Pierre, *Le Cinéma des Français, La Ve République (1958-1978)* (Paris: Stock/Cinéma, 1979).

Kline, T. Jefferson, *Unraveling French Cinema: From L'Atalante to Caché* (Chichester, UK: Wiley-Blackwell, 2010).

Lagabrielle, Renaud and Timo Obergöker (eds), *La Chanson dans le film français et francophone depuis la Nouvelle Vague* (Würzburg : Königshausen und Neumann, 2016).

Leahy, Sarah and Isabelle Vanderschelden, *Screenwriters in French cinema* (Manchester : Manchester University Press, 2021).

Marie, Laurent, *Le Cinéma est à nous: le PCF et le cinéma français de la Libération à nos jours* (Paris; Budapest; Torino: L'Harmattan, 2005).

Marie, Michel, *La Belle Histoire du cinéma français en 101 films* (Paris : Armand Colin, 2018).

Monaco, Paul, *Ribbons in Time: Movies and Society since 1945* (Bloomington, Indiana: Indiana University Press, 1987)

Montarnal, Jean, *La 'qualité française' : Un mythe critique ?* (Paris : L'Harmattan, 2019).

Montebello, Fabrice, *Le Cinéma en France depuis les années 1930* (Paris: Armand Colin, 2005).

Morari, Codruța, *The Bressonians: French Cinema and the Culture of Authorship* (Edinburgh: Edinburgh University Press, 2017).

Morin, Edgar, *Les Stars* (Paris : Le Seuil, 1957).

Morrey, Douglas, *The Legacy of the New Wave in French Cinema* (London: Bloomsbury Academic, 2019).

Neroni, Hilary, *Feminist Film Theory and Cléo from 5 to 7* (New York: Bloomsbury, 2016).

Neupert, Richard, 'Dead Champagne: *Variety's* New Wave', *Film History* 10, n°2 (1998), 219-30.

Nowell-Smith, Geoffrey, *Making Waves: New Cinemas of the 1960s* (New York: Continuum, 2007).

Orr, John, *Cinema and Modernity* (Cambridge: Polity Press, 1993).

Paqui, Guy, *Jean Delannoy : ses années lumière, 1938–1992* (Toulon: Presses du Midi, 2010).

Pauly, Rebecca M., *The Transparent Illusion : Image and ideology in French Text and Film* (New York: Peter Lang, 1993).

Phillips, Alastair, and Ginette Vincendeau (eds), *A Companion to Jean Renoir* (West Sussex, UK: Wiley-Blackwell, 2013).

Phillips, Alastair, and Ginette Vincendeau (eds), *Paris in the Cinema: Beyond the Flâneur* (BFI/Palgrave-Macmillan, 2017).

Pillard, Thomas, *Le film noir français face aux bouleversements de la France d'après-guerre (1946-1960)* (Nantes : Joseph K, 2014).

Prédal, René, *Cinquante ans de cinéma français* (Paris : Nathan, 1996).

Ross, Kristin, *Fast Cars, Clean Bodies: Decolonization and the Reordering of French Culture* (Cambridge, Mass.: MIT University Press, 1995).

Sagan, Françoise, *Avec mon meilleur souvenir* (Paris: Gallimard, 1984).

Schwartz, Vanessa, *It's So French! Hollywood, Paris, and the Making of Cosmopolitan Film Culture* (University of Chicago Press, 2008).

Serrut, Louis-Albert (ed.), *Le Cinéma de Jean-Luc Godard et la philosophie : D'hier à aujourd'hui* (Paris : L'Harmattan, 2018).

Shafto, Sally, *Les Films Zanzibar et les dandys de mai 1968* (Paris: Paris Experimental, 2007).

Temple, Michael, and Michael Witt (eds), *French Cinema Book*, 2nd ed. (London: BFI, 2018).

Tweedie, James, *The Age of New Waves: Art Cinema and the Staging of Globalization* (Oxford: Oxford University Press, 2013).

Vincendeau, Ginette, *Stars and Stardom in French Cinema* (London, New York: continuum, 2000).

Vincendeau, Ginette. *Brigitte Bardot* (London : Palgrave Macmillan, 2013).

Warner, Rick, *Godard and the Essay Film: A Form that Thinks* (Evanston: Northwestern University Press, 2019).

Wilson, David (ed.), *Cahiers du cinéma. Vol.4 1973-1978: history, ideology, cultural struggle*; with an introduction by Bérénice Reynaud (London, New York: Routledge, 2000).

Wimmer, Leila, *Cross-Channel Perspectives. The French Reception of British Cinema* (Oxford: Peter Lang, 2009).

List of Illustrations

While considerable effort has been made to correctly identify the copyright holders, this has not been possible in all cases. We apologise for any apparent negligence and any omissions or corrections brought to our attention will be remedied in any future editions.

Les Quatre cents coups, © Films du Carrosse; *La Pointe Courte*, Ciné-Tamaris; *Bob le flambeur*, Organisation Générale Cinématographique/Cyme/Play Art; *Cléo de 5 à 7*, Rome-Paris Films; *Hiroshima mon amour*, Argos-Films/Como Films/Daiei Kyoto/ Pathe Overseas; *Les Bonnes femmes*, © Paris Film Production; *La Règle du jeu*, Nouvelle Édition Française; *L'Espoir*, Productions Corniglion-Molinier; *La Symphonie pastorale*, Films Gibé; *Jeux interdits*, Silver Films/Mondex Films; *Le Blé en herbe*, Franco London Film; *La Minute de vérité*, Franco London Films/Cines; *The Man Who Knew Too Much*, © Filwite Productions; *Bigger Than Life*, © Twentieth Century-Fox Film Corporation; *Citizen Kane*, © RKO Radio Pictures; *Mr Arkadin*, Film Organisation S.A./Cervantes Films/Sevilla Films Studios; *Monkey Business*, Twentieth Century-Fox Film Corporation; *The General Line*, Sovkino; *Nanook of the North*, Robert Flaherty; *Le Jour se lève*, Productions Sigma/Vog-Sigma; *The Battleship Potemkin*, First Studio Goskino; *The Best Years of Our Lives*, Samuel Goldwyn Inc.; *The Little Foxes*, © Samuel Goldwyn Inc.; *Tabu: A Story of the South Seas*, Golden Bough; *The Garment Jungle*, Columbia Pictures Corporation; *Emil and the Detectives*, Ufa; À bout de *souffle*, Société Nouvelle de Cinématographie/Productions Georges de Beauregard/ Imperia; *Pickpocket*, Agnès Delahaie Productions; *Europa '51*, Lux Film; *The Trouble with Harry*, © Alfred Hitchcock Productions; *Le Beau Serge*, AJYM Films/Coopérative Générale di Cinéma Français; *Le Signe du lion*, AJYM Films; *Paris nous appartient*, AJYM Films/Films du Carrosse; *Les Yeux sans visage*, Champs-Élysées Productions/ Lux Film; *The Defiant Ones*, © Lomitas Productions/© Curtleigh Productions; *Une vie*, Agnès Delahaie Productions/Nepi Film; *Les Cousins*, AJYM Films; *Zazie dans le métro*, Nouvelle Éditions de Films; *Une femme est une femme*, Rome-Paris Films; *Lola*, Rome-Paris Films/Euro International Films; *Le Farceur*, AJYM Films/Roland Nonin; *L'Année dernière à Marienbad*, Terra Film/Société Nouvelle des Films Cormoran/Précitel/Como Films/Argos-Films/Films Tamara/Cinétel/Silver Films/Cineriz di Angelo Rizzoli; *Le Petit soldat*, Productions Georges de Beauregard/Société Nouvelle de Cinématographie; *Tirez sur le pianiste*, Films de la Pléiade; *Le Journal d'un curé de campagne*, U.G.C.; *Et Dieu ... créa la femme*, U.C.I.L./Cocinor/Iéna; *Une partie de campagne*, Panthéon Productions; *Fahrenheit 451*, © Vineyard Productions; *Ascenseur pour l'échafaud*, Nouvelles Éditions de Films; *L'Eau à la bouche*, Les Films de la Pléiade; *Senso*, Lux Film; *Lola Montès*, Gamma Film/Florida Films/Union-Film GmbH; *The Barefoot Contessa*, © Figaro Incorporated; *La Noire de ...*, Filmi Doomireew/Actualités Françaises; *Olivia*, Memnon Films; *La Dérive*, Prods. Cine. De Languedoc; *Jules et Jim*, © Films du Carrosse.

Index